Northern Experience and the Myths of Canadian Culture

In *Northern Experience and the Myths of Canadian Culture* Renée Hulan disputes the notion that the north is a source of distinct collective identity for Canadians. Through a synthesis of critical, historical, and theoretical approaches to northern subjects in literary studies, she challenges the epistemology used to support this idea.

By investigating mutually dependent categories of identity in literature that depicts northern peoples and places, Hulan provides a descriptive account of representative genres in which the north figures as a central theme – including autobiography, adventure narrative, ethnography, fiction, poetry, and travel writing. She considers each of these diverse genres in terms of the way it explains the cultural identity of a nation formed from the settlement of immigrant peoples on the lands of dispossessed indigenous peoples. Reading against the background of contemporary ethnographic, literary, and cultural theory, Hulan maintains that the collective Canadian identity idealized in many works representing the north does not occur naturally but is artificially constructed in terms of characteristics inflected by historically contingent ideas of gender and race, such as self-sufficiency, independence, and endurance, and that these characteristics are evoked to justify the nationhood of the Canadian state.

RENÉE HULAN is assistant professor in the Department of English at Saint Mary's University and the editor of *Native North America: Critical and Cultural Perspectives.*

McGILL-QUEEN'S NATIVE AND NORTHERN SERIES
BRUCE G. TRIGGER, EDITOR

Northern Experience
and the
Myths of Canadian Culture

RENÉE HULAN

McGill-Queen's University Press
Montreal & Kingston · London · Ithaca

© McGill-Queen's University Press 2002
ISBN 0-7735-2227-1 (cloth)

Legal deposit first quarter 2002
Bibliothèque nationale du Québec

Printed in Canada on acid-free paper that is 100% ancient forest free
(100% post-consumer recycled), processed chlorine free, and printed
with vegetable-based, low VOC inks.

This book has been published with the help of grants from the
Humanities and Social Sciences Federation of Canada, using funds
provided by the Social Sciences and Humanities Research Council of
Canada, and the Senate Research Committee of Saint Mary's University.

McGill-Queen's University Press acknowledges
the financial support of the Government of Canada through the Book
Publishing Industry Development Program (BPIDP) for its activities.
It also acknowledges the support of the Canada Council for the Arts
for its publishing program.

National Library of Canada
Cataloguing in Publication Data

Hulan, Renée, 1965–
    Northern experience and the myths of Canadian culture
    (McGill-Queen's native and northern series: 29)
    Includes bibliographical references and index.
    ISBN 0-7735-2227-1 (bnd)

    1. Canadian literature – History and criticism. 2. Canada, Northern, in
literature. 3. National characteristics, Canadian, in literature. 4. Identity
(Psychology) in literature. I. Title. II. Series.
    PS8101.N67H84 2002   C810.9'32719   C2001-901557-7
    PR9185.5.N67H84 2002

Typeset in Palatino 10.5/13
by Caractéra inc., Quebec City

Contents

Acknowledgments

The research for this book was undertaken with the help of a doctoral fellowship from the Social Sciences and Humanities Research Council of Canada and published with a grant from the Aid to Scholarly Publishing Program. The preparation of the manuscript was supported by a Senate Research Grant from Saint Mary's University.

Thanks to the Canadian scholars who shared their expertise and knowledge with me, and especially those who read and commented on earlier versions of this study, including Margery Fee, Sherrill E. Grace, Robert Lecker, John Lennox, Brian Trehearne, Sarah Westphal, Gary Wihl, and John Wolforth, and the Aid to Scholarly Publishing Program's two anonymous readers. Discussions with colleagues and friends encouraged and sustained me as I worked on the manuscript, thanks in particular to Dale Blake, Teresa Heffernan, Shelley Hulan, Susie O'Brien, and Linda Warley. Philip Cercone, Joan McGilvray, Joanne Pisano, John Zucchi, and Lesley Barry of McGill-Queen's University Press were instrumental in seeing the manuscript through to publication. Sincere thanks to Heather Egger, my research assistant and a graduate of the Linguistics Program at Saint Mary's University, for her diligent efforts. Finally, to Michael E. Vance, my deepest gratitude.

Northern Experience and the Myths of Canadian Culture

As long as the north wind blows, and the snow and sleet drive out over forests and fields, we may be a poor, but we must be a virtuous, a daring, and if we are worthy of our ancestors, a dominant race ... Let us, then, should we ever become a nation, never forget the land that we live in, and the race from which we have sprung ... We are the Northmen of the New World.

– R.G. Haliburton,
"The Men of the North" (1869)

... I need wisdom. Wisdom to understand why Canadians have so little comprehension of our own nordicity, that we are a northern nation and that, until we grasp imaginatively and realize imaginatively in word, song, image and consciousness that North is both the true nature of our world and also our graspable destiny we will always go whoring after the mocking palm trees and beaches of the Caribbean and Florida and Hawaii; will always be wishing ourselves something we aren't ...

– Rudy Wiebe,
Playing Dead (1989)

A Northern Nation?

In Canadian literary history and criticism, literature has been to culture as culture is to nation. Literature affirms the presence of culture, and culture in turn grants the nation legitimacy. This correlation of nation and culture can be traced through a shared history that, though not exclusively Canadian, has had significant influence in Canada. When occupied with national culture – or lack thereof, depending on one's point of view – Canadian literary criticism is concerned with the anthropological sense of culture as a way of life. Cultural nationalism affirms this way of life by making reference to cultural products, both of popular culture and "the arts." When attached to national identity in this way, "culture" embraces both cultural products and the idea of a shared way of life. It is this kind of sharing or identity that, despite the hundred years separating them, both R.G. Haliburton and Rudy Wiebe yearn for in the passages cited above.

In his remarks, Wiebe regards the North as "the true nature of our world and also our graspable destiny" (111). The national culture that Wiebe wishes for throughout *Playing Dead: A Contemplation Concerning the Arctic* is a myth both in the sense of an untruth, or false notion, and in the sense of a story that articulates a specific worldview. As Shelagh Grant demonstrates in "Myths of the North in the Canadian Ethos," the most comprehensive and cogent essay on the subject, the notion of "our northern heritage" endures as "an amorphous, obscure, yet recurrent theme in Canadian nationalism" (17).[1] By tracing this theme through myths and images that take particular, historically contingent forms, she argues that they all contribute to the "core myth" that "the vast wilderness regions still impart a distinct character to the Canadian nation, its people, and its institutions" (39).

As northern studies grapples with this core myth, exposing its possibilities and limitations, an important, and I think political, distinction has been drawn between the North imagined by outsiders and the north experienced by its inhabitants.[2] Often framed as a contrast between "myth" and "reality," this distinction continues to occupy northern studies, resulting in the high priority placed on the idea of northern experience.[3] Underlying this distinction is another between "fiction" and "non-fiction," whereby fiction specifically, and literature generally, is sometimes seen to create myth in the sense of falsehood and to contribute to the misrepresentation of northern reality. For example, Farley Mowat, who has been a vocal critic of "the north of the imagination," rails with what seems to be unintended irony against the way the "magnificent reality behind the myth" of the North has been "obscured in drifts of literary drivel, obliterated by blizzards of bravado and buried under an icy weight of obsessive misconceptions" (*Canada North* 6).[4]

"For many, inside Canada and without," write Kenneth Coates and William Morrison, "northern writing is Canadian writing: that is, the embodiment of the physical and human conditions that inform the Canadian spirit and character" ("Writing the North" 5). The "true north" evoked in such writing is a collection of images, ideas, and myths generated within varying, competing, and intersecting forms of representation. Not only is the idea of North represented in every form and medium one could name, but the term itself has been exhaustively and exhaustingly defined. Considered a "relative term" that each Canadian can define for him or herself (Morton 229) and a "territorially shifting concept" in Canadian historiography (Hodgins 12), it has also been defined in geographical terms as a direction, a comparison, a relational term, and quantified as "nordicity," Louis-Édmond Hamelin's statistical formula for determining northernness based on empirical criteria, including latitude, temperature, and population.

The focus on the nordicity of national identity is part of a broader tendency in Canadian cultural history that seeks to unify and to shape collective experience and, in so doing, to smooth over differences. While northern studies stresses personal and local experience, it is part of a larger national discourse that seeks to transcend the personal and the local. Through history, representations of the north have drawn on discourses that are not exclusive to Canada, such as the nineteenth-century Romantic "fascination with the relationship of mankind to the natural environment" (Grant, "Myths" 21). The representation of the north as a possible alternative to urban experience in Canada was not the mimetic response to local experience that north enthusiasts believe but, as Grant demonstrates, an idea that took literary form in the meeting of imported discourses as "[t]he British aesthetic myth blended with the American wilderness myth to reinforce a romantic image of north as expressed first in literature and art then incorporated into the environmental movement of the 1970s" (37).

In *Places on the Margin: Alternative Geographies of Modernity* (1991), Rob Shields describes the representation of the north as a constant tension of "imaginary North" and "ideological North." Shields closely follows Edwin Fussell's thesis describing the double meaning of "the West" in American literature as both "absolute" and "relative." Fussell stresses the way the myth of the West and the frontier articulates America's "difference from" and "continuity with" the East (4). Shields uses the term "frontier" to describe the imaginary North: "a wilderness, an empty 'space' which, seen from southern Canada is white, blank," while the ideological North is that "empty page onto which can be projected images of the essence of 'Canadian-ness' and also images to define one's urban existence against" (165), or as Grant writes, where "the north is often referred to as 'wilderness,' a place beyond southern civilization, agricultural settlement, or urban life" ("Myths" 16). This idea of North as the "last vast North American frontier" in which the "recurring themes in contemporary Canadian fiction" are explored (Mitcham 10) remains, even though the opposition between urban and rural is only a partial account of Canadian experiences. Moreover, characteristics corresponding closely to the imaginary, expanding space of the American frontier indicate how at least one myth of Canadian culture is ironically based on a model derived from the analysis of American culture.[5] Nevertheless, the two definitions put forth by Shields describe the symbolic function of the North in Canada both as an empty space waiting endlessly for definition and as a repository of images defining the official national identity, indicating the persistent "confusion between Northern Canada and Canada as North" (Hodgins 12).

As the boundary demarcating the Canadian north shifts, the meaning of "North" shifts, too: from the relative location of real geographical locations to an abstraction signifying the nation as a whole. The imaginary North constructed within Canadian cultural nationalism can be understood by studying these representations of the geographical north as what W.H. New calls an "aesthetic region." The representation of Canadian geography merges with the representation of the Canadian nation in public discourses, especially in public policy pertaining to issues of territorial and political sovereignty and identity. As the definition of the North expands and its southern boundary becomes less distinct, it starts to describe all of Canada. In Canadian literature, the dominance of realism ensures that real geographical locations north of the sixtieth parallel remain the stuff of literary discourse. As a metaphor, "North" can represent any number of things, from the sense of mystery and the unknown expressed in the works of Margaret Atwood to the very act of writing as articulated by Robert Kroetsch; as a setting, the north can also refer, not just to a specific geographical area, but, in an abstract way, to the wilderness itself.

In literature, people go north to escape, to prove themselves, to learn something, and usually to leave again. The quest leads north to a land of the imagination as well as a land of physical challenge for the adventurous character. As a consequence, the North has been a ubiquitous subject in all types of writing, including literary history. The frozen, empty hinterland, an imaginary and unpeopled place, has been a powerful symbol reflecting Frye's question: where is here? It is this imaginary, empty North that most often represents the nation as a whole: the Group of Seven's North, or the blank white page evoked by many writers. The North represented a source of mystic inspiration to the Group of Seven, affirming the theosophic impulses behind their view of nature, and this sense of the north as mysterious and mystical also informs the national consciousness evoked by critics and north enthusiasts.

In Canadian "folktales, art, and music, an image of the northern wilderness has been indelibly linked to freedom, adventure and challenge" (Grant, "Myths" 20–1), and the related notion of Canada as a northern nation whose citizens possess a free, adventurous "northern character" goes back at least to Confederation. When R.G. Haliburton, son of Thomas Chandler Haliburton and member of the Canada First movement, exhorted the members of the Montreal Literary Club to become the "Northmen of the New World," he signalled two issues that would become perennial in Canadian history and in the representation of the north: the pre-occupation with national unity and the relationship between national identity and the environment. In his speech, "The Men of the North and Their Place in History" (1869), Haliburton, unlike generations who would come after him, felt confident about the nation's future: what unified the new Dominion was the common race of its citizenry, sprung from a mythical North-land they would recreate in the New World. In the epigraph that precedes this introduction, Haliburton's idea of race as a collective identity moulded by the land and the climate slips easily into a definition of nation. Bound by "national ties of blood, and lan-guage" (3), he proclaimed, northern people would unite to "form a New Dominion in this Northern land" (2).

The equation of race and nation at the heart of Haliburton's comments reflects emerging ideas and images of nationhood in the nineteenth century. Reading Haliburton's "The Men of the North," one cannot help but recall the profound influence of the German Romantics on nineteenth-century literary criticism, espe-cially in determining the relative merit of literature from the "sensual South" versus that from the "disciplined North" (Mosse, *Nationalism* 32). Indeed, Haliburton praises the "healthy vigour" of northern poetry as compared to that written in southern climes where "the vigour of manhood is lost in dreamland" (8), and W.A. Foster, who like Haliburton was active in the Canada First movement, calls northern culture "more manly, more real, than the weak marrow-bones superstition of an effeminate south" (*Canada First* 16). As Carl Berger remarks, qualities identified with rugged masculinity infuse the call for the reconstitution of north-ern manly races, built on Haliburton's belief in the "hardness, strenuousness, endurance" that developed from "stoical accep-tance of the strenuous life and the performance of duty irrespec-tive of rewards" (5, 18). These qualities emerged as part of an imperial discourse of masculine dominance and superiority that fostered colonial expansion, in part, by enticing young men to prove their manliness in the empire's service.[6]

In addition to fostering a masculinist narrative of the north, the German Romantic political ideology of nation-formation also had a formative effect on the development of the Canadian state. Of fundamental importance to establishing a nation is "the argument that culture, and more specifically, language uniquely defines a nation" (Chatterjee 8–9), which developed in the German Romantic tradition of literary criticism and historiography at a time when Germans were a stateless people. By imagining the "true spirit of the nation," Romantic thinkers including Fichte and Herder provided a reason for the state's being, and the Romantic view of national origin became intrinsic to the definition of what a nation is (see MacLulich, "Thematic" 22). Modern nation-states, including Canada, nourish the Romantic view of national culture as a sign of the spiritual bond between the nation and the people at the nation's origin, a bond that is "sacred, eternal, organic" and bears "a deeper justification than the works of men" (Chatterjee 18).[7]

Regardless of its European origins, the Romantic view would, ironically, provide the basis for later efforts to sever European ties. In Canada, as in other post-colonial contexts, "[t]he study of national traditions is the first and most vital stage of the process of rejecting the claims of the centre to exclusivity" (Ashcroft et al. 17); therefore, the nation's liberation is seen to depend to an extent on the existence of a separate, distinct national tradition. This liberationist or Enlightenment version of national origin, which is considered to be rooted both in the individual, egalitarian ideals of the French Revolution and in the collective, cultural identity of a people, has an impact on post-colonial nation-formation. National liberation means eliminating the colonial, or to use the masculinized version of the conventional "Mother-Child" colonial metaphor, the "paternal" culture (Surette, *passim*). The influence of British or American culture on national consciousness inspires national resistance and the particularly oppositional form of nation-building whereby the post-colonial nation attempts to rid itself of the dominating colonial power's influence. A national consciousness is required for such official and oppositional purposes.

Canadian national consciousness, in this sense, embraces the post-colonial type of resistance, describing the formation of a distinct national identity. Where history does not provide the circumstances requisite for a common heritage, an "official nationalism" can still be imposed on the people living in a state by an élite wishing to give the state legitimacy (Seton-Watson 148). Describing the North as a common heritage is one attempt to provide such an official narrative of national identity and unity. A national consciousness defined particularly as northern would cement the state's legitimacy by giving it the "deeper justification" required to be a nation. Myths of the north are part of specific Canadian nationalistic discourse that attempts to do this (Shields 162).

The Romantic and the Enlightenment definitions of where national culture originates are not mutually exclusive, for it is the originating story of the nation that justifies the pursuit of national independence in the Enlightenment sense. Such a dichotomy rests on the dual origin of the nation traced to both the Enlightenment and "the romantic and metaphorical tradition in political thought and history" (Bhabha, *Nation and Narration* 1). Yet, in his *Addresses to the German Nation* (1806–15), the Romantic thinker Fichte acknowledges the importance of resistance to the Roman Empire in defining the emerging German nation while also drawing on Herder's argument that language determines national consciousness (122–3). Although the German Romantics take the teleological position that the nation emerges from a shared national consciousness, the "deeper justification" manifested in culture and tradition, they also recognize the importance of politics and history.

Language, culture, and national consciousness are manifestations of the connection between the people, the land, and the nation, according to the Romantics; however, in settler nations such as Canada, the only plausible case of a so-called "organic" connection between people and the land can be for aboriginal people. To satisfy the romantic yearning for a spiritual connection between the nation's people, that is, the settlers, and the land, the "autochthonous claim to the land" belonging to aboriginal peoples is symbolically appropriated in various works of Canadian literature (Fee 18). Because Canadian national identity follows the dispossession of aboriginal people, both physically and symbolically, thinking about Canadian nationalism means thinking about race.

In Canada, where there are official languages and no national language, official culture and many different cultures, national consciousness has often been constructed according to the proposition that "climate and 'ecology' [have] a constitutive impact on culture and character" (Anderson 60). Language does not differentiate Canadian literature from British or American literature, so

nationalists look to place for that difference, and "[o]ur topogra-
phy, climate, and local history are recruited ... to establish the
imaginative distance" from European heritage (Surette, "Creating" 22; see also Kertzer 21). If the environment, the climate, the
place, are all that people in Canada really have in common, then
the influence of place or environment may be used to explain and
to justify the literature's distinct Canadian identity.[8] On this view,
the environment holds the transformative potential to condition
and form a distinct cultural identity, to facilitate acculturation, and
thus to bring political unity. In Canadian literary criticism, this
geographical determinism accounts, at least in part, for the continued interest in the north. In *The Bush Garden* (1971), Northrop
Frye refers to the wilderness and the North together when he
describes how individual identity is conditioned by the regional
environment. Throughout *The Bush Garden*, Frye grounds his reading of Canadian literature in the notion of a collective mythology
that emerges from the environment as reflected by the individual
writer's sensibility (199). "The imaginative Canadian stance, so to
speak," writes Frye, "facing east and west, has on one side one of
the most powerful nations in the world; on the other there is the
vast hinterland of the north, with its sense of mystery and fear of
the unknown" (iii). If the north has "long excited the imagination
of Canadians" (Coates and Morrison, *Purposes* 1), it has been with
that distant, fearful, terrific fascination.

Following in Frye's footsteps, thematic studies uncover patterns
in which the Arctic or the North are often metaphors for "nature"
or "the wilderness."[9] For example, Margaret Atwood's *Survival*
presents the northern environment as a likely setting for stories
of "the awful experience" that characterizes Canadian life (33).
More recently, in *Strange Things: The Malevolent North in Canadian
Literature* (1995), Atwood lampoons the idea of North: "In the
Canadian North of popular image, the Mounties with their bark-
ing dog teams relentlessly pursue madmen through the snow,
prospectors stumble raving out of the bush clutching their little
bags of gold-dust, jolly voyageurs rollick in their canoes, Indians
rescue hapless whites who get endlessly lost in the woods, wolves
devour lone hunters, or not as the case may be; Eskimos, ... well,
you get the picture" (8–9). Atwood's send-up of Northern tales,
however, is also an attempt to account for the symbolic significance it retains: "Canadians have long taken the North for granted,"

she remarks more seriously, "and we've invested a large percentage of our feelings about identity and belonging to it" (*Strange Things* 115). Other thematic studies claim, for instance, that "the Northern Imagination" is the "most exciting creative force in Canadian fiction – French and English" that dominates the "contemporary Canadian literary imagination, distinguishing it from that of other countries" (Mitcham 9, 11).

At the time when thematic criticism was gaining ground in the 1960s, the potential of the north's resources was already the focus of interest in public discourse, leading to concerns over Canadian territorial sovereignty. The north was increasingly described as a source of national wealth and heritage. While vestiges of the Romantic image remain in evidence, it has been gradually overshadowed by this "resource" myth, according to Shelagh Grant, or what Farley Mowat describes as the north's "cornucopia of riches," a myth that was celebrated by politicians throughout Canadian history ranging from members of the Canada First movement to the Diefenbaker Conservatives who were inspired by their leader's vision of "a Canada of the North." The focus of Canadian attention seems to turn northward specifically at moments of intense nationalist feeling. The North was a dominant theme immediately after Confederation, right after the First World War, and again from the 1960s to the mid-1970s when an explosion of publications on the north and the brief ascendancy of thematic criticism coincided with such national events as the Centennial and Expo '67. The specific definition of Canada as a northern nation may not dominate every moment in Canadian history, but it never seems to go away.

By the 1970s, scholars including Kenneth Coates, William Morrison, Shelagh Grant, and Morris Zaslow had exposed the Canadian government's relationship to the north as a neo-colonial one, stating that the "extensive powers of the national bureaucracy, the continued reliance on federal subsidies, and frequent federal intervention in regional affairs all make plain the north's colonial status" (Coates, *Canada's Colonies* 9), and thus signalling the importance of territorial sovereignty in the relationship between the Canadian nation and the so-called Canadian north. What academics remarked in their studies had already been fully assimilated in the public sector. Public discourse from the time of the construction of the Distant Early Warning System to the

voyage of the *Polar Sea* equates the far north, the Arctic in particular, with the outer limit of Canada as a sovereign state – Canada's
frontier – and nature conservationists, such as Mowat, with their
interest in saving "our common heritage," reinforce the connection
between possessing the north and being Canadian.[10]

In such arguments, the relationship of the Canadian north and
"Canada as north" seems transparent, as the "contiguity of the
northern wilderness to the experiences of Canadians" is believed
to have a "special, formative impact on their identity, particularly
as it has developed through their literature" (Senkpiel 135).
This special influence is a matter of emphasis. Why else should it
take precedence over the influence exerted by the United States
to the south, or that of the circumpolar, Pacific Rim, or Atlantic
coastal regions? Like F.R. Scott's poem "Mackenzie River," a
"river so Canadian / it turns its back / on America," emphasis
on the representation of the north and its transformation into an
imaginary frontier by intellectuals as diverse as historians, nature
conservationists, policy makers, and literary critics serves to differentiate Canada's national identity from that of other nations,
especially the United States and Britain.[11]

A sovereign nation must be united, independent, and distinct
from other nations in order to gain recognition *as* a nation. Like
the humanist subject, the nation's characteristics revealed in this
tautology tend to conform to features of traditionally defined
masculine identity. For example, when Louis-Édmond Hamelin
compares the north to "an irresistible itch, which implacably drives
the man to mobility" (9), he describes and reproduces the masculine character of northern narrative. In such stories, "[c]ourage and
strength are needed for survival: this fosters a romantic admiration
for heroic qualities" which are thought to be "encouraged by rigorous northern conditions" (Morley 25). Because having a rugged,
individualistic national character means fulfilling the ideological
requirement for the independence that creates nations, the representation of the north as a source of national identity can be
described as emerging from the ideology of nationhood possessing
culture, language, and consciousness. By elevating a masculinist,
engendered north to the position of "national consciousness," writers and critics enhance Canada's status as a nation while playing
a unifying role in official national discourse.

It is not unusual that "Canadian" literary criticism has been
primarily concerned with matters of national identity and culture,

or that this concern has had a Romantic aspect. As T.D. MacLulich argues, the ideas of the German Romantics are so deeply ingrained in the concept of nation and national literature in Canada that "we hardly notice how pervasively they colour our approach to literary studies" ("Thematic" 21; see also Kertzer; Lecker, *Making*). Therefore, representation which at first appears to present an authentic, mimetic account of the relationship between Canadians and the north must be considered within the context of political ideology.

The relationship of literature to the nation is deeply conflicted and historically contingent. According to Benedict Anderson, readership forms "the embryo of the nationally imagined community" (44). Although the relationship between readership and citizenry is not transparent, as "imagined communities," nations "depend for their existence on an apparatus of cultural fictions in which imaginative literature plays a decisive role" (Brennan 49). Anderson and his followers demonstrate how these cultural fictions differ in content but not in form. Thus, regardless of the substance of stories people tell in order to imagine life as a nation, what those stories say about the nation will always be the same. It will show the attributes that make it worthy of the name and the place in the world order it will secure.

The national model of literary study which organizes literatures by national origin or affiliation suggests a teleological relationship between literature and the nation. Inevitably, national literatures reflect what Robert Lecker calls the assumption "that valuable writing underwrites a national-referential aesthetic" that forges "the connection between writing, culture, and nation" (*Making* 4).[12] This aesthetic resonates with the belief that "every self-respecting nation ought to have its own linguistic and cultural identity" (MacLulich, "Thematic" 19). Within literary studies, attempting to define national consciousness helps to carve out a place for Canadian literature as a subject worthy of study. Such attempts tend to be self-fulfilling, for as long as literary criticism deals with something called Canadian literature, it simultaneously constitutes the "consciously nationalist criticism," one that gives "a convincing rationale for making Canadian literature a separate field of academic inquiry" (MacLulich, "Thematic" 18).

National literatures arise from the discovery of national characteristics, that is, from their own definition. In order for there to be a national literature, there must be characteristics unifying the literature within its national boundaries and distinguishing it from other national literatures; in this way, the emphasis on national culture in Canadian literary criticism signals the endurance of the Romantic ideal. When Northrop Frye concludes that the *Literary History of Canada* (1965) is a "collection of essays in cultural history" (822), he confirms that, if the terms "literary" and "cultural" are not exactly synonymous, their meaning is deeply related. The persistence of the "national-referential aesthetic" seems to bear out Frye's observation. Frye's structuralism, his analysis of myth, his devotion to the pattern of things, was easily assimilated by the generation of literary critics and writers interested in discovering indigenous ways of thinking about Canadian literature. Their search for a Canadian way of life transcending our differences was, as Frye had observed, a cultural pursuit.

This focus on culture has generated an ethnographic impulse in Canadian literary criticism.[13] By placing national culture at the centre of critical inquiry, Canadian literary critics treat Canadian literature as a body of texts that has something to say about Canadian people. In this very broad sense, Canadian literary criticism functions as a form of ethnography, that is, as writing believed to describe a distinct people. This ethnographic impulse may help to account for some similarities between ethnographic and literary studies of the Canadian north. Contemporary writing about the north is deeply influenced by ethnographic theory and method, and the cultural critique offered by contemporary works blends literary and ethnographic theory. A basic ethnographic impulse also underwrites northern studies because much of the writing is ethnographic in focus and because the writing traces a distinction between insiders and outsiders. As a result, northern studies tends to spatialize difference by comparing oppositional terms: inside and outside, north and south, northerners and southerners, us and them.

In particular, the distinction between "real" and "imagined" north has led to the assumption that only real first-hand experience in the geographical north authorizes one to speak about the discursive or imagined North. Talking about "experience" of or in the north claims epistemic privilege. In Linda Alcoff's terms, this use of experience is seen to *determine*, not just *bear upon*, epistemic salience. In this regard, it reflects the importance of experience to the emerging voices of dispossessed peoples in

Canada, First Nations and aboriginal peoples in particular. Spatializing difference in the distinction between the "inside" and "outside," or north and south, suggests that the boundary between them can be crossed. Thus, southern Canadians gain special insight by the experience of going north. Even if the experience is not held to be equivalent to that of inhabitants such as aboriginal peoples, the two are in competition for discursive space. In this way, "experience" as a general concept depends on the articulated experiences of cultural others. Yet, it is hardly conceivable that those who hold up the authority of first-hand experience consciously intend to usurp the experience of northern inhabitants. Northern studies can be "border work" mediating between racial and cultural differences in ways that promote greater autonomy for aboriginal peoples; however, it can also become a fenced-in territory guarded by experienced gatekeepers.

As James Clifford observes, "it is difficult to say very much about experience... Like 'intuition' one has it or not, and its invocation often smacks of mystification" ("On Ethnographic Authority" 128). Despite the opacity of the concept, "experience" unites a variety of discourses. It is the foundation of postmodern ethnography's claim to address power in anthropological inquiry. It is the basis of identity politics. It is also the basis of the weak liberalism that manifests itself as a constant and ultimately universalist self-positioning. As aboriginal voices gain strength, they are concerned with the articulation of experience as aboriginal people. In northern studies, "experience as" a northern inhabitant – and the majority of northern inhabitants are aboriginal – is considered to have the greatest epistemic value while "experience in" the north is next best. The understanding of "experience as" has also led to a general interest in "experience as such." Self-positioning and reflexivity become the stock of critical discourse, and speakers gain epistemic privilege through experience *in* the north rather than experience *as* a northern inhabitant. Thus, authority turns on the epistemic privilege of the cultural insider even when the individual is in fact an outsider. The slippage between "experience as" and "experience in" flattens the epistemic distinction in a way that de-emphasizes racial and cultural differences. Moreover, this flattening justifies the claim that national identity provides the position from which northern experience is best understood. This claim underpins most arguments for the north as part of national heritage, and it emerges from the distinction of "myth" and "reality" permeating northern studies.

Returning to Wiebe's remarks, this longing for experience can be understood as a desire for authenticity. As long as Canadians remain unconscious of their "true nature," Wiebe argues, we will "always be wishing ourselves something we aren't" (111). On this view, Canadian identity is a matter of appreciating who we really are by knowing who we really are not, in this case, Hawaiians, Floridans, or Caribbeans (which may be news to Canadians originating from those places). The idea of a "true nature," like a "true north," confronts the "dilemma of all those who long for authenticity" by identifying with the wilderness and/or Native people: "they can only be real, in their own terms, by turning themselves into something they are 'really' not" (Atwood, *Strange Things* 57).

The inside-outside distinction between those who have experience and those who do not rests on the notion of separate and stable cultures. In anthropology, mediating the inside-outside distinction is the primary goal of fieldwork and initiation. In the post-structuralist environment of literary criticism, however, Foucault's insight that there can be no "outside," that the critic is always inside and outside discourse at the same time, frees the critic from the initiation dilemma. The effect, paradoxically, is a transcendent position. Although some critics limit claims for the epistemic relevance of experience and question related concepts such as accuracy and authenticity, they retain its privilege too. This tendency is particularly noticeable in more recent literary studies in which the grounding of textual authority in northern experience is accompanied by appeals to the authority of post-structural theorists. Given that the grounding of textual authority in first-hand experience suggests a direct correspondence between text and the real, this is a curious pairing.[14]

The reason for this kind of inconsistency may have something to do with the recent rush to embrace postmodern insights. "Post-modernism's accusation against modernism is that it is a liar;" observes Yvonna S. Lincoln, "it promised us truth, but delivered thickly veiled polemic tracts in the name of science" (37). The postmodern condition, understood as a general incredulity, presents a valuable avenue of critique although in practice it presents certain difficulties. Once postmodern critiques revealed realism to be a set of conventions and practices crafted to hold up truth claims, the way was open to new conventions and practices that would dispense with truth claims altogether. As Michael Taussig observes in *Mimesis and Alterity* (1993), the brilliance of the postmodern insight was so blinding that "the beginnings of knowledge were made to pass for actual knowledge" as everywhere, "social constructions, inventions, and representations" were exposed and analysed (xvi).

One response to these developments has been a celebration of textual construction as postmodern writers enthusiastically embrace the self-conscious style marked by reflexivity and intertextuality. In a move that resembles the postmodernist turn in ethnography, recent writing about the North eschews realism by emphasizing intertextuality, self-reflexivity, and dialogics, literary elements associated with postmodernism. Postmodernist writers tend to view an epistemic stance grounded in realism with suspicion and to self-consciously construct an imagined North in the interests of demystifying the geographical north. The result, however, tends to be further mystification. While the anti-realist stance may be liberating for the individual writer, it tends to undermine the distinction between real and imagined worlds that underscores the authority of field experience and on which the critique of realist representation is founded. The tension between desiring to promote greater knowledge of the north and its inhabitants and adhering to forms of representation that put in doubt the very existence of that knowledge permeates postmodern writing.

Moreover, the postmodern celebration of construction, invention, and representation suggests that, as long as readers understand that a text is those things, almost anything goes. However, it is difficult to believe, as many of these writers would have it, that readers ever mistake realist representation for reality itself or that they only understand the difference if it is self-consciously presented by the text. "Only a naive reader would turn to literature for an accurate and authentic rendering of the real," argues John Moss. "Literature gets at truth by other means" ("From Frankenstein" 34). While this is true, what happens when "accuracy" and "authenticity" in literary representation are abandoned is a choice between naive credulity and anything-goes relativism, neither of which offers an ethical approach. Even though, as Taussig reminds us, we forget what we know about the arbitrariness of representation in order to get on with everyday life, that arbitrariness is no excuse for making everything we see in our own images, and it is certainly no excuse for speaking on behalf of others.

There is another reason "why realism matters," as Paisley Livingston argues: readers who pick up a text about a "real" place they have never seen or a "real" people they do not know do so with the belief that they might find out something they do not know, something about what "actually" is. As a result, even if these terms must be carefully mediated, literature holds an epistemic value that entails a responsibility to "the real" because the expectations surrounding realism remain strong.[15] The epistemic stance grounded in philosophical realism that Livingston maintains leads to all sorts of hoary methodological problems. How do we adjudicate the "realism" of an account? What constitutes evidence? What is authenticity? These are difficult questions. Yet, if we are committed to the ethical representation of differences, we are bound to grapple with them. To understand texts as both constructed and responsible to the world outside the text is to realize the ethical and political dimensions of the mimetic function.

The preoccupation with experience means focusing on the cultural relevance of the north in Canada rather than its political relevance. This is a hazard of the ethnographic impulse in Canadian studies generally, but it is also the result of a more general anthropological approach to cultural others. Because aboriginal groups are currently viewed by the mainstream as cultural rather than political entities, the ethnographic view of aboriginal peoples dominates. By concentrating on culture rather than politics, very real inequalities in power can be softened. From the perspective of the dominant culture, this is convenient. In a plural society, cultural differences can always be tolerated and assimilated without conceding much power while political differences cannot.

As the following chapters show, an analysis of gender is a useful method to address issues of political power and difference. Representations of the imaginary North have frequently depended on concepts that are defined by a masculine-feminine opposition. As a geographical location, the north provides writers with the setting for quest narratives and heroic tales of survival. Such stories require their characters to attain qualities traditionally, though not exclusively, associated with masculine identity, including self-reliance, autonomy, and physical endurance. By having these qualities, the individual embraces and embodies the northern "spirit" or "character." A national consciousness shaped by the North tends to encompass the same qualities of rugged, masculine identity. Thus, in writing depicting the north, identity takes on specifically gendered characteristics. These characteristics do not necessarily correspond to sexual difference but to mutually exclusive definitions of gender based on an obsessive reiteration of certain characteristics: independence, strength, individuality as masculine; dependence, weakness, collectivity as feminine. The contingency of both gender and race becomes apparent when these characteristics are studied closely: for example, the gender characteristics of women are often applied to men of non-white races. Tracing these ideas through Canadian literary history clarifies their contemporary usage.

Because the mythology of the North involves representation that draws figures and tropes of gender characteristics, demythologizing the north means rereading these literary elements in light of their historical contexts in order to point out the political and ethical issues arising from the representation of gender difference. This analysis of gender difference follows from the "images of women" criticism which helped inaugurate the second wave of feminism; however, it is informed by the evolution of materialist and Marxist accounts that look to a variety of cultural products for indications of how gender is constituted at a given time. From this point of view, gender is a "complex convention" (Di Stefano 3) that is historically and culturally contingent, or more precisely, a form of ideology (de Lauretis, *Technologies* 9; Di Stefano 56). By turning to these definitions, feminists mark "a shift from the women-centred investigations of the 1970s" to "the study of gender relations involving both women and men" (Showalter 2). Given the persistence of mutually exclusive ways of defining genders, the inclusion of men and "masculinity" in feminist critique was inevitable, for as long as what men and women are is socially constructed through the obsessive differentiation of masculine and feminine characteristics, it will be necessary to critique their binary relation.

In what Sherrill E. Grace describes as "the dominant masculinist tradition of Canadian northern narrative" that is "at once masculinist and racist," the stark masculine-feminine opposition begs a number of questions ("Gendering" 169). Why does the rugged individualism, self-sufficiency, and toughness of a masculine hero require the passivity, silence, and frailty of someone other than the hero, usually women, the landscape, or racial others? Why is it that when others display masculinist characteristics, the representation is considered "subversive"? Why is it that gender and race are yoked together? The history of northern representation, as Grace argues, issues in a "northern narrative of nation" which is "a distinctly Canadian identity comprising hardy, virile masculinity, intellectual, spiritual, and racial superiority (of white, northern European stock), and imperialist authority" ("Gendering" 165). By identifying a "counter-discourse" in which women revise and re-present the tradition of northern heroism, Grace raises the question of whether or not this response can redeem northern representation. Such narratives intervene in the processes of social ascription and cultural practice that assign gender, and undermine the relationship between gender and biological sex, yet their political value has yet to be determined. By simply going north, as Grace acknowledges, a feminist counter-narrative may do little to change the dominant narrative except for giving women access to it. A position structured around opposition can resist the thing it opposes, and perhaps replace it, but its possibilities tend to be limited.

Because gender is a form of ideology, its meaning is never stable; therefore, both "masculinist" and "feminist" narratives are subject to historical and cultural flux. What matters is the meaning these terms take on in a particular context. In the history of northern representation, masculinity is part of the culture of imperialism and nation-building that continues to influence that representation. The new men's studies is useful for explicating the political and social forces contributing to this culture. While the so-called men's movement ranges from masculinist consciousness-raising, in the work of critics such as Victor Seidler, to the New Age misogyny of Robert Bly and his cohort, pioneering critiques of masculinity, such as Andrew Tolson's *The Limits of Masculinity: Male Identity and the Liberated Woman* (1977), acknowledge both the origin of men's studies in attempts to understand the Women's Liberation movement as well as the men's movement's continuing debt to feminism. Like many feminists, Tolson defines gender as the cultural significance of sexuality, a historically and culturally specific significance with political as well as social implications (11). While this definition of the sex-gender distinction accommodates neither the critiques of gender essentialism advanced in queer theory nor the psychoanalytic accounts of how the formation of gender in language precedes the social, its insistence on the formation of social groups and the inclusion of subjects within them may better serve the purposes of this study. In contrast to approaches in which "gender is primarily constructed through the acquisition of language, rather than through social ascription or cultural practice" (Showalter 3), this study focuses not on what makes a person acquire gender but on how existing conventions shape the understanding of gender, that is, not how the person learns to see and be in the world, but how the world sees the person. To that end, the historical differences in the way gender is imagined offer evidence of its construction. For those who study it in these terms, gender is a form of representation, a representation of sexual identity; it has a relationship to biological sex, but is not identical to it. In these terms, forms of "social ascription" may be understood by studying gender both in and as representation. The idea of gender as "performance" and "convention" grounds the comparison with the ideology of north, for as W.H. New remarks in *Land Sliding* (1997), both "the North" and "the Arctic" are conventions, and separate ones, too (119).

The broad definition of gender as social ideology makes it possible to compare gender to other political and social discourses such as nationalism. The relationship between national and gender identity can be traced through three striking correspondences (Parker et al. 5, *passim*). First, as concepts of identity, both articulate relations with others. As relational terms, gender and national identity are derived from their "inherence in a system of differences" (Parker et al. 5) and function to explain and, sometimes, to contain difference. National identity can smooth over unruly constituents within a state by creating a sense of belonging to a community and sharing a common heritage. Ernest Renan first defined the nation in these terms in "Qu'est-ce qu'une nation?" (1882) when he stressed the importance of shared suffering and sacrifice in constituting the nation: "Une nation est donc une grande solidarité, constituée par le sentiment des sacrifices qu'on a faits et de ceux qu'on est disposé à faire encore" (904). The self-sacrifice necessary to achieve such solidarity overcomes differences in rituals such as "dying for one's country," a historically gendered activity that is also "a distinctive form of male bonding" (Parker et al. 6).

Second, national belonging expressed as self-sacrifice has been represented in terms of friendship and love, which are also important

terms in discussions of gender. Benedict Anderson writes that
"the nation is always conceived as a deep horizontal comradeship" (7), and George Mosse demonstrates how that particular
kind of relationship emerged from the eighteenth-century cult of
male friendship (*Nationalism* 30). According to Mosse, European
nationalism "co-opted the male search for friendship and community" in the eighteenth and nineteenth centuries, appropriating
male friendship and manly beauty as symbols of national identity
throughout Europe (76–7, 90). Although the *fraternité* at the heart
of the nation emerges from a representation of the nation as a
collective bond of love which is male-centred but empty of explicit
sexual content, the relationship between the individual and the
nation can be emotional, even erotic; indeed, in his eighth address,
Fichte clearly eroticizes the relationship of the individual to the
nation in order to transcend the erotic when he describes the
nation as an eternal, sacred community, using love as a metaphor:
"Love that is truly love, and not a mere transitory lust, never
clings to what is transient; only in the eternal does it awaken and
become kindled, and there alone does it rest" (117). Literature
celebrating the nation expresses patriotic feeling as a pure love,
and almost any time "the nation is invoked – whether it be in the
media, in scholarly texts, or in every day conversation – we are
more likely than not to find it couched as a love of country: an
eroticized nationalism" (Parker et al. 1). When Carl Berger describes
the nineteenth-century notion that "Canada's unique character
derived from *her* northern location, severe winters and *her* heritage of 'northern races'" (5; emphasis added), he points to the
eroticization of the citizens' relationship to the nation.

Finally, the most significant correspondence between national
and gender identities concerns their expression as politics.
Because "nation-ness is the most universally legitimate value in
the political life of our time" (Anderson 3), especially in calls for
independence and unity, it informs the tactical use of opposition
which is common to all political movements; nationalist politics
"acts as the normative mode of the political as such," so any movement, including those concerned with gender issues, like feminist
and queer movements, will be expected and even "constrained to
take on a nationalist expression as a prerequisite for being considered 'political'" (Radhakrishnan 78). The "immense political
freight" carried by the nation means that "disenfranchised groups

frequently have had to appeal to national values precisely to register their claims as political" (Parker et al. 8). Becoming legitimate in this way is as acute for historically subjugated groups within states, such as those represented by feminist or queer activists, as it is for newly independent states.

The political weight the nation carries as perhaps *the* form of political expression in the twentieth century is nowhere more obvious than in those post-colonial states where, to use Partha Chatterjee's terms, national thought is a derivative discourse (8) that allows the emerging state to find its own place in the world order (168).[16] Because the nation is primarily an ideological concept (Chatterjee 40), imagining specific traits of national consciousness suggests the fulfilment, albeit teleologically, of the nation's ideological requirement for independence and autonomy. The Canadian state sometimes calls upon the notion of a Canadian nation for this reason. The state's need for independence or for unity requires nationalism (Seton-Watson 3); therefore, states aspiring to one of these goals must call upon their status as nations, which is justified by the identification of national consciousness and culture. Renan's definition of the nation as people united by what they have in common resurfaces in the distinction between a state, which is "a legal and political organization, with the power to require obedience and loyalty from its citizens," and a nation, which is "a community of people, whose members are bound together by a sense of solidarity, a common culture, a national consciousness" (Seton-Watson 1).

Even though the nation continues to describe the form the political takes, nations no longer enjoy the sovereign power that nation status once conferred; however, the nation retains conceptual value even as the political power of actual nations declines. With globalization, the issue is no longer the sovereignty of nations, or even peoples: the issue is the future of nations and peoples faced with globalization. With the effective demise of the nation-state through global capitalism (Readings 13, *passim*), sovereignty is increasingly seen to derive from culture. Yet, the issues attached to national literatures and canon-formation seem trivial if not entirely beside the point to an emerging world order in which national myths are becoming meaningless.

Canadian cultural nationalism is a way of creating political unity and legitimacy in a state made up of unruly and diverse ways of being, by imagining what all Canadians share. The myths of the north are and have been a vital source of national character or consciousness. Glenn Gould's original phrase, "the Idea of North," like the composition it comes from, evokes the complex value "North" has in Canadian culture,[17] encompassing geographical, historical, political, and ideological layers of meaning. By uncovering some of these layers, I hope to confront the issues and problems arising from the historiography and literary history of the north, issues and problems which are also fundamental to the position of culture in Canadian studies.

The cultural relevance of the north for Canada is the main subject of this study. Writing about the north is dispersed over many disciplinary and historical contexts and shows an impressive intertextuality, necessitating the interdiscipline of northern studies. Yet, interdisciplinary studies are always susceptible to the problem Paul Rabinow describes: "There is a curious time lag as concepts move across disciplinary boundaries. The moment when the historical profession is discovering cultural anthropology in the (unrepresentative) person of Clifford Geertz is just the moment when Geertz is being questioned in anthropology" (241). In the argument that follows, tracing this time lag in the representation of the north reveals the diversity and contingency of ideas about gender, racial, and national identities. From the Victorian adventure story to postmodern travel writing, the representation of the north features many heroes who exist outside society, a position which can only be sustained by constant flight. In some cases, the hero's opposition to the dark feminine forces of nature or to feminized cultural others signals the opposition of masculine and feminine which comes to define the northern hero and his quest. Postmodern parodying of the quest and the masculinity it defines reaffirms this opposition while seeking to subvert it. In this, the northern hero bears a similarity to the theoretical masculine individual, always aspiring to something that cannot be attained.[18] As textual analysis shows, the inscription of traditionally defined masculinity depends on the exclusion or the opposition of the feminine, represented as the other, the unknown, the wilderness; for this reason, the construction of borders between masculine and feminine infuses the thematic and formal dimensions of Canadian writing on the north. In general, representations of the north trace the binary formation of gender, defining it in terms of opposition.

Any study of this kind requires choices. My first was the decision to study experience, and therefore to emphasize ethnographic rather than aesthetic features of literary representation by discussing it in the context of social science. This decision was made, in part, in recognition of the considerable work on aesthetic features of literature about the north by critics, including I.S. MacLaren, Sherrill E. Grace, and John Moss,[19] as well as the numerous comprehensive studies of Canadian literature that offer insights on the aesthetics of literature about the north. In keeping with my interest in the ethnographic impulse, I selected works from the genres in which I considered it to be strongest: autobiography, ethnography, fiction (including short fiction, novels, and poetry), historiography, life writing, and travel writing as well as texts that cross these generic boundaries. Within and across these genres, the range of techniques from realism to postmodernism reflects the philosophical and historical context of the text. While this approach and the list of genres indicate the interdisciplinary nature of this study, the range of disciplines and cultural products discussed has been restricted somewhat. I have, with a few exceptions, excluded drama, film, hypertext, music, television, and visual arts, knowing that these forms receive attention elsewhere in northern studies. In choosing texts from the genres listed, I have also been selective. While readers will find a broad range of texts discussed in this study, there are many books that I would have liked to include but, regrettably, have had to leave out.

In chapter 1, recognizing that critical appraisals of literature representing the Canadian north have concentrated on aesthetic features and influences to the virtual exclusion of the impact social and scientific disciplines have had on it,[20] I analyse ethnographies written about the people inhabiting different parts of the north, exploring how each text constructs gender both in its depiction of the subject culture and in its construction of the ethnographer's subjectivity. Because ethnography influences the representation of the north both as a source of information that writers draw on and as a model that writers can emulate, it announces many of the characteristics of the representation of the north observed in other genres. Gender becomes a function of ethnographic authority with the establishment of fieldwork as the test of the anthropologist, a pattern which is reflected in the representation of gender roles in the subject culture. Fieldwork requires an initiation into the subject culture which is not only expressed in sexual terms as "penetration" of the culture, but also recalls the quest pattern characteristic of masculine initiation. The ethnographer, regardless of his or her sex, must be masculinized in order to enter and dominate the subject culture, which is thereby feminized – even though, paradoxically, the subject culture may then be depicted as male-oriented. Within anthropology, ethnography becomes and must be overcome as a discourse of homosocial relations, in the words of Trinh T. Minh-ha, a dialogue of "speaking man to man."

Chapter 2 further explores the inside-outside distinction in ethnography by looking at the images of aboriginal people, specifically the Inuit, presented in a variety of genres. Although ethnography represents Inuit culture as under constant threat of physical extinction and as having a gendered division of labour that is necessary for survival, Inuit self-representation in oral and written form does not support many of the facts reported by ethnographers. Inuit writers, especially Inuit autobiographers, record experiences that ethnography either ignores or understates, providing important information to counter the often limited perspective of ethnography. Autobiography accomplishes this revision by fusing personal and political concerns. Gender roles as represented in ethnographic representation are disputed in Inuit writing, which alters the received view that Inuit women are made subservient by the division of labour, and counters the image of the silent Inuit woman that permeates literature, especially fiction, set in the north.

Chapter 3 considers the literary roots of ideas of race and gender that cut across the border of ethnographic and literary representation. In the nineteenth century, ideas such as the racial and moral superiority of northern white people and the physical superiority of men were strongly represented in adventure narratives in which the feminine is either absent or decorative. In northern adventure settings, usually in the Arctic, boys are initiated into all-male communities by accomplishing a series of physical tasks and occasionally by uniting with aboriginal people, either by befriending another boy who helps accomplish the tasks or by becoming embroiled in an erotic triangle including an aboriginal girl. In adventure stories of the period, representations of women or of the feminine are formed in opposition to representations of men. Similar opposition can be found in more recent novels and travel writing about the north.

Chapter 4 returns to the impact of ethnography on the demythologizing and remythologizing of the north in Canadian literature. In travel writing and other forms used by writers who have travelled in the north, the influence of ethnographic texts and theory emphasizes the blurring of genres characteristic of the postmodernist turn. This influence accounts for the emphasis on individual experience, such as fieldwork, as well as the careful attention to storytelling techniques. In the texts examined, a tension lingers between a strong realist strain of representation concerned with articulating the experience of the true north and a postmodernist strain that seeks to destabilize the representation of reality. The epilogue considers the implications of this study for understanding "Canadian culture" and offers some final observations about Canadian cultural nationalism and the role of the north within it. As part of a unifying, national discourse, the north figures in the stories Canadians tell about themselves, and how they imagine the nation is reflected in images representing the north.

The study of the north is primarily thematic, and most works, whether in literature, history, or culture, begin from the belief that the north, in both its geographical and discursive meanings, belongs to Canadians. I believe, on the contrary, that the north has little if anything to do with being Canadian today. Or, at least, its relevance to the majority of Canadians is obscure, a fact that seems to be supported by the many northern studies arguing that the north should be *placed* at the centre of national mythology. Unlike those who call for national awareness of the north, I do not believe that lack of interest in the north means that Canadians have lost a sense of their "true" identity, only that the ideas of culture and national identity at the base of such calls cannot adequately account for the variety of Canadian experiences.

Therefore, I do not wish to defend the claim that literary representation of the north articulates a northern character that all Canadians share. This definition of national identity is severely limited because it rests on the specious notion of national consciousness.[21] I hope to show how the "Canadian identity" based on literary representations of a supposedly northern character is inflected by historically contingent ideas of gender, race, and nation. The representation of the north is a way of imagining the Canadian nation, and as such, it requires analysis that treats it as primarily ideological, especially as it bears on identity.

As more Canadian writers choose to travel north and to write about it, there has been a shift away from the romantic individualism inherent in the quest motif and frontier imagery towards a (Romantic) search for a collective identity. The "true north" sought in these non-fictional, first-person accounts endeavours to place the north at the centre of the would-be national consciousness. The fundamental problem with this view of Canadian literature and, by extension, Canadian identity, is that it is constructed through ideas tainted by reactionary history.

It is important to understand the persistence of nationalist myths like northern consciousness in order to unsettle the stance that spatializes difference in order to reclaim it within the nationalist discourse. Such a stance undermines the kind of nation-to-nation relationship that has led to the emergence of Nunavut. For these reasons, I question the definition of Canada as a northern nation and Canadians as a northern people by showing how this aspect of Canadian cultural history works to unify and to shape experience into a collective identity irrespective of meaningful differences, rather than to create a place inhabited by citizens who have different cultural, racial, gender, and national identities.

CHAPTER ONE

Speaking Man to Man: Ethnography and the Representation of the North

This chapter describes how ethnography creates ideal masculine communities, and explores the extent to which engendering the subject, in this case the north, inheres in ethnographic practice. Although the selected ethnographic monographs concern people who have been classified as Arctic (Inuit) and Sub-Arctic (Innu, Beaver), what is striking is the influence these works, taken together, have had on imagining a north and northern peoples. Like "the Native," the people of the "North" are not always differentiated from each other in literary representation but treated as having one pan-northern identity. It is this uneasy relation between the specificity of distinct cultures and the general description of northern experience that ethnographers have now made central to theoretical inquiry.

ETHNOGRAPHIC AUTHORITY

Although most ethnographers continue to adhere to the realist conventions developed around the traditional fieldwork model, contemporary ethnographic theory has been troubled by what Kamala Visweswaran calls the "'writing culture' critique of anthropological representation" (591): that is, a focus on issues concerning the production of texts, including the problem of what constitutes textual authority. The following discussion of the new or experimental ethnography shows how most experimental approaches explore textual authority while ignoring how that authority is inflected by gender. That ethnographers, both realist and experimental, construct an ideal of masculinity in their descriptions of the subject culture demonstrates how using certain gendered characteristics is an important component of ethnographic authority. Exposing these characteristics helps to explain why gender differences in other cultures are interpreted as they are by ethnographers and points to some common ways in which ideas of the Canadian north are engendered.

In 1982, George Marcus and Dick Cushman published a historical overview of ethnographic practice entitled "Ethnographies as Texts," an inaugural study in the writing culture critique.[1] Calling for a "rhetorical awareness" that would lead to a critical inquiry into the practice of ethnography (58), they outline the way in which "the traditional boundary between factual and fictional modes of writing has been severely strained" (33) in contemporary works. Storytelling – a fictional mode – had begun to blend with anthropological facts as ethnographers became increasingly aware of their position and authority within the narrative, and self-reflexivity became a tool in the rejection of the omniscient narrator of early ethnography.

Clifford Geertz broke with the early positivist tradition by describing ethnography as a "stratified hierarchy of meaningful structures," which is "produced, perceived, and interpreted" by the observer ("Thick Description" 7).[2] But in arguing the social construction of the subject culture, which his positivist predecessors had not, he overlooked the same process at work in the constitution of the observer's culture: others are in the process of being constructed, but the ethnographer arrives fully formed as an individual.[3] By consciously imitating storytelling, experimental ethnographers go even further than Geertz does by recognizing the role their subjectivity has always had in the establishment of textual authority.

To appreciate the challenge posed by the new ethnography, or what has been called the postmodernist turn in ethnography, it is necessary to define the tradition of ethnographic realism that the new or postmodern ethnography claims to replace. Ethnography is a young genre. The term seems to have been translated from the French *ethnographie*, where it appeared in the work of linguist Adrien Balbi as early as 1826, although the *Penny Cyclopedia* (1834) cites the word as deriving from German, translating it as "nation-formation." *Science and Religion* (1836) refers to the "ethnographic family," and the term "ethnography" itself first appears in the English language in James C. Prichard's *Natural History of Man* (1842). Ethnography seems to have emerged in a number of disciplines simultaneously, including geography, linguistics, and anthropology, as the name for writing that describes groups of people.

North American ethnography came into its own in the nineteenth century as a direct result of cultural contact with aboriginal peoples, touching disciplines as varied as geography, law, medicine, and geology. Early ethnographers came from these and other disciplines and professions, and ethnography developed as the 'writing up' of notes taken while doing their jobs. Henry R. Schoolcraft, an American Indian agent, was one of the first of these men to turn his attention to ethnology and ethnography full-time. Another early ethnographer, Lewis Henry Morgan, used his training as a lawyer in his description of Iroquois institutions, *League of the Iroquois* (1851). Influenced by the prevailing assumption that Indians and their cultures were vanishing forever, these and other writers rushed to learn as much as they could. From these interdisciplinary beginnings, ethnography gradually became the specialized writing of scholars trained in anthropology, and by the end of the nineteenth century, largely due to the influence of Franz Boas, it was the focus of rigorous standardization. The conventions of ethnographic realism, as it came to be known, were established at this time in order to distinguish ethnography from other forms of writing.[4]

Ethnographic realism resembles its literary counterpart only to the extent that both are concerned with matters of accuracy and truth in representation; in literary terms, ethnographic realism is actually closer to the nineteenth-century concept of naturalism.[5] Its accepted conventions emerged with the appearance of the fieldwork model, especially the fieldworker's attempt to provide an account of the whole world or form of life under study (Marcus and Cushman 29). Anxious to distinguish their genre from popular works by travel writers, nineteenth-century ethnographers developed a detached, authoritative narrative tone, intended to resemble scientific discourse.

One of the conventions of ethnographic realism was the "marked absence" of the narrator as a first-person presence and the use of the omniscient third-person point of view, "manifest only as a dispassionate, camera-like observer" (Marcus and Cushman 32). As Marcus and Cushman point out, the third-person point of view "heightens the sense of objectivity projected by the text" while it "helps to sever the relationship between what the ethnographer knows and how he came to know it" (32). Thus, early ethnography created a paradox wherein the style of writing obscures the field-worker's experience even though fieldwork experience forms the foundation for the authority of the account. Anthropologist Sally Cole describes how writing acceptable ethnography still involves this alienating "discursive shift" from the "personal, subjective, and sensual experience" of fieldwork to the "post-field experience of producing a scientific monograph" whose "authority 'resides in the absolute effacement of the speaking and experiencing subject'" (121; see also Moore, "Interior" 127–8).

Other characteristics of ethnographic realism that developed with the increasingly central role of fieldwork include suppression of the individual in favour of the whole, organization of the text by cultural unit, generalization, use of jargon, and exegesis (Marcus and Cushman 32–6). These specific techniques are incorporated in the four common realist conventions identified in the analysis of Franz Boas and Diamond Jenness later in this chapter: 1) the absence of the author from the text; 2) the emphasis on minute detail described in documentary style; 3) the description of the "Native point of view"; and 4) the interpretive omnipotence of the fieldworker, which ethnographer John Van Maanen calls the "godlike pose."[6] Each convention asserts the central authority of the ethnographer as the one who obtains and communicates the truth about the culture in the most accurate way possible.

Ethnographic realism camouflages representational techniques by leaving the author out of the text. In this way, it resembles the marginal positivist strain of epistemology which, Lorraine Code points out, depends on excluding anything outside its own paradigm in order to make truth claims (16–17). Code's critique targets academic philosophy concerned with epistemology, but a similar process of exclusion operates in other academic disciplines as well. The result is an illusion of certainty, the "godlike pose" or, as Donna Haraway calls it, the "god-trick" (*Simians* 191). Craig Owens' critique of realist aesthetics, "Representation, Appropriation and Power," is that the resulting mystification supports an authoritative claim to truth. Filmmaker and critic Trinh T. Minh-ha raises the same issue in *When the Moon Waxes Red* (1991), summarizing her position with a call for critical reading: "By putting representation under scrutiny, textual theory-practice has more likely helped upset rooted ideologies by bringing the mechanics of their workings to the fore. It makes possible the vital differentiation between authoritative criticism and uncompromising analyses and inquiries" (42; see 38). As Norman K. Denzin notes, "Trinh seeks to undo the entire realist ethnographic project which is connected to such terms as lived experience, authenticity, verisimilitude, truth, knowledge, facts, and fictions" (59). By unmasking authoritative texts by understanding the assumptions underpinning authority, including the supposed transparency of ethnographic realism, Trinh does not assume that "rooted ideologies" are stable, homogeneous, and unified sources of power; rather, she argues that they may not be what they seem.

The innovations of postmodern ethnography target these issues by calling attention to the constructed nature of all descriptive accounts and by challenging the idea of ethnography as simply the "writing up" of fieldnotes. Advocates of the new ethnography, such as James Clifford, call for the demystification of the narrator's authority through dialogue, intertextuality, and self-referentiality: the new ethnographer, in other words, poses as a storyteller who stresses his own subjectivity in an attempt to expose his authority over the text and the subject culture. "Informed by the notion of culture as a collective and historically contingent construct, the new ethnography claims to be acutely sensitive to cultural differences and, within cultures, to the multiplicity of individual experience" (Mascia-Lees et al. 12).

The emergence of postmodern ethnography allows ethnographers to question the unity of the speaking subject by favouring "dialogics, polyphony, and heteroglossia" (L. Turner 239). Drawing on Bakhtin's "Discourse in the Novel," James Clifford defines "heteroglossia" as an "ambiguous, multi-vocal world" in which "people interpret others, and themselves, in a bewildering diversity of idioms" ("Ethnographic Authority" 119),[7] thereby challenging anthropology's idea of separate, stable cultures studied by members of other separate, stable cultures. Yet, despite such evidence of the close relationship that has always existed between ethnography and literature, interventions based on interdisciplinary contact with literary theory tend to be met with resistance.

To preserve the crumbling disciplinary boundaries, ethnographers have set up a dichotomy between literary and scientific poles, or as Paul Atkinson calls them, the "humanistic" and the "sociological," and hastily qualify terms such as "fictional" and "literary." Atkinson's *The Ethnographic Imagination* (1990), for example, addresses this problem with an assertion that paying "attention to the 'literary' or 'rhetorical' features of sociological texts in no way undermines their scholarly credibility and status" (1). Atkinson studies conventions used by ethnographers and foregrounds the creative features of the text; that is, the elements of ethnography that resemble fiction. He views the ethnographic genre as only one of the "many ways in which cultural representation has been accomplished throughout this century" (4), an assertion that acknowledges the convergence of social science and literary theory in the analysis of cultural representation. With this recognition, Atkinson justifies his own methodology and supports the validity of reading social science as literary representation. Marcus and Cushman take a different tack by insisting on "blurring the distinction" between fiction and ethnography in order to preserve the conceptual integrity of both genres.[8] In contrast, Steven Webster criticizes their failure to consider how ethnography might actually resemble a fictional genre ("Realism and Reification" 44).

Critics of the postmodernists note that, despite their seemingly radical departure from tradition, postmodernists are "conventionally authoritative in their presentational styles and analyses" (Sanders 93). Indeed, it is not difficult to see that postmodern ethnography is more style than substance, or that the new ethnographic theories preserve a methodology grounded in an epistemic position that is now facing numerous attacks. As Trinh T. Minh-ha asserts in *When the Moon Waxes Red*, reflexivity in anthropology does not alter the relationship between ethnography and the reality it creates if that reflexivity is used only as a new device to perpetuate a traditional epistemology (46–7).[9] Nor does understanding the ethnographer as a unified entity called the subject contribute to renovating ethnographic authority as postmodern ethnography claims to, especially if, as Stephen Tyler claims, it "describes no knowledge and produces no action" (123). Because this "experimental moment betrays a greater concern for poetics than for politics" (Enslin 541), it is precisely this sort of claim by postmodern ethnographers that makes their work problematic for a politically grounded approach such as feminism. The self-reflexive text does, however, serve the postmodern goal of displacing epistemology in favour of rhetoric, creating, as Jane Flax notes, one great conversation (32). For example, when author Robin Ridington describes his book, *Trail to Heaven* (1988), as "a commentary on the ideas and assumptions of the thoughtworld we call anthropology" (ix), his personal, self-reflexive style attempts to assess his impact as observer on his own observations. Yet, throughout the text, he occupies the position of objective observer typical of ethnographic realism by retelling the Dunne-za people's tales in English, transcribing their words verbatim as though no mediation, analysis, or interpretation was involved in the task. The translation of the author's subjectivity into textual practice is filled with such pitfalls.

Even when experimental ethnography alludes to its own textual construction, it inevitably relies on the narrative authority of the storyteller over that construction and, consequently, the observer's authority over the presentation of the subject culture. The focus on ethnography, the "writing up" of experience, by anthropologists such as James Clifford may also simply justify anthropology's interdisciplinary contact with literary theory: that is, concentrating on the status of ethnography as writing rather than on the science of anthropological method gives institutional credibility to going outside the discipline. Indeed, George E. Marcus answers the charge that there is "little direct reference to power, class struggle, inequality, and the suffering that has moved history" in experimental ethnography by arguing that the ethnographic project is "so obviously directed" towards such issues that its engagement with them "should go without saying," and he claims that ethnography can be "articulate with Foucaultian and Gramscian ideas" without being founded on "the trope of power" (*Ethnography* 75).

To feminists, power is not a trope. As Frances E. Mascia-Lees, Patricia Sharpe, and Colleen Ballerino Cohen have argued, postmodern ethnography works to secure a position within the academic institution, as questioning ethnographic realism becomes a means of making a place for one's work in relation to ethnographic tradition and securing one's niche within the discipline. It is ironic that postmodern ethnographers find this place by collapsing ethnography into literature and literary theory, since the inception of ethnography was characterized by its attempts to distinguish itself from literature, especially travel literature.[10]

The legitimation crisis in anthropology has produced a critique of the founding assumptions of ethnographic authority, and contemporary ethnography must deal with a tension between supporting a theory that highlights its own role in generating reality without abandoning the idea of the independent reality that it seeks to describe.[11] As Martyn Hammersley observes, ethnography continues to tend towards a "naive realism" (50). Even postmodern ethnography claims to represent a set of facts, no matter how fragmented their presentation might be, and the storyteller model admits the author's creative role without undermining the "story's" truth claims. As a result, ethnographic realism continues to influence postmodern innovations: a single perspective still emerges through the ever-present, self-conscious narrator, who is constructed as both storyteller and hero of his own quest.

The quest pattern shapes the experience of fieldwork, and fieldwork has been the authorizing test of the anthropologist. As Van Maanen writes in *Tales from the Field*, "[a] lengthy stay in an exotic culture (exotic, that is, to the fieldworker) is the central rite of passage serving to initiate and anoint a newcomer to the discipline" (14). The quest provides the ethnographer simultaneously with an identity within the text and an identity within the profession, and Mascia-Lees, Sharpe, and Cohen link the quest motif to the romanticism of some ethnographers (25).[12]

The typical description of fieldwork experience follows this pattern: the hero (ethnographer) becomes separated from his own society in order to enter an alien world, and becomes initiated into that alien world. Upon return, the hero shares this experience with readers either by creating the feeling of "being there," so that his or her experience becomes the readers' experience, or by establishing intimacy with readers through a confessional style. Although this style breaks with traditional ethnography's rejection of the personal, the confessional storytelling model, for all its promise of experimentation, still relies on the notion of an accurate and independent reality reflected in the ethnographer's confession. "Thought of initially as a type of story, the ethnographer's journey of discovery and self-discovery/revelation constitutes an account of personal development. It has features of a quest – a sort of voyage of search, adventure and exploration" (Atkinson 106).

Initiation means a transformation from cultural "outsider" to cultural "insider," from innocence to experience. In ethnographic discourse, this means getting in touch with the "Native point of view." When Clifford Geertz reasserts the romantic notion of empathy in understanding the Native point of view, he returns to the positivist foundations he previously challenged by looking to the authentic in the subject culture – the something essential beneath the other skin which must be articulated. By displacing the observer's impact on the culture represented, Geertz takes the constitution of the ethnographer as subject for granted, just as his storytelling colleagues do.

Trinh T. Minh-ha, on the other hand, insists that the subject, not just the subject culture, but the entire notion of subjectivity, must be reevaluated through experimentation, otherwise, "[l]eft intact in its positionality and its fundamental urge to decree meaning, the self conceived both as key and as transparent mediator, is more often than not likely to turn responsibility into license" (*Woman* 47–8). Responsibility becomes licence when authors conceal their own textual construction while maintaining the belief that the truth about the culture in question can be located and, once located, revealed. Most ethnography involves this conflict between the desire to expose the naked truth about a culture and the desire to ensure the text's authority by concealing the means by which this truth is constructed.

Ethnographic realism and postmodern ethnography both involve an attempt to get to know other cultures, to bring the other out of obscurity. Despite commitments to portray fairly or "objectively" one culture to another, ethnographers cannot resist the specificity of their own experiences or the expectations of the readers' reception – as the gestures towards the ethnographer's subjectivity in postmodern texts suggest. In both moments, ethnographers mediate between the subject culture and the culture of the reading audience, a configuration whose first assumption is the ontologically given nature of both cultures. Marcus and Cushman observe that ethnographic realism relies on "the idea that there is a reality independent of the researcher whose nature can be known, and that the aim of research is to produce accounts that correspond to that reality" (43). While postmodern ethnography views "culture as a collective and historically contingent construct" (Mascia-Lees et al. 12) and is intended to undermine the discrete, ontologically given culture suggested by ethnographic realism, in practice, both subject culture and receiving culture are assumed to have a single, locatable story, not a variety of stories. Finding this narrative focuses the various methods of ethnographic practice. Moreover, as I have argued, claims to objectivity made by both realist and postmodern ethnographers do not extinguish the individual author's desire for textual authority and institutional support.

Desire becomes masculinized metaphorically in the discourse of fieldwork where the subject culture is often described as a body to be "entered" or "penetrated" by the concerned outsider who must undergo a complex process of initiation – as in Geertz's description of ethnographic interpretation as "the penetration of other people's modes of thought" ("The Native Point of View" 235). The sort of language I describe here is too ubiquitous to summarize adequately. It is, however, implicit in many accounts of ethnographic practice, even Paul Atkinson's description of ethnography as the "constantly rehearsed dialectic between 'in-' and 'outside'" (163). By uniting with the culture in question, "getting inside" if you will, ethnographers pass the initiation while the satisfying notion of their own individuality remains intact.

GENDER AND ETHNOGRAPHY

The sexualized language of ethnography points to the centrality of gender relations in the traditional initiation model of fieldwork. When Trinh T. Minh-ha describes anthropology as "speaking man to man," she recognizes the traditionally triangulated ethnographic model consisting of male anthropologist, a readership comprised of male colleagues, and a textualized, feminized subject culture. By looking at this relationship through a reading of Eve Kosofsky Sedgwick's *Between Men: English Literature and Male Homosocial Desire* (1985), especially its description of the continuum between 'men loving men' and 'men promoting the interests of other men,' one recognizes how the desires informing anthropological method are satisfied in the creation of a shareable beloved, the subject culture.

According to Sedgwick, male bonds construct all social interaction in a male-centred culture; that is, the type of culture presumed by most ethnographers in light of their own cultural backgrounds. The most basic manifestation of homosocial bonding is the erotic triangle, a hierarchical arrangement of male rivals, friends, or partners united by a common desire for a female object. While Sedgwick's thesis concerns literature, anthropology provides an illustration of a similar bonding at work when it involves the suppression of women's experience in order to develop theories about what unites men. Women, at once invisible and much too visible in their absence, are the collective term of reference for the all-male world, as Sedgwick explains with reference to a literary context: "It has been clear that women had a kind of ultimate importance in the schema of men's gender constitution-representing an absolute of exchange value, of representation itself, and also being the ultimate victims of the painful contradictions in the gender system that regulates men" (134). The roots of this exclusion run back through the history of ethnography, and they indicate the extent to which gender identity shapes ethnographic method. From anthropology's early days as a discipline, as Lynnette Turner's "Feminism, Femininity, and Ethnographic Authority" (1991) shows through the example of nineteenth-century ethnographer Mary Kingsley, women ethnographers have used their writing to appeal to male mentors and to disavow their gendered identities publicly, effectively excluding themselves, because in a discipline defined by a tradition of masculine perspectives, ethnographic authority is "defined as a male prerogative" (L. Turner 248). These roots are so strong that, a century after Mary Kingsley, contemporary theorist Paul Atkinson asserts that most ethnographic texts are still apt to "construct and presuppose a male perspective" (146).

The case of ethnographer Sally Cole's professional development as told in "Anthropological Lives: The Reflexive Tradition in a Social Science" (1992) is instructive. Cole describes how, as a feminist, she undertook her research with the desire to "minimize the resultant hierarchical nature of the traditional relationship between the anthropological researcher and the subject" (115). Because she wanted to produce a collaborative project, she chose the life history as a model that would allow individuals in her subject culture to speak for themselves. When she approached her professors with the idea, however, she was told she "would have to do 'more than' life histories in order to do anthropology" (117). "Life histories, they said, are too individual, idiosyncratic, subjective, anecdotal; the data they represent is non-comparable, non-generalizable, non-scientific" (117). Although she continued to search for a means of integrating her own experience, Cole went on to pursue a standard research project that would help in the "task of producing an ethnography that would pass the examining board that would license me as a professional anthropologist" (118).

Stories such as Cole's do not belong to the distant past of ethnographic practice, nor are they merely the product of institutional adherence to the methods of ethnographic realism she describes. On the subject of gender, especially the integration of feminist approaches, the new ethnography is dismissive, even hostile, as James Clifford's appraisal in the introduction to *Writing Culture* (1986) indicates: "Feminist ethnography has focused either on setting the record straight about women or revising anthropological categories... It has not produced either unconventional forms of writing or a developed reflection on ethnographic textuality as such" (20–1). Rejecting feminist ethnography allows postmodern ethnographers to occupy the position they claim as the most inclusive approach to the discipline when, in fact, they seek to exclude any approach but their own. Feminists from Nancy Hartsock to Judith Stacey, who suspect the impulse behind postmodern theory to be a will-to-power, show how "the postmodern claim that verbal constructs do not correspond in a direct way to reality has arisen precisely when women and non-Western peoples have begun to speak for themselves and, indeed, to speak about global systems of power differentials" (Mascia-Lees et al. 15; see also Hartsock; Stacey), suggesting that postmodern ethnography's rejection of feminism works to preserve its institutional position, not to mention the institutional position of anthropologists such as Clifford.[13]

To expect that the mere inclusion of women in a profession will profoundly alter the way things are done is to assume an inalienable difference rooted in the gender of the author alone, or as Gayatri Spivak warns, to assert the "simple alterity" of women ("The New Historicism" 291). Representations of the north, as the subsequent chapters show, display no such simple alternate position. Despite this fact, there has been a critical development in ethnography of Inuit cultures signalled in the work of such social scientists as Barbara Bodenhorn, Jean Briggs, and Ann Fienup-Riordan, and in the life histories collected by Julie Cruikshank and Nancy Wachowich. While ethnography by women brings different perspectives to the subject of study, it must gain authorization through already-established conventions, and it must submit to the scrutiny of an audience whose criteria have been formed in a historically male-centred professional environment. Therefore, any text written in an ethnographic mode reveals gender expectations at play because, in a tradition defined by masculinist perspectives, gender itself becomes a category of ethnographic authority.

Indeed, as Lynnette Turner observes, "the construction or negotiation of authority is where the difficulties and ambivalence of gender inhere" (239). Some feminist theorists, Marilyn Strathern among them, suggest that ethnography can be written from a standpoint that accepts the partial nature of truths in the fieldworker's experience (34). "Not inclined to sidestep or ignore the difficult issues of power and cultural difference," write Sally Cole and Lynne Phillips, "feminist anthropologists seek to come to terms with them" (5). But while ethnography can be read as a collection of partial perspectives, Cole's own story shows that it is not always written authoritatively or institutionally approved as such. In the discussion below, Naomi Musmaker Giffen's work stands as an example of how ethnographic authority depends on certain patterns and conventions that are alien to her synthetic and comparative method. This may be the reason why her work does not enjoy the authority of the single perspective narratives written by Diamond Jenness. That these conventions depend on 1) an exclusion of women from the culture represented, and 2) an initiation model based on the masculine quest pattern, indicates how gender assumptions influence the practice of ethnography.

For most of this century, ethnography about northern peoples has been produced as the result of fieldwork carried out by individuals trained in anthropology or sociology, although its appeal extends beyond those disciplines. In general, contemporary ethnographers are more aware of the literary tools at their disposal than they once were, and many are engaging in the experimental style of the new ethnography. Writers from outside the social sciences have also had an impact on recent ethnography, and traditionally defined literary genres are increasingly read as ethnography, illustrating how "different historical moments engender different strategies of reading" (Visweswaran 597). However, as the following analysis shows, the new interdisciplinary and experimental approaches have not completely eradicated the theoretical assumptions that underlie ethnographic realism.

FRANZ BOAS AND NORTHERN ETHNOGRAPHY

Ethnography and travel literature are the most prolific and author-itative genres contributing to the way Canadians envision the north. Ethnographies such as Diamond Jenness's *The Life of the Copper Eskimos* (1922) and Hugh Brody's *The People's Land: Eskimos and Whites in the Eastern Arctic* (1975) head the list of popular books describing Inuit culture from the point of view of the professional or amateur anthropologist. In this section, my read-ings of selected ethnographic texts will show how traditional ethnography encodes gender expectations, specifically, how the subject culture comes to represent the feminized object of the ethnographer's masculinized desire. By creating a world of men, by excluding women's experience, and by grafting his own (West-ern) gender assumptions on to the roles of both women and men, the ethnographer reflects and anticipates the expectations of the receiving audience.

The history of ethnographic theory and the history of northern ethnography meet in the legacy of Franz Boas (1858–1942). Before Boas arrived in North America, anthropologists and ethnologists generally took a holistic approach to cultural systems, assuming human nature to be constant and all societies to be part of the universal progress towards civilization. As the editors of Boas's collected ethnography, Ronald P. Rohner and Evelyn C. Rohner, explain, Franz Boas criticized the notion of "psychic unity" behind theories of cultural evolution, especially the comparative basis on which societies could be placed along a hierarchical scale of development (xvi). "Cultural improvement is relative," he argued; "it is not an absolute, with Western man representing the apogee" (qtd in Rohner and Rohner xviii). Charging that ethnol-ogy was ethnocentric and speculative, Boas called for an empirical approach to anthropology that stressed the importance of field-work. The fieldwork Boas undertook was dedicated to presenting the subject culture from the culture's own point of view (Rohner and Rohner xxiii). In this, it differed from the work of other nineteenth-century ethnographers, whose methods were an undisciplined attempt to collect as much as they could about

Native life because they believed it was about to become extinct. This "naive ethnocentrism" allowed them to select data that would support their theories (xxiv).

The Rohners describe the Kwakiutl of the North Pacific Coast as Boas's "first love" (xxiii); however, Boas was also the first anthropologist to study the "Central Eskimo" of Baffin Island and Hudson's Bay. Although the data for his work in *The Central Eskimo* (1888) and in volume 15 of *The Bulletin of the American Museum of Natural History* (1901) was collected during his visits to the north, Boas seems to have been more concerned with collecting artifacts for presentation in museums than he was in joining the daily routine of his subject community. Nevertheless, in these accounts, Boas originated conventions of ethnographic realism such as scientific tone, attention to minute detail, and narrative omniscience.

Although Boas is credited with "the scientization of anthropology" (Krupat, *Ethnocriticism* 65), Rohner and Rohner charge that his commitment to empirical and inductive approaches applied to fieldwork, not to the "writing up," and assert that his own writing does not always foreground his fieldwork experiences (xxix). *The Eskimo of Baffin Land and Hudson Bay* (1901), a 570-page tome, illustrates the importance to Boas of minute detail, with a text devoted to physical descriptions and illustrations of the pieces collected by military officers during contact with the people of the region. Except for a reference in the two-page introductory section, the author's presence can rarely be perceived in Boas's work, and no references are made to his fieldwork. Using the detached tone and omniscient perspective that would become standards of ethnographic realism, he describes common practices and stories to account for Inuit social organization. In this characteristic passage, Boas uses a passive verbal construction to introduce information on myths: "A few additional notes relating to the Sedna and Omerneeto myths have been obtained. It is believed that ..." (483). How the myths were "obtained," by whom, and from whom disappears in the all-seeing perspective of the narrator. Boas makes few remarks on his own experiences in the region; instead, he explains each observation without reference to the methods used in the field or the interpretive process involved in determining the meaning of data. As a result, the account presents the subject culture the way it is when, to use Geertz's words, "only

God is looking" (*Works* 141; qtd in Jacobson 2). In this passage from *The Central Eskimo*, as in others, there is a resemblance between ethnographic narrative and the realist novel, a genre whose popularity coincides with the prolific period in Boas's career: "When the sun has reached such a height that the snow begins to melt in favored spots, a new life begins at the stations. The skins which have been collected in the winter and become frozen are brought out of the store room and exposed to the sun's rays. Some of the women busy themselves, with their crescent shaped knives, in cutting the blubber from the skins and putting it away in casks" (59–60). Boas encouraged the separation of ethnography and literature by insisting on the scientific basis for ethnography; his rejection of the personal in ethnographic accounts and his choice of narrative conventions contributed to the founding of what Marcus and Cushman call "realist ethnography" (Krupat, *Ethnocriticism* 70–1). These conventions, thought to expunge the "literary" from ethnography, ironically, also solidified the importance of both the authoritative voice of omniscience that postmodern ethnographers now oppose and the role of the ethnographer as cultural exegete that postmodern ethnographers now celebrate by returning to the literary. Because the kind of fieldwork Boas advocated depends on initiation into the subject culture, it simultaneously encourages the sexualized metaphor of cultural contact contributing to the engendering of ethnographic authority. Ethnographers to come, including Diamond Jenness, would follow his example.

DIAMOND JENNESS
AND NORTHERN ETHNOGRAPHY

Diamond Jenness (1886–1969) remains an influential figure in northern studies. The Canadian Museum of Civilization's 1993 exhibition "Diamond Jenness and the Inuit" was a tribute to the longevity of his career. In quotations, footnotes, and bibliographies, the authoritative voice of Diamond Jenness continues to be heard in matters concerning the north. For example, Rudy Wiebe's *Playing Dead* attributes its opening story to Ipakuaq and Uloqsaq, but their stories are quoted from Jenness's reports. While Jenness's purposes were "scientific" in the sense of the word in his day, his work has since become part of the structure of north-south relations in Canada, and it provides an authoritative basis for the representation of the north and its people. I have chosen *People of the Twilight* (1928) and *The Life of the Copper Eskimo* (1922) rather than the more recent collection compiled by Jenness's son because of their earlier publication and popularity. As narratives circulated shortly after the fieldwork was done, these books are foundational texts that influenced attitudes towards the north.

Early ethnographers such as Jenness did not acknowledge the clearly literary source of their descriptive methods, even though the literature they produced from fieldwork structured their experience around the familiar quest pattern of separation, initiation, and return. Initiation functions at a symbolic level: the world the ethnographer enters – the sexual overtone of the verb has been recognized already – may seem to immerse him, but that world reflects his own vision. Some cultures appear through the gaze of the male ethnographer as all-male or at least as structured around a strict division of labour in which males are privileged. Women are peripheral in such accounts, or they are treated as unreliable informants, even when they are asked to tell their stories. In most cases, a collective yet almost exclusively male subject is presented as desirable.

Diamond Jenness invokes the quest pattern in *People of the Twilight* (1928) through a series of references to his journey away from civilization (7, 129). These allusions are integrated into ethnographic convention with reference to the process of initiation. Jenness notes almost wistfully: "little by little civilization slipped from me and I settled down to the routine of Eskimo life" (95). In another instance, leaving civilization fulfils a methodological requirement as Jenness refers to "the purposes for which [he] had shaken off civilization and adopted the Eskimo life" (129). Jenness leaves out an important qualification in these passages, namely, that "settling down" or "adopting the Eskimo life" in his narrative does not mean initiation on even grounds; rather, it means being received with honour in most households, offered a special place to sleep, given food, and served as a guest. He also benefits on several occasions from the labour of the others, mostly women, who provide such services as cooking his food and building his snow shelter.

Despite a lack of interest in the community's women, especially the tendency to ignore them as potential informants, Jenness's text contains glimpses of women's experience. The most shocking of these anecdotes, for they amount to textual asides rather than detailed observations, concerns the practice of infanticide. The birth of a baby girl at the moment of migration seems unfortunate to both Ikpuck (also known as Ipukkuaq, Ikpukkuak, and Ikpuquaq) and Jenness because "[a] boy would have augmented the ranks of the hunters; but a girl, well she was only one more to support" (207). At this point, instead of returning to earlier observations concerning the Inuit division of labour, according to which women provide a range of specific services, Jenness emphasizes the difficulty of Inuit life. In other places in the text, women go sealing (93), make clothes (57), prepare and serve food (31 and *passim*) and tend the lamps (57).

Even in the passage describing the worthless girl, Jenness contradicts himself and recognizes women's labour when he describes how mothers resume their harsh tasks almost immediately, sometimes only hours after giving birth (208); despite all this, the potential life of a female is seen by Jenness only as a burden on the community's economy. After recounting how the new parents "had crushed out its little life and laid the body on the wind-swept snow" (207), and noting that he knew of four mothers who had killed their infants at birth, Jenness offers the following justification: "Terrible as their crime may seem, they should not be condemned too hastily. Every society has devised some method, conscious or unconscious, for checking the full and unrestricted growth of its population; and infanticide, the simplest of them all, was in past ages the most widely spread" (207). After this statement, Jenness shifts the responsibility from the parents to the mother alone who is seen as having no choice given the difficult life of the Inuit people (209). Jenness does not comment further on the fact that the infant killed was a girl; rather, he moves from the specific example of an unwanted girl to a general discussion that does not refer to the sex of the babies at all. Jenness thus avoids commenting on or documenting a practice that was a subject of controversy: the extermination of female children. One must look to another text by Jenness, *The Life of the Copper Eskimo* (1922), for specific comments on gender preference, in which he rationalizes by alluding to the difficulty of survival in the north: "Boys, in fact, are seldom exposed, for they will support their parents when they grow up" (166). Jean Briggs calls this particular justification the "common belief" that "a boy grows up to be a hunter – a provider – whereas a girl is only a drain on her parent's household until she marries and moves away to be useful to her husband's household" (266–7). Briggs disputes this belief by pointing out that infanticide was only practised regularly by the Netsilingmiut and that her fieldwork showed no widespread preference for male children (267).

The absence of the women's experience in the account of infanticide is striking. Ikpuck's wife, Icehouse, goes immediately to visit the bereaved mother while the men seem to pay no further attention to the matter (207). The meaning of Icehouse's gesture and the mother's response are left out and seem almost invisible to Jenness, so the account points to an entire area of experience outside the ethnographer's view and indicates how selective his vision is: only the stories of men interest him, and even they are subjected to a trivial comparison with Aesop's fables and to the assertion that he did not pay much attention to their stories at all (142). Gender bias surfaces again when Jenness describes how widows are considered to be a "burden" on the others (159).

Jenness again ignores the content of women's experience even as he directly refers to it. When two consecutive husbands reject a nameless fifteen-year-old girl, presumably because she did not take to married life, Jenness and his companions convince her family not to marry her off for another year (57). The girl's resistance to her community's gender expectations is not pursued in the text; neither is it part of Jenness's stated focus in telling her story.

Jenness narrates a similar incident in which Icehouse's anger turns to laughter after he upsets his tea on the best of the sleeping robes (113). Jenness does not mention apologizing for the accident, nor does he indicate why her indignation melts away, even though her interception of a smile and a wink shared by Ikpuck and Jenness only makes the situation worse. If one reads across the text, however, to Ikpuck's harsh rebuke of Icehouse for quarrelling with a neighbour, another interpretation emerges. On that occasion, Ikpuck orders Icehouse to sleep in an empty tent rather than join the warm bodies on the sleeping platform. When she protests, he banishes her naked from the tent. As with the fifteen-year-old girl, Jenness makes himself the women's champion by finding her in another family's tent and by assuring her safety if she returns. Icehouse's words, "Ikpuck is too angry with me. I am afraid" (182), articulate her position within the family and society. The last comment on the incident describes Icehouse as "unusually quiet in the morning" (183), and it is difficult to read this observation or her general submission as anything but a sign of subordination. Jenness's claim that "[m]arriage involves no subjection on the part of the woman" (162) collapses in this story as well as in the description of a fight during which Ikpakuak beats his wife with a "tomahawk" while she butts him in the stomach with her head (162). Whether or not women were truly powerless is difficult to tell. What matters is Jenness's representation of the events in which women are overpowered by Inuit men and must be rescued by white men. Such anecdotes reveal him and his companions as chivalric interlopers.

The chivalric role depends on the availability of a woman in distress, and the resigned, silent Inuit woman who fulfils this role is a ubiquitous stereotype in ethnographic texts. In *People of the Twilight*, she surfaces in the person of Sculpin, a young girl whose smile and laughter make her a favourite with the white men, who also call her Jennie. Described as more intelligent than the others, Jennie "knew how to keep out of our way," writes Jenness, "and spent many quiet hours in a corner mending the rents in our clothing, or gazing at the pictures in our books" (57). Servitude, silence, and usefulness are Sculpin's attractive qualities.

Besides constructing a gender ideal through Sculpin and representing the general subordination of women through Icehouse, *People of the Twilight* internalizes the homosocial bonds arising from a traffic in women with its justification of "wife-swapping." Jenness takes a radically relativist position on the practice, commenting: "The people were not really immoral, for they were doing no wrong according to the standards of life handed down to them through countless generations; and the transfer of wedlock was not made indiscriminately, but according to definite regulations" (53). He goes on to recognize the way the practice allows men to form bonds with one another, gaining access to hunting territory or assuring safe travel in strange places (53–4). In *Life of the Copper Eskimo*, he refers to the way men "cement their friendships" through the practice (239). Jenness stresses the instrumental value of exchange from the men's point of view while indicating how women use the same practice to get from one man what they cannot obtain from another.

The division of labour that Jenness describes emerges from assumptions about gender identity and differentiation grounded in his own culture. Women's work, integral though it is to the hunt, assumes a subordinate position in a hierarchy of useful tasks. The exclusion of women's experience reflects the general tendency to undervalue women's roles, a tendency which is most graphically demonstrated in the rationalization of infanticide. Most of all, the representation of the division of labour underlines a bias emerging from a Western notion of masculinity. As John S. Matthiasson has explained in his critique of the anthropological accounts of Inuit life, ethnographers studying the Inuit have been "men of adventuresome spirit who were enamoured of the hunt itself" and who equated control of the hunt with social dominance (73). While he does not name Jenness in particular, Matthiasson observes how the experiences of most ethnographers supported their assumptions because their involvement in the community's daily life was limited to the activities of the men (73–4).

But no limitations are recognized in the narrative, which displays all the expectations of its generation through the single, all-seeing subject who records life by creating the "pretense of looking at the world directly, as though through a one-way screen, seeing others as they really are when only God is looking" (Geertz, *Works* 141; qtd in Jacobson 2). Jenness's authoritative accounts emerge from his experience in the field and from the organizing principle of the work: his journey into "Eskimo life" from "civilization" seeks to discover something about Inuit culture, but his writing reveals how important subjective interpretation – including gender blindness – is in forming his observations of Inuit life.

THE ROLES OF MEN
AND WOMEN IN INUIT CULTURE

In "Histories of Feminist Ethnography," Kamala Visweswaran traces the contribution of women in the social sciences from 1880 on. She shows that the fieldwork model, though preferred, is not the only method in anthropology, not even in Jenness's time, indicating that the claim to objectivity made in texts such as *People of the Twilight* should be reevaluated through a reading of different texts. Naomi Musmaker Giffen's roughly contemporary *The Roles of Men and Women in Eskimo Culture* (1930) erodes the authority of

the individual fieldworker's experience by demonstrating how
that authority depends on its own textualization. In an early example of the standpoint method, Giffen assembled all the "partial"
perspectives she could locate in ethnographic monographs in
order to give approximate, not final, conclusions. In one instance,
after speculating that curing fish falls to the women because "the
use of the needle is invariably associated with feminine pursuits,"
an assumption grounded in her own culture, Giffen notes that
"another partial explanation" could be that the women usually
catch the fish in the first place (14). Instead of presenting an observation as the "truth" about the culture, Giffen leaves interpretation
open to possibilities that may not appear immediately, and by so
doing, she (perhaps unwittingly) highlights the textual and representational characteristics of ethnography. Most important, her
work shows that the dominance of the fieldwork model has been
contested at different historical moments.

Despite the radical difference between Giffen's method and that
of the texts she analyses, she too naturalizes many of the assumptions about Inuit culture that her male colleagues make. On the
troubling issue of infanticide, she writes: "it is easily understood
why male children are highly prized while girls, who are considered to some extent as 'unproductive consumers' are often killed
at birth" (1–2; emphasis added). Like Jenness, Giffen assumes
survival is the motivation for infanticide. In another instance, she
accepts that "petting-songs" or lullabies are "naturally" the way
women tend to express themselves. Giffen's comments are part
of a general pattern in anthropology about the Inuit. As Jean
Briggs's research shows, the impression that male children were
more highly prized than female was created in the suggestion
that female infanticide was widely practised when in fact it was
not (267).

Nevertheless, Giffen's tendency to reflect the assumptions of
her time, and to identify with male authority figures – even when
her analysis contradicted then – does not diminish the challenge
her little-known work makes to the contributions of her contemporaries. Nor does it undermine her conclusion that the Inuit
possessed a "relatively sophisticated point of view" on the division of labour, because they readily perform each other's roles
(83). Where many of her contemporaries defined the division of

labour as if it were an inviolable separation of genders, Giffen showed the division to be highly permeable. Giffen's work may not be as influential as Jenness's – his reports are probably the most often-quoted documents on northern life, and his observations continue to influence southerners seeking contact with northern peoples – but her method challenges the single perspective of his authority as well as the strict division of labour ethnographers believed the hunting society to be.

In *The People's Land* (1975), Hugh Brody employs many of the conventions of the realist form established in the tradition of Boas and Jenness and grounds his truth claims in his fieldwork in the north. *The People's Land* fits somewhere between the scientific accounts of Boas and Jenness and rhetorical new ethnography proposed by James Clifford. Later, Brody situates his work within the experimental mode of the new ethnography, describing *Maps and Dreams* (1981) as "a book of anecdotes as well as a research report, its structure being the result of an attempt to meet two different needs" (xxiii); that is, "a need for scientific detail, evidence that must stand the test of scrutiny by academics and cross-examination in uncomprehending or hostile courtrooms" and a need "to bring to life unfamiliar points of view" (xxiii).

Brody presents the challenge that comes with "the writing up" of fieldwork experience, and it is this aspect of his work that I wish to emphasize here. At issue are the rhetorical and literary methods used to make experience accessible to readers, not the experience itself which is undeniable, for, as Clifford remarks, "it is difficult to say very much about experience… Like 'intuition' one has it or not, and its invocation often smacks of mystification" ("On Ethnographic Authority" 128). Therefore, it is important to distinguish between the author as a person with his own history, and the author as the persona constructed in his own text. As narrator in *The People's Land*, Brody is only minimally present in the text, creating the impression that readers are visiting a world while they participate in its textual construction. The text assumes the self-effacing tone of a scientific paper, the same assertive voice that makes a heavy claim to truth, and renders a global perspective as if the position of the narrator, who consistently refers to himself generically as "the social scientist," is outside or above the reality described. Brody substantiates facts by referring to informants who are either anonymous, or else identified by generic function as the "white government worker," the "young Eskimo," or the "oldtimer" (these are Brody's terms).

Theorist Paul Atkinson observes how the use of synecdoche masks the analytical process at each level of the ethnographer's project and sets up a "strong narrative contract" between the writer and the reader (62). Many proponents of experimental ethnography, including Geertz, rely heavily on this literary device as well as on metonymy, though they do not use these literary names.[14] The intimacy suggested between ethnographer and informant through the use of this trope covers up unequal power relations, making it difficult, as Graham Huggan observes in his discussion of Brody's writing, to tell if he speaks with or for others (66). By contrast, the use of synecdoche in autobiography written by Native people voices political concerns.[15]

Representations based on synecdoche are easily refuted. One can obviously reject Brody's generalizations about hunters by rejecting his narrative construction of characters. Another problem inherent in the idealization of individual hunters is that it may set false expectations. If readers take the informant to be truly representative, they will expect all other informants, or worse, all Native people to be like the person represented, and they may blame or pity those who do not meet this standard, an attitude towards aboriginal peoples that Brody himself identifies in *The People's Land*.

Suppressing the text's representational apparatus and confidently presenting the authentic or essential nature of the subject culture is, as we have seen, a convention of ethnographic realism that establishes the ethnographer's authority. The illusion of authority presents the ethnographer as spokesperson reading the text written by the subject culture itself; however, it also involves persuading readers that superior (scientific) knowledge of that culture authorizes the ethnographer to speak on its members' behalf. The omniscient narrator takes this position, looking through the "one-way screen" Geertz describes. With the narrator's superiority established, the text looks like a mirror of the subject culture's authentic life.

Despite a slightly more visible authorial presence and rhetorical awareness in *Maps and Dreams* than in *The People's Land*, the pressures of ethnographic authority cause Brody to fall back on the strategies of realism when he approximates the Boasian "Native point of view" and disappears behind an omniscient perspective.[16] Postmodern method fails to acknowledge that ethnography is synthetic and that there is no innocent place outside representation, no innocent place beyond the relationship of self and others from which to judge (Said 216), but as transcendent observer, the realist ethnographer assumes the existence of such a position and occupies it by manipulating conventions of ethnographic realism. The author's subjectivity, shown in his approval, displeasure, admiration, and disappointment, gleams on the surface of the narrative without any direct interrogation of its impact on his interpretation.

Nevertheless, *The People's Land* identifies powerful and pervasive stereotypes of the north and the people who live there, and raises important issues about how northern people are represented in Canada. Brody alerts readers to the colonizing gaze of white northerners in their desire to fix the "Native" within a convenient image. A chapter on "White Attitudes to the Eskimo" analyses the "white" image of the Inuit as both "tough and benign" (77). White northerners are said to disdain their individual Inuit neighbours while holding on to an ideal of the "real Eskimo" (86). Their admiration for an abstract Inuit-ness, which idealizes the land and the traditional but *now extinct* life of the Inuit, allows them to judge real live "Eskimos" according to harsh and artificial standards. Those who cannot live up to these standards are lamented for having lost their true identity. In general, fatalism, guilt, and paternalism are said to inform white nostalgia for the disappearance of the Native way of life (54–5).

It is ironic that Brody should expose the paternalistic attitudes of whites towards post-contact aboriginal societies as he appears to lament the toll contact has taken on tradition. As in many anthropological accounts, a traditional way of life is constructed and its passing documented. Traditional life has been deformed by contact (190): trapping destroyed Inuit self-reliance (133); carving is a "consequence of southern domination of Eskimo economic life" (134); current drug and alcohol problems among Inuit people are the result of the transformation of their economy, which has left the young with nothing to keep them occupied. The basis for these conclusions seems similar to some drawn in early ethnography, but what is important here is the way Brody shifts the emphasis of northern ethnography from physical survival stressed by earlier ethnographers to cultural survival, thus mapping an important shift in attitudes towards aboriginal societies.

In her book *The Nelson Island Eskimo: Social Structure and Ritual Distribution* (1989), anthropologist Ann Fienup-Riordan describes how the emphasis on survival in the work of ethnographers actually excludes the social conditions and values attached to the hunt.[17] In the same way, John S. Matthiasson argues that the gender of the researcher explains the presumed male supremacy in Inuit culture. Noting that with only a few exceptions, those ethnographers who have studied the Inuit have been men, Matthiasson suggests first of all that "[i]t is possible that for them control of the hunt also meant social dominance" and, second, that "the very fact that they were male limited their observations to the sphere of male activity. They were not as privy to the female realm, and so could not describe it as they could that of the male" (73–4). While Matthiasson does not blame them for their blindness, he does call their observations "skewed and male oriented."

Many anthropologists now question the hierarchy of labour thought to be associated with hunter-gatherer societies. They argue that the division of labour is produced by the anthropological model employed because, in fact, the sexual division of labour in many northern communities shows flexibility that many anthropological studies fail to notice. Jean Briggs writes: "There is nothing holy to [the Inuit] about the sexual division of labour; neither is there, in their view, anything inherent in the nature of either sex that makes it incapable of doing some of the jobs that the other sex ordinarily does" (270). Barbara Bodenhorn's "'I'm Not the Great Hunter, My Wife Is': Inupiat and the Anthropological Models of Gender," makes this point based on the observation of "unexamined assumptions about the meaning of hunting, marriage and gender" (55) in studies of hunter-gatherer societies. Such assumptions suggest that ethnography's construction of gender roles reflects the ethnographer's own background and prejudices.

As theories of ethnography blur the boundaries between genres in light of the travel writing and other works of non-fiction that present information about other cultures, it becomes increasingly difficult to define what ethnography is, except to say that it is writing by professional ethnographers. Marie Wadden, a journalist and writer who is perhaps freed of the expectations placed upon a writer trained in social science, offers a look at Innu culture in *Nitassinan* (1991) by telling the story of the community's political awakening in the face of military encroachment on its land. Rather than concentrating on the hunt, *Nitassinan* focuses on all aspects of the daily life of the community, which means that instead of portraying one individual "informant," she lets a variety of characters into her text: a teenager named Makus shows her the sweat lodge he built (19); a young mother, Manimat, prepares a carpet of boughs in her home (169); a hunter, Ben Michel, brings home the first goose of the season (35). Early in the narrative, Wadden confesses to the practical and cultural reasons that caused her to stick close to camp instead of following the hunters: "I didn't accompany the men on their hunting while I was at Penipuapishku-nipi. It would have been highly unusual for a woman to do this, and I also knew I would have trouble keeping up with them, as they often travel long distances on snowshoes in search of game" (18). This revision means articulating the experience of women, and the result is a depiction of Innu community life that balances the usual "authentic" way of life constructed around a stereotyped version of the hunt that Matthiason critiques.

By reporting the words of the Innu community, men, women, old, and young, *Nitassinan* describes part of their world. It does not shy away from the obvious and continued effects of contact on the Innu whose traditional lifestyle mixes technologies; it rejects the fatalist and self-serving opinion of non-Natives and government agencies that "because the Innu have adopted some of the ways of European-Canadian society they no longer have a distinct culture, and therefore no legitimate claim to their land" (43). The political activism of the Innu provides a compelling example of a politically radical circumstance: the Innu, a people who do not accept the authority of the Canadian constitution over their people, wilfully submit themselves to it in order to bring about real change.

Read as ethnography, *Nitassinan* is a study in what Linda Alcoff refers to as "the practice of speaking with and to rather than for others" (23). Wadden tells her version of Innu resistance to low-level flying as she reports the views and arguments of the people around her. Experience underpins some of her authority, as it does in a realist text; for example, in one chapter she tells how she heard the terrific noise created by low-flying jets and how she managed to get it on tape. However, the text extends the realist ethnographic form by devoting more space to the experience of the other witnesses in the community. Wadden's authority is granted in the consent of these voices as when Janet Michel endorses Wadden's right to use her tape recording with the remark: "They never believe us when we say this happens, but maybe now they will, when you play that on the radio" (38).

By giving precedence to the speech of the Innu, by using each person's real name, and by quoting directly, Wadden uses the dialogic form favoured by anthropologists such as James Clifford in "On Ethnographic Authority," which calls on different cultures to "form complex concrete images of one another" without forgetting that such representations are made "in specific historical relations to dominance and dialogue" (119). *Nitassinan* achieves this without obscuring its representational apparatus or losing sight of the independent reality it describes, not only because of the heightened awareness of the ethnographer's subjectivity but also because it is as detailed and careful as Boas first insisted ethnography should be. Wadden's work seems to answer feminist concerns and to support Sally Cole's argument that ethnography should be "not only about the anthropological self but also about context – about the subjectivity and historical specificity of the field experience as well as the social and political realities of the lives of anthropological subjects, the traditional Other" (125). Rejecting realist conventions for a more effective form of realism involves the delineation of that context. As narrator, Wadden is ever-present with explanations of how she came by the knowledge she has, what she did in certain situations, what personal connections gave her access to Innu homes and confidence; moreover, she refuses to universalize the feelings of individuals or to paraphrase their conversations. Her book meets the challenge posed by Edward Said to "see Others as historically constituted" (225) by looking at a culture and a struggle in all its particularity of detail and historical specificity.

Saqiyuq: Stories from the Lives of Three Inuit Women (1999), the result of collaboration between Nancy Wachowich, Apphia Agalakti Awa, Rhoda Kaukjak Katsak, and Sandra Pikujak Katsak, is similarly concerned with the historical dimension of culture. In "Introduction: The Life History Project," Wachowich meticulously details her method, including the methodological difficulties raised by translation of both language and form and the need to achieve "the balance between the need for these testimonies to remain as much as possible in the women's own words, and the need for life histories to be comprehensive and 'reader friendly'" (9). Wachowich describes the means of communication used, including post, phone, fax, and e-mail (9), the editorial decisions made, such as the exclusion of material that the women "did not want included in the public account" (10), and the effort "to bridge Inuit and non-Inuit knowledges" by adding contextual information (10). The stories told by three generations of women are not offered without mediation, but neither are they represented only through the observer's interpretation. *Saqiyuq* attests to the growing acceptance of diverse social scientific methods and to changing attitudes towards life history since Sally Cole's difficult experience. The individual stories offer insight into the lives of Inuit women in different historical moments. Read together, they also offer powerful evidence of the way cultures change over time.

Apphia Agalakti Awa, who was sixty-two years old at the beginning of the project, tells stories that witness the changes during her long life: "I went down to Iqaluit to have my baby"; "Arvaluk and Simon went to School"; "Inuit were given numbers." Many of her stories contest the early images of women in ethnography. For example, when she tells how her adoptive father arranged a marriage for her without her consent, she describes "crying and screaming" when her husband got into her bed the first time and how he waited until she was menstruating to initiate sex (39–40). She recalls "being so upset after it happened" and trying to fight off her husband, saying the "[i]f it was today ... I would report that I was raped by my husband" (40). This testimony, like her statement that Inuit women had children by Qallunaat (or white) whalers because "[i]t was their husbands' idea to trade their wives for stuff" (118), contest the image of the passive, acquiescent women in the ethnography that is contemporary with her experiences, particularly the accounts by Jenness. As her daughter, Rhoda Kaukjak Katsak, and granddaughter, Sandra Pikujak Katsak, continue with their memories of their own lives, they describe the different expectations and roles of women in each generation. Like Awa, they trace the history of the community: visiting the relatives exiled to Grise Fiord, camping on the DEW line, going away to school. With each generation, resistance to the influence of Qallunaat culture gains strength. As a member of the generation sent away to school, Rhoda Kaujak Katsak describes making her first political statement in a poster for Pierre Trudeau's visit to her school. The poster depicted Trudeau talking to a walrus who asks "What the heck is he saying?" (173). Sandra Pikujak Katsak, who at the time of recording had not yet married or had children, questions Christianity as part of her resistance to Qallunaat culture: "It is like they tricked us into Christianity, into believing the same things they believed in" (243). These stories affirm the lack of power Inuit had over aspects of their own lives as well as Katsak's feeling that "they spent all those years trying to change me into a Qallunaaq, and they couldn't" (200). Now, learning about the old culture, the things she should have learned as a child, she asks "looking back and hearing my parents' and grandparents' stories, what is so bad about my own culture, what is so wrong with Inuit culture, that it has to be removed?" (200).

As Naomi Musmaker Giffen's momentary internalizations of masculine bias suggest, writing ethnography requires the negotiation of gendered expectations. Gender expectations inhere in ethnographic method with its reliance on narrative techniques such as the initiation model and on realist conventions such as the omniscient narrator, which enhances the author's credibility and authority. The gender bias responsible for the misrepresentation of the division of labour within hunting societies thrives in northern ethnography with influential ethnographers creating an all-male world through a series of important exclusions. In the choice of male informant, the reliance on synecdoche following that choice, and the omission of women's experience, ethnography has built a male-centred world out of the north, a world in which the exigencies of survival explain most social practices, especially those concerning the social organization of the hunt. Although produced in different contexts, these ethnographies demonstrate a singular perspective that is grounded in cultural assumptions that must be contested.

While the tendency towards "naive realism" (Hammersley 50) undermines ethnographic representation, postmodernism does not correct its vision. The new generation of ethnography theorists tend to replicate strategies for creating authority that are inherited from the realist tradition, and as Henrietta Moore observes, "in focusing on how 'other' cultures are represented by anthropologists, the discipline has paradoxically managed to distance itself from a more radical critique of the consequences of this debate for an ethics of anthropology" ("Interior" 128). Ethnographers might have had good reason to take the postmodernist turn, given the inaccuracies inherent in failing to consider the observer's biases and cultural assumptions; however, postmodernist ethnography creates tension between the independent reality it describes and the textual construction of that reality. Despite these difficulties, the ethnographies described here remain influential both as authoritative sources of information and as examples of representational method.

CHAPTER TWO

"Everybody Likes the Inuit": Inuit Revision and Representations of the North

Non-Inuit writing on the north is often preoccupied with two supposed elements of Inuit experience: Inuit access to the Stone Age past as a "contact-traditional" hunting society, and Inuit access to an exotic spirituality. The first element is part of a general trend in the representation of aboriginal people: "real Inuit," like the "real Indians" Louis Owens refers to in *Other Destinies*, are always considered to be part of the past (4). Writers attracted by the idea of the hunt, such as Barry Lopez, are particularly susceptible to this tendency and disseminate masculinist images of the hunting society and how it functions, with men dominating the cultural landscape because they hunt big game. As John S. Matthiasson observes, most literature about the Inuit works this fantasy into "an image of the chauvinistic male hunters dominating their women and trading them back and forth as if they were property" (73); such literature fails to notice the role played by women in the men's hunt or the fact that women hunt sometimes as often as men do. What interests these writers is not how the society works or what hunting represents within the culture; rather, it is the rugged individualism that can be displayed in such deeds, as in the staged hunting scenes in Robert Flaherty's *Nanook of the North* (1922). The importance of the second supposed attribute of Inuit culture, traditional spirituality, can be observed in highly personal travel writing about the north, narratives in which the individual fulfils a quest for self-knowledge or greater wisdom through contact with aboriginal people.

Travel writing, like ethnography, tends to portray Inuit men as hunters, interpreters, and guides, and to leave women out of the picture, creating an image of a culture dominated by masculine pursuits. Yet in their dealings with whites, Inuit men are made subordinate to those who hire them; that is, they occupy the role Inuit women have been assumed to play in Inuit culture. Frequently depicted as poor, defenceless creatures, they undergo a symbolic emasculation that allows them to play a subordinate, passive role, as the feminized counterpart of the masculinized explorers and travellers. The north described in such accounts has been usurped by white men as a playground for their own masculinist fantasies; it is what Margaret Atwood calls "[t]he Robert W. Service North of popular image [which] is assumed to be a man's world; even though the North itself, or herself, is a cold and savage female, the drama enacted in it – or her – is a man's drama, and those who play it out are men" (*Strange Things* 90). By speaking "man to man," to reiterate Trinh's phrase, realist ethnographers cast their subjects in the same way.

Inuit self-representation tells a different story. Both traditional stories and contemporary writing represent Inuit men and women in ways that challenge non-Inuit representation. By merging their traditional conventions with European literary forms such as autobiography, Inuit writing plays a historical role in preserving details of past traditions, a pedagogical role in addressing and educating outsiders, and a political role in making statements on behalf of Inuit.

Images created by ethnographic studies have defined aboriginal peoples, and especially notions of what is traditional in their cultures. Even the term "traditional" synthesizes many perspectives, including those of the ethnographer's culture. Reading these books is an encounter with the images that have allowed sustained paternalism, even neo-colonialism, in Canada's governing of the north.[1] In the wake of the new ethnography and the debate over who speaks for whom, most ethnographers would now insist on the difference between these two practices; nevertheless, the distinction between speaking about others and speaking for others is, as Linda Alcoff shows, often blurred (9).

The debate concerning who speaks for whom in literature can be polarized, with one side advocating the absolute creative freedom of writers and the other insisting that writers should depict only their own experiences. Some writers of the north refuse to become embroiled in this controversy at all, by refusing to write about the

Inuit or to report their words. This well-meaning attempt to avoid appropriating the voice of others can have the same effect, however, if the voice of northern inhabitants cannot be heard. These issues bear on the reception of writing by Inuit to be discussed later in this chapter because non-Inuit writers effectively "speak for" Inuit both by reaching an audience that Inuit writers may not have access to and by influencing how that audience will receive Inuit writing.

This criticism is not an argument against the practice of speaking for others; instead, it is a warning of the impact that speaking for others can have in the absence of dialogue, that is, when some have no voice – as has been the case, historically at least, with aboriginal writers. I argue that when Inuit writers speak on behalf of other Inuit it is often in the interest of giving voice to collective concerns. Without a modified version of speaking for others, Robin McGrath would not be able to say that Agnes Nanogak represents the storytellers of the Western Arctic in her collection ("Introduction" xii), nor would Heather Henderson be able to say that Minnie Aodla Freeman "speaks for" her people (62). Without the practice of speaking for others, aboriginal people would not find voices that could reach the people who need to learn most, and non-aboriginal people would continue to imagine aboriginal people according to prevailing stereotypes; thus, "speaking for others" cannot be rejected outright. Inuit self-representation, autobiography in particular, seems to reflect Linda Alcoff's observation that sometimes it is politically expedient to have a spokesperson speak on one's behalf (13).

REPRESENTATIONS OF THE INUIT
BY NON-ABORIGINAL WRITERS

Long before anthropologists such as Franz Boas appeared, Norse sagas (*ca* 1001–05) depicted the people the Vikings encountered in North America as "ill-favoured," troll-like creatures (Dickason 52), although these people may not have been Inuit but Beothuks. In the sixteenth century, Europeans believed that the Inuit were cannibals (Dickason 52, 56). The Inuit do not fare much better in explorers' accounts. In *A Journey to the Northern Ocean* (1795), Samuel Hearne observes that the Inuit are "but low in stature, none exceeding the middle size, and though broad set, are neither well-made nor strong bodied" and have "a dirty copper colour" except for some women who are "more fair and ruddy" (108). Although Hearne's description is unflattering, his attitude to the Inuit in his famous account of the massacre at Bloody Falls is one of pity, not scorn. In this passage, Hearne refers to the Inuit as "poor Esquimaux," "poor unsuspecting creatures," "poor unhappy victims," and "poor expiring wretches" (98–101). Throughout the passage, Hearne depicts the Inuit as helpless, innocent victims of a vicious and treacherous attack.[2]

Such are the images of the Inuit offered in one of the earliest texts studied as Canadian literature. Since Hearne cannot speak the languages of those he encounters, he does not make a study of the whole culture, as later ethnographers would, yet the minute detail in descriptions of Indian and Inuit implements, weapons, dress, and customs in his text resembles what would later be called realist ethnography and, indeed, provided a source of ethnographic information before other studies were made. Hearne's observations reflect his dealings with aboriginal peoples in the specific context of exploration; however, as McGrath suggests, the images created by his observations left a legacy for writers to come. The powerful image of the helpless, dying victims of Bloody Falls is not countered within Hearne's narrative because he had very little contact with the Inuit and refers to them infrequently, except to compare details of tools and armaments with those of the Indians who accompany him. A reason for this absence is offered by Alan D. McMillan's *Native Peoples and Cultures of Canada* (1995), which shows that when Hearne and his Chippewyan companions travelled across the barrenlands, the area was inhabited only by other Athapaskans, for the Inuit had not yet moved into the region (280).

With the exception of David Thompson, the eighteenth-century explorers had little or no contact with Inuit. Although it refers to passing places where "Esquimaux" have had encampments (258–9), Alexander Mackenzie's *Voyages from Montreal* (1801) contains no report of contact with Inuit. Because his various Indian guides were enemies of the Inuit who took pains to avoid meeting them (257), Mackenzie resorts to reporting what other aboriginal people have to say about them: 'Esquimaux' are "treacherous" (284), "very wicked and malignant" (245), and murderers of men and abductors of women (255).[3] These remarks are emphasized when Mackenzie narrates the antics of a guide who mimics "various indecencies, according to the customs of the Esquimaux, of which he boasted an intimate acquaintance" (253).

Despite the war-like images presented by the Indian guides on these expeditions, the predominant attitude towards Inuit in exploration literature is not antagonistic. Calling the Inuit "a people with whom we are very little acquainted," *David Thompson's Narrative 1784–1812* (1916) refers to the Inuit as "very industrious and ingenious" and "cheerful and contented" (14). Two further passages repeat these terms as Thompson compares the Inuit favourably with the Indians (16, 352): "Nothing can oblige an Indian to work at anything but stern necessity; whereas the Esquimaux is naturally industrious, very ingenious, fond of the comforts of life so far as they can attain them, always cheerful, and even gay" (16). By the early nineteenth century, Hearne's hapless Inuit at Bloody Falls had developed into a stoic, slightly tragic, contented, and peaceful people.

Because explorers such as Hearne, Mackenzie, and Thompson were engaged in the service of empire-building and mercantile capitalism, their interests were primarily geographic and their accounts of aboriginal cultures are not anthropological in the sense of those provided later by scientists such as Boas and Jenness. Paradoxically, the explorers are frequently less prone than the anthropologists to interpret Inuit life through their own cultural biases, and tend to offer what are admitted to be opinions rather than explanations. However, certain characteristics featured in the representation of Inuit people are strikingly similar to the ethnography that would come later.

Arctic exploration intensified during the nineteenth century with the excitement surrounding Sir John Franklin's unsuccessful attempts to find a Northwest Passage, and continued in the twentieth century with the race for the Pole (see Bloom *Gender on Ice*). In one of the intertextual moments characterizing the representation of the north, Sir John Franklin describes how he and his men reached the place Hearne called Bloody Falls, where they find what they believe to be evidence of the attack Hearne witnessed (350). The authority Franklin grants to Hearne's conclusions perhaps accounts for the attitude of his narrative towards the Inuit, which reflects the innocent and afflicted images of Hearne's journal. Franklin seems sceptical concerning the Indians' constant warnings that the Inuit will overwhelm and kill them all, and he wonders what would happen only if "the Esquimaux were as hostile to strangers as the Copper Indians have invariably represented them to be" (343). Despite the fears of his Indian guides, Franklin characterizes the "Esquimaux" as a "harmless and defenceless people" (265) and a "persecuted nation" (289). When the Inuit flee at their approach, leaving only a terrified old man who is too frail to escape, Franklin's scepticism seems justified (351–2). As David Woodman's excellent study *Unravelling the Franklin Mystery: Inuit Testimony* (1991) shows, published accounts of the Franklin expeditions do not depict details of further contact with the Inuit.

Contact between white explorers and Inuit increased during the nineteenth century, and explorers, having learned the lessons of the Franklin expedition, gradually began to adopt Inuit methods of travel, dress, and diet in order to increase their chances of survival and success. In these texts, Inuit are not as alien, though they are still regarded as a primitive people. As W. Gillies Ross reports, Margaret Penny encountered "kind-hearted Esquimaux" (21) on Baffin Island in the winter of 1857–58 and recorded that she was "much pleased with the poor natives" (22) who she appears to have befriended. Like Hearne, Penny used the term "poor" repeatedly to describe the Inuit – "poor creatures," "poor people," and "poor natives" in her brief descriptions. In sharp contrast, Elisha Kent Kane, who led an expedition in search of Franklin, records many encounters with groups of Inuit in *Arctic Explorations* (1856), but describes those who come aboard his ship as "rude and difficult to manage" (207). By his own account, Kane treats the Inuit as inferior, ordering them about, detaining them, granting them leave to go only as he wishes, and always suspecting them of theft. In one instance, some women accused of stealing are stripped, tied, and marched thirty miles on his orders (366). Inuit reports of the Franklin expedition's cannibalism were met with horror and disbelief by the English and account for the more hostile view of the Inuit that emerged at the time. For instance, Charles Dickens dismissed such reports on the grounds that the Inuit were "covetous, treacherous and cruel" (qtd in Beattie 60).

Despite the hostile reception of Inuit testimony to Franklin's fate, a stereotype of the Inuit as primitive yet pleasant and happy developed in twentieth-century travel literature. In *Glimpses of the*

Barren Lands (1930), Thierry Mallet, the fur-trading inspector for Révillon Frères, praises his Inuit friend Kakoot for doing his work "cheerfully" (93) and for being "the most intelligent and the most prosperous" in the region (85). Signalling the preoccupation with Inuit survival which still dominates representations of the north, Mallet passes most of his time pondering Inuit gravesites and envisions a day when "Indians and Eskimos would vanish" as whites moved in (33).[4] The book ends with the dramatic tale of a young Inuit girl who, despite the death of everyone in her company, keeps travelling "with the unfailing courage of her race, until death, at last, mercifully struck her down" (142).[5]

Travels in the north increased in the 1940s and 1950s as enthusiastic plans for northern development stimulated nationalist feelings about the region in the rest of Canada. In 1943, Malcolm MacDonald, a member of Parliament determined to make Canadians "North-conscious" (viii), published *Down North* after two brief visits. MacDonald describes many aspects of Inuit material culture, arguing that the Inuit are a "distinct people and society" who risk being destroyed by "civilization" (202), and recommending policies to preserve "all that is best in Eskimo character and custom while adapting them to the inevitable changes of those times" (203). MacDonald's paternal attitude reveals itself in his choice of descriptive verbs: Inuit "dawdle" and "gossip" (155) and are seen "gesticulating and chattering in incomprehensible gibberish" (63). His efforts to make Canadians aware of the north is a striking example of how the north has been appropriated to the ends of official nationalism.

One representation dominates this period: that of Inuit as primitive people threatened with extinction by the inevitable arrival of civilization. Mrs Tom (Ella W.) Manning's *Igloo for the Night* (1946), an account of the author's years spent with her husband on the British-Canadian Arctic Expedition, records the encroachment of civilization as observed by a middle-class woman. In her preoccupation with social etiquette, Mrs Manning acts as the civilizing feminine presence that oldtimers fear on the frontier: as more women arrive and houses are built, one oldtimer complains to her that the north has become "too civilized" (206). (Decades later, Hugh Brody observed in *The People's Land* [1975] the same nostalgic regret of "oldtimers" for the "life of nature" that had given way to the "life of culture.") Manning, who displays a keen interest in cleanliness and manners, is appalled by a group who are "dirty, ragged, and untidy ... especially the women and children, although a fatter lot I've never seen" (139). In another instance, she marvels that, despite the lack of discipline applied to Inuit children, they are "polite and well-mannered" and grow up to be "for the most part, such charming people, obedient, cheerful, courteous" (55). These comments underline her assertion that the "Eskimos are a happy people" (140).

Manning's book is typical of the post-war trend of travel accounts written by the wives of Arctic adventurers. Most of these books, including American Miriam MacMillan's *I Married an Explorer* (1951), Laura Beatrice Berton's *I Married the Klondike* (1954), and Jean W. Godsell's *I Was No Lady ... I Followed the Call of the Wild* (1959), record the lives of women who follow their husbands north. In their roles as feminine helpmates to their masculine partners, these women reproduce the binary structure of their relationships in the world they describe. Thus, descriptions of the Inuit contain implicit and explicit comparisons between the civilized and uncivilized, as when MacMillan judges that the Inuit, although a "primitive people[,] appear to be as bright and intelligent as the educated persons of a civilized world" (139).

The strict definition of gender roles structures Jean Godsell's book which, despite the title's claim to the contrary, records the domesticating influence of a "lady's" presence in the north. By her own account, Godsell spends much energy creating a social scene that resembles southern life, throwing a Christmas party (75), organizing a dance (63), and making sure to cut the crusts off the sandwiches made by the Inuit women (59). In contrast to her genteel ways, Natives are seen as primitive. One Native character "grunts," "sneaks," and has a "crafty look in his beady eyes" (64). Although she laments the end of northern isolation, Godsell regards the history of the north as a history of white pioneers, each of whom "stood out, stark and alone, on his own pinnacle for opening up the Northland," and she concludes that "pushing back the frontier, was a job for individualists" (208).

Although she blames the degradation of the Native people on contact with whites (in an ironic demonstration of her point, all the Native people who attend her dance contract smallpox) and speaks out against residential schooling (109–10), Godsell describes little of Inuit culture, apart from her references to female infanticide and ancient blood feuds (132), for which she draws on Hearne's description of Bloody Falls. In these passages, the Inuit are primitive, albeit innocent, objects of paternal care; thus, they are represented in the position of subordination Godsell and wives like her occupy in their own lives, and racial difference reflects gender difference.

Other women and men from Canada, the United States, and Europe writing about their travels and experiences in the north in this period also constructed their narratives around a civilized-uncivilized binary. Thus, the Parisian author of *Kabloona* (1941), Gontran de Poncins, chooses to study the people of the Central Arctic, the Netsilik, specifically because "they inhabited regions so remote and difficult to reach" and "still lived their primitive life of thousands of years ago" (4–5). For de Poncins, as for Jenness and others before him, the voyage north means gradually shedding the civilized self: "I, a child of civilization, had wandered in the course of a few weeks into the stone age" (xxvi). *Kabloona* emerged from the diaries and notes taken by de Poncins during his visit to the Central Arctic in 1938, at the historical moment that produced the modern ethnographic method based on field-work – the era dominated by the legacy of Franz Boas through the careers of his students Margaret Mead, A.L. Kroeber and others. The Netsilik exemplify the "uncivilized" mind, the "elementary being" (26) because, according to de Poncins, they cannot "participate in an exchange of ideas," do "not think at all," and possess "no capacity for generalization" (109). As one who can "think" and "generalize," the Cartesian de Poncins considers himself to be only fulfilling a task the Netsilik are incapable of performing themselves.

Travel writing of the 1940s and 1950s shares certain tendencies with the fiction of the period, especially the use of the voyage north as a self-imposed exile away from feminizing civilization which allows the male protagonist to become an idealized masculine individual. The rough, violent, inarticulate men in fiction such as Harry Bernard's *Les jours sont longs* (1951), André Langevin's *Le temps des hommes* (1956), and Hubert Evans's *Mist on the River* (1954) encounter aboriginal people who are an extension of a brutal and exacting natural world. In *The People's Land* (1975), Hugh Brody observes that the white inhabitants of the north he encountered during his stay still viewed Inuit people living beyond civilization as "an embodiment of the land" (82).

By the 1960s and 1970s, travel to the Arctic was becoming common, and a number of Canadian writers including Al Purdy, F.R. Scott, Farley Mowat, James Houston, and others made the voyage. In 1968, Jack Warwick introduced his study *The Long Journey: Literary Themes of French Canada* with the statement that "[t]he North is well known to the English reading public as a region of adventure and challenge," and he sets out to find "how it impinges on the French-Canadian consciousness" (3). While the comments I will make here do not even approach the comprehensiveness of Warwick's study, I would like to compare the representation of aboriginal people, a topic Warwick does not go into in detail, in realist texts set in the north by Yves Thériault and Gabrielle Roy. In doing so, I wish to further destabilize the notion of northern experience and representation as evidence of a distinctive "Canadian" culture. Indeed, views on the north in Québécois culture indicate how supple the borders of culture are.

The first critically acclaimed novel about the Inuit, Yves Thériault's *Agaguk* (1963) depicts Inuit culture as the violent, primitive continuation of the Stone Age. As Warwick points out, Thériault's interest is in creating a character who is an individual, a rebel even, and suggests that this view is "not of the Eskimos as they are, but as they used to be" (121). Yet Warwick does not claim, as John Moss did later, that *Agaguk* is an "authentic representation" of Inuit life (*Reader's* 325); rather, he stresses the author's moral purpose which is concerned less with ethnographic detail than with the symbolic. In its attempt to show the Inuit as part of nature, *Agaguk* presents stereotypes of Inuit characters as remnants of a brutal Stone Age. Inuit life is primitive, and Inuit actions are instinctual. Agaguk is portrayed as a savage who, when his wife, Iriook, gives birth, is consumed with fear and rage, believing she is possessed by an evil spirit. Throughout the novel, Thériault depicts a hunting society in which Inuit women are subservient and life is filled with gratuitous violence and brutal ignorance. The castration and cannibalism performed on RCMP officer Henderson seems to be included mainly for shock value, as is the treachery exhibited by Chief Ramook when he murders his own people and frames his own son. As Jack Warwick argues,

Thériault uses the Inuit to dramatize themes of personal freedom and individuality, and his revival of the "noble savage" serves that purpose (121–2).

In Thériault's next novel, *Agoak* (1975), contact is shown to have eroded the division of labour by gender, and the ideal hunting society has been corrupted by civilization. The narrator describes Agoak as far removed from Agaguk and the world "de froide misère et de presque sauvagerie" (19). In this passage, the narrator describes Agoak's accommodation of white ways in a baffled tone: "Lui, l'Inuk versé comptable de banque, préférant les vête-ments de Blancs et la nourriture des Blancs, et ayant délaissé depuis longtemps le mode de pensée esquimau" (21). Thériault seems to lament the disappearance of the real Inuit along with "la prescience qui avait été longtemps l'arme la plus efficace de l'Inuk, et qui expliquait plus que toute autre chose son incroyable et quasi miraculeuse survie à travers des dizaines de milliers d'années dans un pays soumis à un climat impossible à décrire tant il est cruel, destructeur, implacable, inexorable" (25). This loss is most acute in the case of women, who signify an even closer link to nature: for instance, the reaction of Judith at Agoak's leaving is "instinctive, nullement raisonée" (16). As the Inuit women who once patiently endured the role of "bête de somme, d'esclave, de femelle soumise" take on modern ways (15), their emancipation represents an even greater loss of culture. Civiliza-tion, in Thériault's fiction, ruins the culture by disrupting the roles that Thériault presents as natural.

Cultural loss is central to Gabrielle Roy's *La rivière sans repos* (1970), which thematizes the dilemma of encroaching modernity in the rape of an Inuit girl, Elsa, by an American soldier. The rape takes place in an atmosphere of cultural shift after Elsa and her friends walk home from the movies, linking their arms as girls in films do (3). The rape scene plays on the impact of the cinema as Elsa is "stupéfaite au point de séparer mal la réalité du buisson, de l'histoire d'amour vue à l'écran plus tot dans la soirée et dont ceci pouvait sembler la suite" (127) and feels "tout était cependent tel qu'au cinéma, étrange, lointain, à peine vraisemblable" (126). The son conceived in this act becomes a symbol of the ambiva-lence of acculturation as Elsa takes on the daily routines of white people, sheds her own customs, and becomes confused: "Elle était une personne toute changée. Elle aussi maintenant croyait en des choses comme l'ordre, la discipline, l'heure" (151). It is difficult not to read Roy's text as a metaphor of north-south relations, with the Inuit girl representing the north and her aggressor, the south. However, the novel's opposition of a north defined by association with the feminine and the Native to a south associated with white masculinity does not facilitate the masculine quest; rather, it symbolizes cultural contact. Roy's romantic image of Inuit culture threatened by modernity and miscegenation reveals a concern with the survival of collective identity. Thériault's *Agoak* also views acculturation as detrimental to Inuit culture, especially to the strict gender roles depicted in *Agaguk*, but the concern is still focused on the individual's quest. Rather than representing this quest in terms of physical endurance and survival, however, these novels concern the threat that contact with other cultures poses to the traditional way of life. Because the novels emphasize cultural survival, the individual's story also symbolizes collective experience. This narrative differs somewhat from the quest conceived as a contest between the rugged individual and the harsh, unforgiving environment.

Contemporary works set in the north no longer depict northern people as part of the natural environment or as remnants of the Stone Age; rather, novels such as Rudy Wiebe's *A Discovery of Strangers* (1994) and travel writing such as Aritha van Herk's *Places Far from Ellesmere* (1990) attempt to describe aboriginal culture in its own terms by inquiring into and trying to represent Inuit points of view. In this endeavour, such texts resemble ethnographic accounts, yet, while the representation of Inuit people has also veered away from some of the images used in the past, it is still characterized by a preoccupation with cultural survival and an emphasis on traditional and pre-contact culture.

THE INUIT IN CHILDREN'S LITERATURE

Survival and extinction are the two predominant themes in children's literature and school textbooks about the Inuit, mirroring those in books for adults. Children learn that Inuit culture is "a miracle of survival" (Shemie 3) because "they accepted what life brought them and improvised when it fell short of their needs" (Siska 11). A stress on the environmentally sound lifestyle of the hunting society gives a slight twist to the survival theme, as children learn how the Inuit "took from the land only what they needed to survive" (Siska 8). However, they also learn that the Inuit way of life is disappearing, a message reflected by titles such as Jan Reynolds' *Frozen Land: Vanishing Cultures* (1993).

Encouraging children to learn about the Inuit before their way of life vanishes, as Reynolds' text does, replicates the "dying Indian" motif prevailing in other genres. Canadian readers would have encountered the motif in the work of Confederation poet Duncan Campbell Scott, especially his article "The Last of the Indian Treaties" (1906) in which he remarks that the "Indian nature now seems like a fire that is waning, that is smouldering and dying away in ashes" (110). In the most hopeful convergence of the survival and extinction themes, the Inuit are said to have "found new ways of surviving in the Arctic," although few of the old ways survive "except their art" and although "the lives of the people of the ice have been changed forever" (Siska 46).

If, as ethnographer John S. Matthiasson writes, "[s]chool children from around the world know about the romantic people who lived in igloos and hunted sea mammals for food" (9), it is because Inuit culture has been used (along with other aboriginal cultures) to teach difference, and now tolerance of differences. It is not only the ethnographer's view of Inuit culture that children encounter: Inuit literature itself has been classified as children's literature, as Robin McGrath explains, probably because much of it is illustrated (see *Canadian Inuit*). As a result, adult readers have had a tendency to read it as such and to dismiss the literary value of traditional stories. Indeed, most writing transcribed from Inuit oral tradition has been categorized and taught as children's literature.

Both spiritual and material aspects of Inuit culture are usually represented in adventure stories written for a young audience, as Inuit characters intervene in the conflict between the (white) individual and the environment by offering the means of survival, and by guiding the individual on his journey to freedom and self-discovery. In C.W. Nicol's *The White Shaman* (1979) and in James Houston's *Spirit Wrestler* (1980), the spiritual transformation of the hero forms the basis of the plot. The Welsh-born hero of *The White Shaman*, Richard, has mystical experiences of increasing intensity throughout the narrative, culminating in his sacrificial death. Most of these experiences occur when he is alone hunting, such as the time when he suspects that "he had sprung from a form that had feared land, and that this thing, remnant within him, drew him to the Sea Mother" (112). Each time Richard has such an experience, he describes it in terms of his knowledge of Inuit traditions; as a result, his initiation into manhood runs parallel to his gradual assimilation of Inuit spirituality, until the narrator acknowledges the successful transformation: "His was a meta-morphosis of the spirit, with Tik gone, and Tikkisi emerging as one of strength. The slate was wiped clean by shock and amnesia, and Richard Tavett, once known as Tik, had indeed become Tikkisi, but while Tik had always been searching for self, the thought that such a problem should even exist never crossed Tikkisi's mind. He was. He lived" (150). Richard's successful initiation is an affirmation of self. By mimicking Inuit spirituality, he gains access to an ontologically given status ("He was. He lived") which means that he no longer has to worry about becoming. Because he is a "white shaman" mimicking Inuit identity, Richard-Tikkisi is freed from problems of self-definition because Inuit identity is not achievement; it simply is. And Richard simply is a man. Shaman status also allows him to transcend the troubling ethical consequences of his actions. As Tikkisi, he possesses the power to will things into being, and his threats against Philip become real-ity. While his mentor, Ipeelee, warns him against abusing his power, he does not blame Tikkisi for Philip's death, and Tikkisi never comes to terms with the role he has played in that event.

James Houston's *Spirit Wrestler* features the voice of Shoona, "a shaman of the northern Paleo-Asiatic type, one of a long line of shamans so ancient that we can only guess when their order first began" (305). Houston based the experiences of Shoona on knowl-edge gained during twelve years living among the Baffin Island Inuit where, he claims, "[a]ll the events and shamanistic practices recounted here were not unusual" (305). Shoona's story is nar-rated by a northern service officer who receives the story myste-riously from Shoona's spirit and who mediates his position as a medium for Shoona by asserting that "[t]he important thing is that the story of Shoona's life was given to me" (14).

Shoona narrates from a first-person point of view, but his story is framed by the events following his arrival at the service officer's door. At the end of the book, it becomes clear in the framing narrative that Shoona has been dead throughout his communication with the officer. While his power as a shaman, tested throughout the story, seems to be articulated in this communication, it does not alter the fact that Shoona is one more dead aboriginal person in Canadian literature whose story has had to be told by a white.

While children's literature romanticizes Inuit traditions of the past as authentic and laments their contamination by such influences as television, literature for young adults focuses on timeless spirituality. By romanticizing tradition, texts for young people give Inuit culture a pure, ahistorical form that functions as a static repository of difference and identity.[6] Maintaining a notion of Inuit cultural purity, as represented in the images of smiling Inuit and igloos illustrating children's books, allows Canadians to foster an image of the Inuit as innocent and afflicted, a passive, feminized image that dates back to Hearne's description of Bloody Falls.

INUIT REPRESENTATION

A study of Inuit representation through their literature makes an appropriate and necessary complement to the preceding chapter, given that their literature has been used for ethnographical purposes. Indeed, as members of a society living in neo-colonial conditions, the Inuit occupy a privileged position in relation to representational issues; that is, as Donna Haraway would say, they are on to the god-trick, the "denial of the critical and inter-pretative core of all knowledge" (*Simians* 191). Aboriginal people have what post-colonial scholars call "a capacity, far greater than that of white settler societies, to subvert received assumptions about literature" (Ashcroft et al. 144). However, aboriginal writing is valuable beyond how it illuminates non-aboriginal literature and the "received assumptions" the post-colonial theorists mention; the task of literary criticism of aboriginal writing should be understanding its own features, not embedding it in a national or post-colonial canon. Criticism of aboriginal literature should also examine how, just as land is appropriated by the Canadian state, so is the experience and imagination of aboriginal writing appropriated by non-aboriginals. In this context, the uniqueness of the Inuit case lies in the way Inuit culture has been depicted by national discourses of identity.

As early as the 1960s, some anthropologists questioned the accuracy of depicting the Inuit as culturally homogeneous and distinct. While they argued that a contact-traditional lifestyle was emerging in response to rapid social change, the representation of Inuit art and literature, especially by museums, continued to focus on the past life of Inuit culture, commonly figured through a focus on the hunt and the theme of survival (see Matthiasson *Living on the Land*). Today, although Inuit self-representation has evolved, museum exhibits have not, tending still to reflect southern Canadian interest in artifacts from the traditional material culture; in other words, the story of the Inuit as told by another culture for another culture.

With institutional approval to back their position as authorities, anthropologists, explorers, and even curators have come to play a significant role in defining what is authentic about the traditional culture (Harry 148). In this process, they continue to be led by a consuming interest in survival.[7] Traditions – identified, preserved, and, in some sense, created by outsiders – are valued because they are believed to have survived from the pre-contact past. The preference for past tradition, evident in the popularity of Native storytelling, "places Native people in the museum with all the other extinct species" according to Daniel David Moses (Moses and Goldie xiii). In the same way, anthropologists approach Inuit literature as emerging from the Stone Age.

While non-Inuit writers have historically depicted Inuit in ways that enhance and serve their own narrative intentions, Inuit representation deals with local political and material concerns, indicating the tendency Arnold Krupat notes of Native American fiction towards "homing in rather than moving out" through the quest (*Ethnocriticism* 114; see also Bevis). Speaking for others within the culture comes to be an act of political as well as aesthetic representation. This feature of Inuit writing has affinities with post-colonial literature as theorized in *The Empire Writes Back*; for example, in the way African writers stress the social relevance of their work and its importance in the community rather than the individual's career (Ashcroft et al. 126).

Inuit writing does not affirm the attributes conferred by outsiders. Unlike writing about the north by southern Canadians, which situates the north and its inhabitants neatly within the Canadian nation, Inuit writing refuses to invoke a national position; nor does it celebrate its own "Canadianness" or "nordicity." In fact, Inuit leaders usually address Canada on the nation-to-nation basis indicated in John Amagoalik's promise after the 1984 First Ministers' conference to "continue to have discussions with the government of Canada on Nunavut" (qtd in Petrone 264). While Inuit leaders do not reject Canada, they have also maintained the clear sense of separate, ethnic nationalism that led to the creation of Nunavut in 1999.

While contemporary representation of the Inuit romanticizes Inuit culture and homogenizes differences in timeless images, Inuit writing tends to present a complex integration of the insider's information and the outsider's expectations. As members of a minority, the Inuit bear the burden of explanation: southern writers write as if they can imagine the Inuit to be whatever they want, but Inuit writers write knowing they have a responsibility to themselves as a misrepresented or unrepresented constituency. The pressure to explain oneself to those with more power, whose position means not having to know or even to listen, a privilege that exercising tolerance implies (Spelman 182), typically falls on the members of the marginal group. In this abstract sense, the struggle for self-representation accompanying the struggle for self-government in Inuit and other First Nations communities resembles the discovery of subjectivity by other marginalized groups, including women in various societies. Yet Inuit literature in English is distinct in that its political form reflects the traditional belief that words can bring events into being, and it serves a practical political purpose by addressing the national culture in one of its official languages.

Anthropologists seem to agree on the status of Inuit culture as "a way of life that is rapidly vanishing" (Briggs 262) or, more dramatically, "for which the death knell has already been tolled" (Matthiasson 12). When Inuit suggest that their culture is dying, however, their meaning is quite different, because it is inspired by a desire for continuity and renewal, not a wish to commemorate what is past. Many older Inuit people fear that their culture will die with them, and their initiative to maintain continuity has produced collections such as Mark Kalluak's *How Kabloonat Became and Other Inuit Legends* (1974). An example of what Robin McGrath calls "authentic literature," this collection attributes each story to its teller and cites Kalluak as editor and translator. Included in the collection are a variety of tales about traditional figures such as Kiviok, Mahaha, and Kaugyagyuk, as well as traditional stories of orphans and animal spouses.

The stories preserved at the insistence of the older generation do not corroborate observations made in ethnographies; in fact, traditional stories dispute many assumptions held by outsiders, especially those concerning gender roles, passivity, and innocence. The notion of Inuit culture as a pure and dying one allows for the naturalization of gender categories in the writing of outsiders. By concentrating on their perceptions of what constituted traditional Inuit life in the past, outsiders can project naturalized gender differences onto Inuit culture, and, in the worst cases, describe gender in terms which are comforting to those confused about changes in contemporary gender expectations.

The diversity of modern and traditional accounts by Inuit challenges any account of fixed, stable gender roles. For example, while Inuit Alice French mentions female infanticide in her autobiography and echoes Jenness by explaining that a girl was "of little value until she married and brought home a hunter and trapper" (4), traditional stories do not indicate a stable gender hierarchy. Similarly, Jenness's acquiescent Jenny and subservient Icehouse are nowhere to be found in the traditional stories collected by Kappi, Kalluak, and others. Neither are the pliant, silent, Inuit women who populate the adventure stories discussed in chapter 3: Houston's Panee, Horwood's Nasha, or Kelley's Anu. Traditional stories feature strong women, women who act without men, and women who, far from needing to be saved, save others. "The Huntress" tells of a wife who learns from an old woman that her husband is tired of her and plans to kill her. The wife not only escapes him, but travels to another shore where she saves a town from a terrible ogre (Nanogak, *Tales* n.p.). In both "Mother Bear and Two Sons" and "Raven Who Took a Sea Gull Wife," a deserting husband who leaves his wife for another woman is killed when the original wife decides to take revenge (Kappi n.p.). "Flying Sledge" tells of a girl who refuses to take a husband because she is a successful hunter herself and who, when she agrees to marry an orphan boy, is carried away with him on a magic sled as a reward for her act (Kappi n.p.).

Traditional stories restrict no activity to one sex or the other. Instead, the stories suggest, as ethnographer Jean Briggs argues, that "[t]here is nothing holy to [the Inuit] about the sexual division of labour; neither is there, according to the Inuit, anything inherent in the nature of either sex that makes it incapable of doing some of the jobs that the other sex ordinarily does" (270; see also Fienup-Riordan). Despite the interesting opposition these stories make to anthropological accounts, problems arise when moving from the representation of Inuit life in traditional stories to the way Inuit people actually live; these are the problems posed by reading for anthropological meaning and value. Because realist ethnography is based on fieldwork, hence observable data and phenomena, such works of the imagination are often left out. Indeed, Jenness makes it quite clear that stories do not interest him (*People* 142). A literary critical approach can help account for the contribution oral and written literature makes to culture. While Inuit literature attempts to represent real experience, it is not the transparent window realist ethnographers seek, the window on the real life of the Inuit as they are "when only God is looking."

THE RECEPTION OF INUIT WRITING

One of the major critical positions undermining the reception of literature by aboriginal peoples is the assumption that aboriginal writing carries a primarily anthropological value. Aboriginal cultural expression of any form has been judged for its value as artifact, perhaps because scholars continue to believe that Native cultures are about to become extinct (King, *All My Relations* xiv; Hall 79). Traditional stories have been collected like the other bits of material culture furnishing museum displays that commemorate the death of aboriginal culture. Transferring ownership of culture through ownership of artifacts to the state allows the nation to consolidate its ownership of the land, for, in the words of Michael Walzer, the connection between people and the land remains a "crucial feature of national identity" (44). Native culture must be swept aside for this to happen, and as Margery Fee's important essay argues, the transfer of cultural material from aboriginal to Canadian ownership is analogous to appropriation of land ("Romantic Nationalism" 17). Both actions help build the nation's institutions.[8]

Literary criticism has played a role in this colonization. In his introduction to an issue of *Canadian Literature* devoted to Native writers, W.H. New describes how popular perceptions, including those of literary critics, deny the literary value of writing by Native people: "Native speakers, writers, singers, and tale-tellers have long contributed creatively to tribal culture. Indirectly they have contributed to national culture, too, but to the degree that the nation did not, would not, listen, their activities were regarded (when acknowledged at all) as primitive, pagan, curious, quaint, and collectible rather than as intrinsically artistic" (7). Writing by Native people, like most issues pertaining to Native peoples, is treated as a point of reference for the national culture, something to be accommodated, tolerated, and sometimes assimilated. Rather than consider how aboriginal writing, art, or politics is constituted through its own conventions and methods, many assume the aboriginal culture to be ontologically given; it can be appreciated or collected without explanation or interpretation. As Frank Davey argues, even the dedication of special issues such as the one New introduces "becomes a lavish token of kinds of criticism that have not occurred in preceding regular issues," acting as "a token compensation for a continuing exclusion" (70–1).

The myth of the north as a national heritage tends towards this sort of tokenism with its appropriation of aboriginal cultural products such as Inuit art. As part of what Benedict Anderson calls the "totalizing classificatory grid," imposed by the "state's real or contemplated control[,] peoples, regions, religions, languages, products, monuments, and so forth" become part of the nation's treasures (184). In a startling example of Anderson's identification of the relationship between census, map, and state, the Canadian government began its bid for northern sovereignty by sending in the Geological Survey and by issuing serial numbers to all Inuit people on disks worn around the neck.

PROBLEMS WITH AUTHENTICITY

Inuit literature in English, once excluded by the anglo-Canadian academy because of challenges it presented to received notions of form and genre, has been newly acknowledged. Inuit literature, with its ancient oral tradition and varied contemporary forms, can only be considered a new or emerging one in the limited context of this new reception. Inuit texts in English merge conventions from oral and written Inuit literature with forms from other literary traditions in order to preserve tradition and to accommodate modernity (see Petrone *Northern Voices*). As a result, what they require is the "ethnocritical" approach advocated by Arnold Krupat and described as "complex interactions between a variety of Western discursive and analytic modes and a variety of non-Western modes of knowing and understanding" (*Ethnocriticism* 43–4). By drawing on diverse critical approaches, critics can listen to the voices of subjectivities and communities in process without making those voices refer back to national culture. This is the task set for those who wish to study aboriginal people's literature in an ethically defensible manner.

Individuals often describe their own experience with the intention of being accurate, and realism is an important tool in this representation; however, emphasizing authenticity means reading texts only for their mimetic function, for the reality they are supposed to reflect. Because most literature written about the north represents people inhabiting the north, it is possible to refer to that literature as ethnographic, regardless of its affiliation with fictional, scientific, or historical genres. Native literature is expected to present the real Native point of view as if that point of view were unmediated and readily accessible to the aboriginal writer. In critical discourse, this expectation may arise from the heavy investment in realism made by other forms of writing about aboriginal peoples, especially in the north, including ethnographic monographs, Westerns, and adventure stories. As I argue in chapter 1, the turn away from realism towards postmodern ethnography has not altered this situation substantially. In the preceding chapter, "realism" was discussed in the context of "ethnographic realism" and the postmodern responses to it.

Ethnographic realism, as Marcus and Cushman observe, relies on "the idea that there is a reality independent of the researcher whose nature can be known, and that the aim of research is to produce accounts that correspond to that reality" (43); this configuration depends on the ontologically given nature of culture. What happens when the "subject culture" uses realism to speak out? The realism deployed by Inuit authors functions in different ways to represent the north and to express different concerns about the north.

Anthropological readings of aboriginal literature, that is, those readings that treat Inuit literature as if it were ethnography by focusing on the description of the culture, ignore literary value and value authenticity. At a time when postmodern ethnography and post-structural literary theory challenge the real, aboriginal literature is expected to provide "real" anthropological and historical detail, and this expectation suggests, according to Thomas King, that "race imparts to the Native writer a tribal understanding of the universe, access to a distinct culture, and a literary perspective that is unattainable by non-Natives" (*All My Relations* x). Given the intense desire to be heard expressed by Native writers, positing incommensurable perspectives seems untenable, and King calls it "a romantic, mystical, and in many instances, a self-serving notion" (xi).

It is therefore necessary to distinguish between the assumption that revising myths and stereotypes of Inuit culture is useful and the assumption that Inuit authors access some essential truth about their culture by virtue of being Inuit. The latter assumption reflects the "dying Indian motif" that aboriginal writing seeks to undermine. The difficulty with outsiders' versions of Inuit life is not that they are more or less authentic, but that they have been received as authentic. Images of Inuit have been controlled, historically at least, by non-Inuit, as Victoria Freeman writes: "While many books have been written about the Arctic or about Inuit people, very little of what has been written has reflected an Inuit viewpoint: Inuit and non-Inuit alike have seen Inuit culture reflected through southern eyes" (266). Inuit representation seeks to change this situation by providing images to counter prevailing stereotypes and by revising traditional forms. When Inuit writers use realism, it functions quite differently from ethnographic realism; when the real is represented by a subject culture, realism is used both as a claim to authority and as a counter-discursive move against the representation provided in the writing by others.

For a long time, talking about Inuit culture has meant talking about Inuit traditions as they were before contact. As a result, Inuit literature in English has been expected to reflect only an idea of the authentic, or the past, in northern experience. In *Canadian Inuit Literature: The Development of a Tradition* (1984), a book dedicated to proving that Inuit culture is not dying but changing (53, *passim*), Robin McGrath identifies several problems arising from the stress on authenticity in Inuit literature written in English, besides the fact that it tends to relegate Inuit culture to the Stone Age. The reception of Markoosie's *Harpoon of the Hunter* (1970) illustrates the first danger of reading traditional stories only as representations of the authentic: because reviews of the novel emphasized the mistakes in the text, they failed to assess or, in some cases, even address the literary value of the story (83–4). The second danger arises when Inuit writers borrow songs and images from other cultures: as in the case of Mary Panegooshoo's "Where Are the Stories of My People?", readers may assume they are reading a traditional Inuit story when the text draws on an African one (112).

Inuit literature challenges the supposed transparency of the authentic text; indeed, it calls for a new meaning of authenticity. "Authentic literature," in Robin McGrath's estimation, names the storyteller and any translators involved, lists the languages the story may have been filtered through, identifies any additions or omissions, and retains inconsistencies in the translation. In other words, an authentic text of traditional aboriginal literature looks something like a critical edition. It is not enough to accommodate Inuit literature through tolerance, McGrath argues; instead, she advocates subjecting Inuit literature in English to "the same academic attention that we give literature by English-Canadian or French-Canadian writers" (702).

INUIT AUTOBIOGRAPHY

Inuit literature's accommodation of modernity, which undermines the stability of the "authentic," reflects intersecting linguistic, historical, political, and social pressures. Inuit literature written in English merges oral and written, Inuit and European, and past and present traditions. It has been characterized as attempting to preserve tradition and to accommodate outside influences. For example, some of the earliest Inuit writings in English, autobiographies written by the Inuit of Labrador, show the ambivalence towards identity indicative of the cultural métissage that Dale Blake explores in "Women of Labrador: Realigning North from the Site(s) of Métissage." Some writers used the autobiographical form to espouse English culture while disowning aboriginal identity.

In *Northern Voices* (1988), Penny Petrone traces Inuit autobiography back to testimonials recorded by Moravian missionaries as early as 1776 (58), and continuing in Inuktitut after a written form was developed (103). Writing one's life story began as a religious imperative, encouraged by Christian missionaries, and, as such, early examples tend to show the author's appreciation for and assimilation into the new, colonizing culture. For the missionaries who solicited works by Inuit people, the autobiography testified to their success in converting aboriginal people (57). To them, English ancestry, Christianity, and English literacy, not aboriginal heritage, authorized individuals as writers. In *Woman of Labrador* (1982), Elizabeth Goudie tells how her son was named Robert Bruce to celebrate her husband's Scottish background (53), yet speaks of "Eskimos" with a distance that denies her own Inuit heritage. Almost one hundred years earlier, Goudie's great-aunt, Lydia Campbell, distanced herself from her mother's Inuit identity in her *Sketches of Labrador Life* (1893) by apologizing for her father's choice of bride: "Then of course they had to take wives of the natives of this country. There were very few white men here, much less women" (8). When Campbell describes the decline of the Inuit, which she blames on alcohol and tobacco, she never includes herself among the afflicted population – although she is half Inuit.[9] Dale Blake notes that Campbell's sense of racial identity is "oblique" (168), for although her autobiography is "generally suggestive of Inuit oral myths and legends, with their humour, violence, excitement, superstition, and often unhappy endings" (169), it also relies heavily on Christian themes. In a passage that must have pleased her Anglican clergyman, Campbell engages her religious values by writing that when the Inuit were more plentiful, the "poor souls had no religion whatsoever, besides the rum bottle and biscuits and butter" (11). Campbell concentrates on her father's tales of his home in England (7–8) and continues to describe the poor "Eskimo" as if she has no connection to them (10–11, 29). These two autobiographies show signs of colonial acculturation through identification with the authority figure endorsing the work, and disavowal of the aboriginal mother. At the same time, one hears the voices silenced by ethnographers like Jenness, the voices of Inuit women speaking about their own experiences. As Blake suggests, the two books provide a complex representation of and engagement with aboriginal heritage. The three generations of women who tell their stories in *Saqiyuq: Stories from the Lives of Three Inuit Women* (1999) also provide a history of changes in Inuit communities in the twentieth century, especially with respect to women's roles.

Autobiography became increasingly political in the twentieth century, yet the tradition of white sponsorship continued, albeit with quite different motivation, in publications such as Anthony Apakark Thrasher's autobiography, *Thrasher … Skid Row Eskimo* (1976). According to the book's foreword, Thrasher was first encouraged by his lawyer to write his story, and he wrote it while waiting to stand trial for manslaughter; later, two journalists made it their job to "collate what was essentially a loose-leaf diary into narrative form, authenticate that narrative as thoroughly as possible and expand it" (x). Sceptical about the accuracy of his statements, they verified every detail before publication. In their search for the "facts," they ignored the account's narrative form and literary characteristics; indeed they claim responsibility for changing Thrasher's story into narrative.

Like his contemporary, Minnie Aodla Freeman, who also produced an autobiography, Thrasher first left the north to attend a training course; like Freeman, he suffered the culture shock of coming south. But unlike Freeman, who took a job in Ottawa, Thrasher was deposited in a skid row motel in Edmonton and never got much further. He remembers beatings he received, liquor he drank, and women he slept with, as well as incidents also experienced by Freeman, for example, learning how to cross the street at the traffic light (72–3). While his story concentrates on the sordid aspects of street life, its political subtext can be observed in his nostalgic memories of life in the north and in comments concerning changes to Inuit way of life. Describing his difficulty coping with life in the south, Thrasher writes: "My people in the North were struggling with the same problems. Southern ways were spreading into the Arctic, and my people knew nothing of these new habits and customs, and couldn't grasp many simple things that the white man had accepted for decades" (75–6). Thrasher makes his experience of alienation a political statement on behalf of other Inuit. He idealizes his past life and promotes a view of the Inuit as "a docile people, trusting and loving" (161). By presenting himself as a victim, he undermines his responsibility for his actions, including the death for which he ends up being convicted, so his account seems problematic at best.

There are many narrative inconsistencies in his book; for example, he claims he "read in a medical book that alcohol slows your body's blood pressure down, and gives you resistance to heat," right after he writes: "I couldn't read labels at all, and I ended up chewing laxatives like candy" (75). If these are exaggerations, they suggest that Thrasher's autobiography might be better understood in the tradition of the song duel, just as *I, Nuligak* (1966) can be better understood as a meeting place for the autobiographical form and the structure of the Kaujjarjuk legend (McGrath, *Canadian Inuit* 103). Thrasher's boastful exaggeration and his unreliability can be read as participating in the general one-upmanship of the song duel form, described later in this chapter, that allows for both the settling of an account and the proof of one's masculinity. However, *Thrasher ... Skid Row Eskimo* has been read as a window on the miserable life of urban aboriginal people rather than a book with possible literary merit.

Alice French's *My Name Is Masak*, published the same year as *Thrasher*, features the same integration of romanticized views of traditional life and sordid scenes of the effects of acculturation. French concentrates on her childhood, especially life in residential school, but her autobiography also preserves details of material culture, such as a passage in which she describes the use made of a whale carcass (70). In both the French and Thrasher autobiographies, the author tells the life story of the community while telling her or his personal story, and this gives the autobiography a broader political significance.

Although autobiographies provide valuable ethnographic information to contradict the often skewed perspective of ethnographic representation, they are not simply artifacts of a culture. As products of close collaboration with white editors, the autobiographies by Campbell, Goudie, and Thrasher are what Krupat identifies as "Indian autobiographies" rather than the "autobiographies by Indians" which are self-written and edited (*Ethnocriticism* 219). How much influence can be attributed to editing is uncertain. The editor of Lydia Campbell's sketches admits in the preface to "omitting only a sentence or two of no particular interest," yet although more subtle narrative blanching could have occurred, signs of Inuit culture persist in these texts. For example, Lydia Campbell concentrates on the errors of her youth, because Inuit women are taught that it is "unseemly to discuss their accomplishments, although it is quite acceptable to recall the errors of childhood and adolescence" (McGrath and Petrone 316). French's *My Name Is Masak* and Minnie Aodla Freeman's *Life*

Among the Qalunaat (1978), though more recent, also deal primarily with childhood experiences. As the cases of *Thrasher ... Skid
Row Eskimo* and *I, Nuligak* show, autobiographies written by Inuit
form a continuum with Inuit oral tradition, and, as *Life Among the
Qalunaat* and *My Name is Masak* show, their authors act as political
spokespeople for the community.

Freeman's *Life Among the Qalunaat*, perhaps the best-known Inuit
autobiography, exemplifies the important political function of Inuit
literature written in English. According to Heather Henderson,
Freeman "speaks for" her people (62): by "[m]oving beyond the
personal to the public and political, she becomes a spokeswoman
protesting injustice" (65). Because the "egotism" needed to write
autobiography is antithetical to Inuit ways, Henderson argues,
Freeman subverts autobiography by using her life story to voice
the collective experience of her people. But Henderson need not
submit that the Inuit way, that is, one not driven by ego needs, is
the authentic experience underwriting Freeman's authorization as
a spokeswoman. One has only to look at the content of the book
to understand it as literature with a political value. In fact, Freeman
makes her book's thesis plain when she laments the passing of
the Inuit culture she knew, writing "I miss my dear people who
are becoming stranger, even to me, covering their familiar ways
with another culture" (217).

In passages like this one, the self represented is not without
individuality, but it is identified with the rest of the community.
This is the "part-to-whole" relationship that Krupat has called the
"synecdochic self," one marked by a sense of the self "in relation
to collective social units or groupings," rather than the more
prevalent North American notion that each person possesses an
interiorized self separate from other distinct individuals (*Ethnocriticism* 212). It is clear that people who do not revere individualism would not represent themselves as rugged individuals,
and this may be the most important factor contributing to the
differences between Inuit and non-Inuit representations of the
north and the people in it.

Throughout her autobiography, Freeman demonstrates her connection to her community by documenting experiences bearing
on political issues, such as the racial prejudice expressed by a
teacher who refers to students as "you natives" (195), or the
stereotype contained in the white vision of Inuit as "smiling

happy people" (194). In an ironic account of how images of the Inuit are made, she describes how she was used to represent the north, while working at the Department of Northern Affairs as a translator: "I found myself one day in a building with a lot of big cameras. Then I was made to put on a parka in the middle of July, when the temperature outside was eighty degrees. It would not have been so bad inside the building, but up I went, right to the roof, where the sun beamed down. A man made a movie of me while I drank ginger ale. I understood that I was advertising the ginger ale" (41). While the irony in the situation gives the passage its humour, Freeman underlines her feeling of exploitation by following it with the understated yet painful observation: "Seeing my picture on the back of Pure Spring Ginger Ale trucks made me feel uneasy" (41).

In another moment when an event in her life takes on a political meaning, she tells how she was asked to pose for a photographer by sitting at a desk with something in her hand, and then later discovered her picture in the newspaper: "The story read: 'Eskimos buying bonds, keeping up with progress,' some remark like that. I felt sick. I had no idea what bonds were. My parents had never even heard about them, let alone buy them. Today my father still has no idea what bonds are, though he has been working with Northern Affairs for the last thirteen years. I felt sick because I was being used to show the qallunaat in the South how well the Inuit are treated in the North" (65). In such passages, Freeman speaks of her own experiences while placing them in the collective context.

Autobiographies, especially those by women, record experience that other accounts downplay or ignore, and for that, they are important as ongoing revisions of ethnographic documents. Lydia Campbell's autobiography contradicts fictional love stories involving white men and Inuit women by describing the cruelty of one Englishman towards his Native wife (27), and by telling a cautionary tale about how a woman who died "under her husband's care" haunted him after he took up with a young girl (14). Meanwhile, her admiration for her sister, Hannah, acknowledges the abilities that go unnoticed in images of passive, silent Inuit women: "I wish there were more Hannahs in the world for braveness. She brought up her first family of little children when their father died, taught all to read and write in the long winter nights, and hunt with them in the day, got about a dozen foxes and as many martens" (6). When Alice French describes how her grandmother Susie runs the household, she adds that many women acted as heads of the household in her community (60). According to French, women also decided who should marry whom (76).

The responsibilities outlined by French stand in sharp contrast to the lack of freedom described by her contemporary, Elizabeth Goudie. Goudie describes the difficulty she had adjusting to her life as a trapper's wife: "I was young and liked gay life. I liked dancing and visiting friends. Jim thought I ought to stay at home with him. Life was very dull for me at first but I got used to it. It was the custom for the man to run the home, the women took second place. A woman could have her say around the house but about the main things in life, the man always had his say. His word went for most everything" (50). Goudie complains of boredom in several instances, as part of her construction of her life as one hardship after another.[10] The discrepancy between Goudie's version of women's place and Alice French's version may be attributed to regional cultural differences or the greater degree to which the Labrador Inuit mixed with Europeans, but it is clear that they stem from different values, with Goudie's experiences most closely resembling those reported by ethnographers.

Although Minnie Aodla Freeman's autobiography does not describe the enforcement of the division of labour according to gender roles, it does articulate certain expectations affecting Freeman during her youth. In one instance, she describes the kind of woman Inuit men dream about as "gentle, kind and understanding" (187); in another, her father's advice suggests that women are expected to take the responsibility for making their marriages work (201). In matters of gender, she wants guidance, and she equates her confusion about gender expectations with the loss of her Inuit identity. At residential school, as she approaches puberty, she experiences a kind of culture shock when she realizes that, in her absence from the community and her family, she has not been trained in the appropriate womanly tasks (140). She feels that her development has been stunted. Yet, she is just as confused and alienated when her period arrives while she is at home in her community, and she complains that no one will tell her what is going on (145).

Introducing Armand Tagoona's *Shadows* (1975), George Swinton recognizes how the fusion of political and personal narratives as well as the ongoing revision of traditional forms meet as the "self becomes part of history – autobiography is extracted from the myths and legends and becomes projected into, and renewed in, myths" (n.p.). *Shadows* consists of twenty-three plates, with commentary by the artist, autobiographical segments, and a number of stories. As Tagoona tells his life, he represents the history of his region and his people with understated clarity: "I am often asked how the Inuit felt about being brought into settlements. It is not an easy thing to talk about; the Inuk himself is not sure how he feels. I myself have lived in settlements almost all my life but I tasted a little 'out there' in the Inuit camps in winter. I love it 'out there'" (n.p.).

Increased interest in the north and activity in the field of communications created an explosion of writing about and by the Inuit in the 1960s and 1970s. Many collections of traditional stories appeared, including those by Kalluak, Kappi, and Nanogak, and many Inuit writers published in northern periodicals such as *Inukshuk, Nunatasiaq News, Inuttitut, Inuit Today, Inummarit, Inuit Monthly,* and *Keewatin Echo.* While this activity continued into the 1980s, a number of anthologies also appeared, including *Paper Stays Put* (1980) and *Northern Voices* (1988), as well as the first study of Inuit writing, McGrath's *Canadian Inuit Literature: The Development of a Tradition* (1984).[11] Illustrated autobiography, such as Normee Ekoomiak's *Arctic Memories* (1988), continues to be an important genre in Inuit literature.

Ruth Tulurialik's *Qikaaluktut: Images of Inuit Life* (1986) precedes Alootook Ipellie's *Arctic Dreams and Nightmares* (1993), but both are examples of the importance of the illustrated text in Inuit representation. Tulurialik's text performs the ethnographic function of cataloguing and interpreting culture. It provides definitions (for example, the passage "Tukipqutaq" indicates the word's denotation of a rock marking a good fishing spot) and stories of cultural practices (significantly, those on traditional birthing do not mention infanticide). Other sections – "The Bay," "Minister," and "Bad Policeman" – describe modern features of northern life, as Tulurialik demonstrates the coexistence of ancient and modern ways.

In *Arctic Dreams and Nightmares* (1993), the stories inspired by the ink drawings collected in the book are intensely personal, but they draw on stories and images from oral literature instead of adopting the western autobiographical form. In fact, Ipellie introduces his book as a "smorgasbord of stories and events, modern

or traditional, true or imagined" (xix). Like the Inuit culture represented in ethnography and other forms of writing about the
Inuit, Ipellie's Inuit culture revolves around survival. However,
unlike other representations, Ipellie's celebrates the "resilient culture" (xiv) for standing up to the "constant threat of cultural geno-
cide" (xv). In the contemporary world, survival means cultural
survival: "It is the will and the perpetual pride of our elders that
has helped us to retain the old myths, stories and legends so that
our present generation can absorb them and pass them on to future
generations" (xiv). Part of the goal of Ipellie's work is to continue
their work, and by featuring traditional figures like Sedna or
stories like "The Woman Who Married a Goose," the Inuit world
he creates represents the traditional alongside the modern use of
technology and several references to contemporary events.

In "When God Sings the Blues," the narrator's "spirit journey"
occurs after he performs a secret chant allowing his spirit helper
to travel to the Magical Kingdom where God dwells. The god
depicted is an ironic portrait of the Christian God brought to the
Inuit with contact. Known by his Inuit name, Sattaanassee, which
means Satan, this god possesses a "large array of fax machines"
and a "high-powered telescope" with which to look in on human-
ity (48). Sattaanassee's power comes from technology, yet another
ironic comment on the influence of contact on Inuit belief. More
concerned with the money going into his coffers than anything
else, the economic recession sends Sattaanassee into a depression,
causing the narrator to invite him to a blues jam to cheer him up.
The satire on the Christian religion is complete when the Arctic
audience is entertained by Sattaanassee singing the blues. By
borrowing a form (blues) from southern black culture, Ipellie
demonstrates the elasticity of cultural meaning, the way cultures
intersect and influence each other. His work employs satire, which
is a convention of Inuit oral literature, to comment on the aspects
of modernity that continue to affect Inuit life.

INUIT POETRY

I call forth the song ...
I draw a deep breath ...
My breast breathes heavily
As I call forth the song.
– Akjartoq (qtd in Colombo 44)

"There is no such thing as Eskimo poetry," wrote Edmund Carpenter in 1971, "there are only poetic acts by individual Eskimos" (13). Carpenter's remarks are some of the first in the criticism of Inuit literature as literature. Much of what we know as Inuit "poems" are actually traditional oral songs, chants, and prayers transcribed, collected, and translated by ethnographers, and, therefore, Inuit poetry is subject to the problems of authenticity discussed earlier.[12] While ethnographers who collected traditional songs and stories were moved to do so by their fear that the Inuit traditions were dying, Richard Lewis collected poems for his anthology *I Breathe a New Song* (1971) – whose title alludes to the fact that the Inuktitut word for "to make poetry" means "to breathe" – in order "to help preserve a culture that began to disappear in 1955" (6).

Although Inuktitut does not have an equivalent for the verb "to create," Carpenter describes the Inuit idea of poetic creation thus: "Poet, like carver, releases form from the bonds of formlessness: he brings it forth into consciousness. He must reveal form in order to protest against a universe that is formless, and the form he reveals should be beautiful" (14). Inuit poets are not concerned with representing the landscape, Carpenter asserts; rather, they interact with the environment, which "requires a creative human act before the world explored becomes a world revealed" (15). There is no distance between the poetry Carpenter describes and the prayers and chants of the oral tradition. The poetic brings things into being. In Inuit culture, writes Joseph Epes Brown, "[t]o name or speak of a person, a being, or some phenomenon in Nature, is to make really present that which is named, or indeed is actually to call forth the spiritual essence of that which is named" (142–3). In this Iglulik poem, sung by Aua, the hunter sings for strength "Words Which Make Heavy Things Light":

> I will walk with leg muscles
> which are strong
> as the sinews of the shins of the little caribou calf.
> I will walk with leg muscles
> which are strong
> as the sinews of the shins of the little hare.
> I will take care not to go toward the dark.
> I will go toward the day.

> (in Petrone, *Northern Voices* 7)

Characterized as they are by the repetition of words, phrases, and images, traditional Inuit poems collected and translated for English readers give a sense of the diversity of Inuit culture even if, by taking written form, they cease to be part of the oral tradition. Collections of examples from the oral tradition are synecdochic statements on the culture because they can only evoke the tradition they belong to.

The traditional hunting songs and weather chants that are primarily narrative indicate the male-dominated hunting culture non-Inuit imagine the Inuit to be. In Orpingalik's "My Breath," also collected in Petrone's *Northern Voices*, the speaker mourns his former strength, remembering his hunting prowess and lamenting the state his woman is in:

> Sad, I would that my woman
> Were gone to a better protector
> Now that I lack strength
> To rise from my couch.
> Unaya-unaya. (24)

The representation of gender difference also inheres in certain distinctly Inuit forms such as the song duel. Song duels, which are also called nith songs, drum songs, or satirical songs, are a form which seems to be unique to Inuit culture. In these, the poet or singer responds to a challenge or challenges another by deriding himself, someone else, a group, or a type of behaviour (McGrath, *Canadian Inuit* 48). Song duels use irony and satire to various ends depending on the purpose they serve, which may include settling disputes, gently criticizing another, accusing another, or binding the friendship between song brothers; they are also intended to amuse listeners. Song brothers engage in duels also to prove their masculinity, and their derisive remarks usually focus on the hunting and sexual prowess of the adversary.

Once they are preserved on paper, these Inuit traditions are claimed within the national literature. In his preface to *Poems of the Inuit* (1981), John Robert Colombo admits that his interest in the Inuit is closely related to his "concern for things Canadian" and his belief that "the oral art of the Inuit adds a distinctive element to the national mosaic" (7). The Inuit represent that absolute difference and identity which justifies the definition of Canada

as a multicultural mosaic; moreover, the cultural diversity represented by Inuit poets is as distinctly Canadian as the work of
canonical poets: "Aua, Netsit, Uvavunuk, and Orpingalik are new
– and strange-sounding – names to place alongside those of Saint-
Denys-Garneau, Raymond Knister, W.W.E. Ross and Sir Charles
G.D. Roberts, their better-known contemporaries. Yet the mix
could occur only in Canada and the two groups of singers have
much more in common than is immediately apparent" (7).

   Despite Colombo's enthusiasm, however, relatively few contemporary Inuit writers choose poetry as a genre in which to
express themselves, preferring the rhetorical advantages of the
essay, speech, and even short fiction. Those who do write poetry
have reached an audience beyond their community in literary
anthologies such as Penny Petrone's *Northern Voices: Inuit Writing
in English* (1988). As Petrone remarks, contemporary Inuit writers
devote much of their talent to journalism, and "with a new political consciousness, unknown to their ancestors, they are writing
a literature of opinion and information, largely derivative and
imitative of western models, reflecting the new realities of political
and social change" (201).

   What little contemporary Inuit poetry there is uses forms and
treats themes common to the oral tradition, as the poems collected
by Petrone indicate. Robin McGrath argues in her essay "Oral
Influences in Contemporary Inuit Literature" that the form and
content of Inuit poetry may change, but it is still firmly rooted in
the oral tradition. For example, Liz Semigok's "My Cooking Pot"
(1988), which was written first in Inuktitut, then translated into
English, offers thanks: "Grateful am I when it boils something"
(285), and William Kalleo's "The Known Mysteries of Seals" (1982)
has the repetition of the hunting chant: "Hunting seals / Hunting
different seals" (253). McGrath makes a convincing case for satire
as the emerging Inuit form in English, and poems such as Alexis
Pamiuq Utatnaq's "Blood Thirsty Enemies" (1974) exemplify the
satiric impulse of much Inuit writing:

> Our Enemy
> Our enemy
> They're so many
> Our blood they spill
> They make us ill

Help us, oh God
From their piercing rods
Our sworn foes
Those mosquitoes.

(in Petrone, *Northern Voices* 166)

In this poem, the surprise ending gives pause, reminding readers that, in the Arctic, mosquitoes pose an ever-present threat, as Ivaluartjuk sang in "Cold and Mosquitoes" (1929); however, these mosquitoes also signify invaders from the south too, the image of bloodsucking pests being a particularly evocative one in times of increased resource exploitation.

Ivaluartjuk is just one poet who is also a storyteller and whose work therefore connects directly to the oral tradition. Mary Carpenter Lyons uses poetry and storytelling to voice contemporary political concerns. In "Nunavut? –Denendeh? = Northwest-erritories" (1988), the speaker calls on the land to give its people strength to face the "distant men" who watch them die and "Who sit and build / invisible, governing walls." The poem concludes with the lament: "O greatland, you are leached by white lies / Lip-serviced, not loved" (in Petrone, *Northern Voices* 273). Like the poets of the oral tradition, Carpenter uses the "simplicity of tone, language, and subject matter, all of which combine to suggest the depth of importance of brief moments of emotion" (McGrath, *Canadian Inuit* 45).

As with traditional stories, the reception of Inuit poetry in the south has been deeply influenced by the value of its anthropological content. As part of the essential, sacred culture, poems are treated as artifacts to be collected and preserved. Robin McGrath describes how attempts to popularize Inuit poetry have resulted in "all Inuit poems [being] regarded as sacred, unspoiled flowers that were simply to be admired in a passive way, never subject to the intense light of criticism" ("Inuit Literature" 702). McGrath argues that "Inuit poems in English are not just anthropological enigmas, but are works that are accessible to anyone who brings curiosity and a little imagination to their reading of poetry" ("Reassessing" 19). Unlike the novel, autobiography, and essay, Inuit poetry has not developed primarily through contact with non-Inuit, and it retains strong ties to the oral tradition, but Inuit poems written in English also address a non-Inuit audience. As

Petrone remarks, "the sacredness of the word has marked all Canadian Inuit literature. And young Inuit writers today continue to believe, as their forefathers before them, that in language will they find the true meaning of their ancient northern homeland" (202). The reception of Inuit poetry also demonstrates the popular appeal of anthropological material that the proliferation of ethnography seems also to confirm. Inuit literature in general, and Inuit poetry in particular, has been received this way because the representation of traditional culture confirms preconceptions of the Inuit as a remnant of the Stone Age. These preconceptions include the centrality of hunting in the culture, the cultural significance of survival, and the domination of women within the division of labour, the very same notions that are challenged by contemporary Inuit writers, poets, and storytellers.

In the national discourse that places northern experience at the centre of national identity, Inuit culture can be considered a sort of apex of Canadian nordicity; after all, the Inuit inhabit regions that fulfil Louis-Édmond Hamelin's ten criteria of nordicity. In a 1972 survey, Canadians described Inuit in terms of the noble savage, as a people possessing a pure ideology under threat of southern civilization (Hamelin, "Images" 8), and Hugh Brody observes similar attitudes in *The People's Land*. Inuit culture can be claimed within national discourse, whether that discourse is based on the concept of nordicity outlined by Hamelin or the multicultural values described in government documents.

Images of Inuit life in painting, carvings, and photographs represent "Canada" in public places and publications. Inuit culture plays a dual role in national myth as both the ultimate of identification and the ultimate of difference. That is, as the most northern culture, it represents the idea of north in the Canadian identity, and as a culture under anthropological study, it represents the difference that multiculturalism claims to accommodate. Early criticism of Inuit writing reflects a preoccupation with anthropological content and relevance, and this preoccupation establishes expectations in the non-Inuit audience concerning gender and national identity, which are countered by Inuit writers in their revisions.

While non-Inuit tend to depict the Inuit as ideal Canadians, inhabiting the territory of Canadian national difference, Inuit writers are concerned with the collective experiences and problems of Inuit, not Canadians. As Minnie Freeman's discomfort with the use of her image in advertisements indicates, non-Inuit representations of Inuit do not reflect these concerns. Most importantly, writing by Inuit does not refer to the Canadian identity of the north, recalling Thomas Berger's often quoted observation that its inhabitants view the north as their homeland, not as the national heritage of the multicultural state.

In recent years, multiculturalism has replaced biculturalism as the official discourse of the Canadian government. To understand the ideological ambivalence of multiculturalism it is unnecessary to look further than government publications concerning the renewal of the constitution, which advance tolerance as the multicultural ideal at the heart of Canadian identity. When a 1992 publication asserts that Canadians are "recognized around the world for the values we cherish – tolerance of differences and respect for different cultures and minorities; generosity; compassion for the less fortunate; freedom and opportunity for the individual" ("Our Future Together" 1), it seems clear that the "we" refers to Canadians who share the same things, including the ability to tolerate differences and to respect other cultures. Paradoxically, the "we" does not encompass the object of tolerance, so the passage actually excludes those who are "different" while claiming to accept them. Moreover, the text remains silent about what these cultures are actually different from and thereby implies that the majority members do not have ethnic, gendered, or otherwise defined identities. Such categories (gender, ethnicity, race) serve as repositories of difference that the norm somehow transcends. Whatever the norm tolerates defines it. Both Leslie Monkman (5–6) and Margery Fee ("Romantic Nationalism" 29) identify a similar binary opposition in the constitution of Canadian identity by recognizing how aboriginal difference comes to define the (white) Canadian norm.

The most salient point in the critiques offered by Monkman and Fee concerns the function of aboriginal culture as a point of reference for defining Canadian culture. According to Fee, national models of Canadian literature, and writers who espouse them, have been known to romanticize "the Native" as a means of consolidating ownership of the territory claimed as Canada. Such a romantic image and endorsement of what the Native point of view has to offer readers introduces William Mowat and Christine Mowat's *Native Peoples in Canadian Literature* (1975): "Possibly this book asks the impossible: it asks the reader to step outside his own ethnic consciousness and to walk a mile in Indian moccasins... If the reader is able to shun any sense of paternalism or superiority that he may hold, if he is able to open himself to upside-down concepts of time, and to fresh relationships with people, society, and the land, he may find his perceptions of Indians and Eskimos jolted but enlarged" (1). In other words, the Native point of view will provide what the national culture, here represented by "non-Indians," lacks. Aboriginal culture plays the same role for Canada that white women have played for white men by representing the "other" by which the "self" can be defined. Mowat and Mowat are right about one thing, however: it *is* impossible to step outside one's own ethnic position in the way they desire, and it is even less desirable to pretend one can. As Linda Alcoff argues, there is an important distinction between the mistaken notion that one can transcend the epistemological and discursive contexts one inhabits as a critic and the potential of "positionality" characterized by continuous shifting between and within those contexts.

Romanticization results from fixing "the Native" in a national image, because to fix something as complex as culture it is necessary to settle on a limited range of attributes. In a well-known passage quoted in Petrone's *Northern Voices*, Inuit writer and politician Nellie Cournoyea sums up the role of the Inuit in Canada: "They glamorize and romanticize the Inuit ... and give us status the others don't have. Canadians like to talk about us eating frozen meat and living in the cold. It gives Canada something that other countries don't have. Everybody likes the Inuit" (286).

The result is a romantic image that characterizes the representation of Inuit culture in Canada as well as the reception of Inuit writing. In the case of Inuit culture, the Native as reference point defining Canadian culture collapses into the north as reference point defining Canadian national consciousness. The Inuit have been imagined as ideal Canadians, as those who can pass on the "autochthonous claim" (Fee, "Romantic Nationalism" 18) to both the land and the north. However, the self-determination of Nunavut will continue to trouble this easy equation of north and the Canadian nation.

"To Fight, Defeat, and Dominate": From Adventure to Mastery

In *The People's Land* (1975), Hugh Brody describes the myth of the frontiersman, for whom going north is "going away from the constraints and inhibiting social forces that restrict self-expression 'at home'" (47). From Samuel Hearne to Albert Johnson, the history of the north has been "the saga of a few heroic individuals" (17), a history made possible by a dual image of the north as both the frontier utopia "where man can yet pursue a personal dream – where he can hope to be individual" (Mitcham 17), and as the frozen wasteland represented in the phrase "the land God gave Cain" (Mowat, *Canada North* 6).[1] Northern experience, for most of us, is an intertextual meeting of such stories, myths, and images in which aboriginal peoples are figures and symbols, not the complex relationship to the land and to others that it is for northern inhabitants. While the Inuit in particular have been fetishized as northern Canadians and as racial others accommodated by the multicultural state, it has been against the historical background of colonization and dispossession. The shape of this history was determined by ideas about what it is to be a "man," both in anthropological and social terms.

In the literature examined so far, the imaginary and ideological north displays certain features: male community, an individual quest, conquest of nature, and flight from civilization. Some of these features bear a resemblance to the American frontier in Western novels. The idea in Canadian literature of the frontier as an outward-moving expansive space with its hero who "lights out for the frontier" can be attributed to the literary influence of America. The geographical frontier in Canadian history does not typically move westward as Frederick Jackson Turner's famous thesis postulated; rather, as Northrop Frye observed, the existence of a frontier between "civilization" and "nature" creates an inward-turning mentality. Instead of "lighting out," most Canadian individuals look in. As Frank Norris shows in his study of Ernest Thompson Seton and Sir Charles G.D. Roberts, when American Klondike stories were gaining popularity as dime novels, Canada did not develop a similar genre (54). America had frontier literature; Canada had animal stories (59). The tradition of wilderness story in Canada, of which the stories of Ernest Thompson Seton, Grey Owl, and Farley Mowat are a part, differs from American frontier literature in a number of ways.

The derivative nature of the frontier myth may be enough to explain why this particular view of northern experience cannot describe a "distinct culture" for Canada. While scholars including Shelagh Grant, Wilfred Eggleston, and Rob Shields have examined the idea of a "frontier" to the north and west of Canada, Bruce Hodgins' definition of the north as a "territorially shifting concept, somewhat *analogous* to the frontier" cogently describes the conceptualization of the north in Canadian history (4, emphasis added). This is not to say, however, that the literary representation of the north does not contain elements which liken it to the literary representation of the frontier; on the contrary, a similar type of hero figures prominently in both.

MYTHOLOGIZING THE NORTH: ADVENTURE BOYS AND RUGGED INDIVIDUALS

Heroic, rugged individuals, usually male, people the literature set in the north, and they usually share common characteristics. "They are out encountering the land–" writes Margaret Atwood, "they penetrate it, they open it up, they stake it out, they grapple with it, they fight with it, they wrest its secrets and its treasures from it, they win or lose" (*Strange Things* 97). Whether it is an American draft dodger lured north by an ad in a magazine, like the hero of Thomas York's *The Musk Ox Passion* (1978), or a sensitive, penitent veteran, like the hero of Fred Bodsworth's *The Atonement of Ashley Morden* (1964), the northern hero leaves his southern home and sheds his past in order to find freedom and self-affirmation.[2] This quest is heightened in adventure tales which add particularly dangerous settings and events to the voyage. Because adventure takes place in exotic settings far from home, it represents freedom from social connection, responsibility, and moral reason, that is, "a breaking of the social contract" (Green, *Adventurous Male* 71).

The challenge presented by the endless possibility of the frontier or by the intractable forces of nature creates opportunities for heroism. "In the adventure tale," Martin Green observes, the person "responds to that challenge with a series of exploits which make him/her a hero/heroine, that is, eminent in such virtues as courage, fortitude, cunning, strength, leadership, and persistence" (*Great American* 1). As noted in chapter 1, ethnographers who become the heroes of their own stories participate in this tradition of representation by idealizing the "cherished outward-bound, lone-wolf, muddy-boots image" (Van Maanen 74) of the northern hero who continues to be male, white, and alone. In exploration literature, this figure embraces the landscape as he follows rivers ever deeper into his sublime Mother Nature, naming them like a New World Adam; later, he can be found penetrating virgin wilderness like the American frontiersman.

As Annette Kolodny has demonstrated, the dichotomy drawn here between the primeval and the civilized, or the wilderness and the settlement, especially in representations of the American frontier, is deeply "gendered" (*Land Before Her* 5 and *passim*). Kolodny's research describes the "psychosexual dynamic of a virginal paradise" (3) in early American literature as an effect of the masculine desire to dominate and to possess a feminized environment, and she thereby challenges Turner's influential vision of American expansion by exposing the frontier as a gendered concept. Kolodny argues that the frontier, as "geographical locus" for this fantasy, pushed westward as women arrived and masculine desire was frustrated by the influence of women on frontier society (4). Linda Ben-Zvi supports and updates Kolodny's reading by applying psychoanalytic terms: "The myth of the frontier, then, becomes not only the historical account of conquest, but also the psychological tale of masculine individuation, separation, and schism" (219). The literary genre appropriate to this "psychological tale" is the adventure, and its motif is the quest.

In *Desert, Garden, Margin, Range: Literature on the American Frontier* (1992), Eric Heyne frames the discussion of frontier literature

with the assertion that crossing the frontier, conceived as a territorial border or margin, constitutes the American national rite of
passage (7). Heyne's critique recognizes the gendered aspect of
initiation: to fulfil the frontier myth the American hero must be
masculine, although, as the narratives examined in this chapter
suggest, biological maleness does not guarantee success on the
frontier. It is in the complex articulation of his initiation in the gap
between wilderness and civilization, not in the identification of
his biological sex, that the hero aspires to masculinity.

"Adventures," writes R.S. Phillips, "like exploration and travel
narratives set in Victorian Canada, are generally masculinist" (46).
Indeed, the concern of adventure narratives with masculinity has
been remarked by every scholar who has ever written on the
subject. Because adventure narratives set in the Arctic depict idealized forms of masculinity, they are integral to the formation of
other masculinist narratives representing the north. In this
respect, they continue the tradition of American frontier literature
and bear a striking similarity to the popular genre of the Western.[3]
Observing this similarity, Aron Senkpiel shows how the north in
Canadian literature has come to signify an imaginary border that
heroes cross from civilization to freedom (137–8).

The adventure hero, perhaps more than any other type of hero,
exemplifies the masculine as a status achieved by successfully
acquiring recognized traits. As Genevieve Lloyd argues, manhood
has been conceptualised throughout Western history as a matter
of accomplishment (86), and while the content of the characteristics
associated with masculinity change with the times, the acquisition
of such characteristics remains essential to forming masculine
identity. As a result, men can never be "at home" with masculine
identity; rather, they must constantly aspire to an identity based
on an externalised sense of self by continuously proving themselves
worthy (Seidler, *Rediscovering* 149).

Literary representations of masculinity as this kind of attainment
tend to structure identity around a quest. According to Mircea
Eliade's seminal study *Rites and Symbols of Initiation: The Mysteries
of Birth and Rebirth* (1958), there are two compelling cases for the
specifically gendered form of the modern quest narrative and for
the importance of initiation in the development of masculine
identity.[4] First, although Eliade is concerned primarily with so-
called "primitive societies" in which initiation rites have religious

significance, he also considers the secularized versions of initiation in modern society in which "initiatory themes remain alive chiefly in modern man's unconscious" and are expressed in the production and reception of literature (134). These initiatory themes are based on the common cross-cultural features of the initiation of pubescent boys and include a "test of courage, resistance to physical suffering, followed by magical transformation" (82), wherein physical ordeals are heaped on the initiate leading to great suffering and symbolic death into new life (30). Second, when Eliade demonstrates how themes in modern literature reflect rituals in societies throughout the world, he suggests a connection between the quest in modern literature and the quest pattern in the initiation of males, suggesting that stories of the quest as we know it are echoes of such ceremonies. The events and patterns represented in adventure narratives written for boys lend support to his suggestion.

By differentiating male from female initiation, Eliade's study demonstrates the specifically masculine character of the quest pattern or motif in Western culture. In most traditional societies, female initiation is signalled by the mysterious beginning of menstruation, which occurs at different times for different individuals. Most female initiation involves separation from the society, like the early stage of male initiation, followed by a moment of being welcomed into the community as a woman (43). However, although female initiates may undergo tattooing, mutilation, and other painful rituals preceding re-entry into society, the series of physical ordeals, torture, and other tests of endurance that boys must pass are largely absent from female initiation. In most initiation ceremonies, boys do things while girls have things done to them. As a result, it would be impossible to equate the development of the quest pattern or motif, which involves "doing things," that is, fulfilling certain physical tasks to achieve a certain goal, specifically with archetypal female initiation or with the social construction of femininity in those societies.[5]

In its modern, secularized form, the quest narrative provides an imaginary opportunity to take on tasks which prove one's masculinity – which might explain the proliferation of adventure stories aimed at boys and young men. Masculinity is defined in opposition to femininity, to Native people, to nature, all of which represent the primitive, or to childhood, a primitive state, which is why male characters in juvenile adventure literature always try to act like men rather than boys (Green, *Great American* 6–7). Late nineteenth- and early twentieth-century adventures often also align attaining gender identity with demonstrating patriotism and serving national interests. As boys learned how to be men by reading adventure stories set on the frontier, they also learned to imagine themselves taking up the challenge "to advance that frontier – against native populations or natural barriers – to extend the domain of civilization" (2).

In America and Britain, adventure became "the energizing myth of empire" (Green, *Great American* 4), its didactic function emphasizing the importance of turning boys into good citizens of the British empire or into young men willing to settle on the American frontier (Bristow 19; Green, *Great American* 8; Moyles 49). During this period, attitudes towards boys reflected concerns British social reformers had about educating the "rough lads" or working-class boys in London. The situation of the rough lads presented upper-class reformers with a paradox: the primitive nature represented by rough lads was both romantic and dangerous. In order to contain it, upper-class men opened social and athletic clubs and established "vertical bonds of comradeship across class lines" (Koven 365) intended to improve the working-class children. At first produced in a cross-generational setting, these goals were also set in cross-cultural and cross-racial situations in which missionaries established paternal relationships with aboriginal people.

At the end of his study of the British adventure genre, *Empire Boys*, Joseph Bristow observes that narratives for boys place too many opposing demands on their idealized heroes and must find extraordinary means of smoothing over narrative inconsistency (226). Bristow analyses narratives by Conrad, Stevenson, and Kipling to demonstrate the relationship between perpetuating a specific form of masculinity consistent with the notion of "the great man" and safeguarding the interests of the British empire, but Canadian literature also includes stories containing convenient plot twists and implausible events in order to allow the hero to display his individuality. The tension between opposing social pressures – for example, the young heroes are expected to display both moral restraint and unrestrained, even unscrupulous individuality – requires concealment to ensure the unity of gender identity, a concealment of fissures that Eve Kosofsky Sedgwick also identifies in novels concerned with masculine identity (119). For example, in Caspar Whitney's "The Winged Snowshoer of the North Land," the narrator can live out his solitary heroism only after so alienating his Indian servants that, in a very unlikely turn of events, they abandon him in the middle of the wilderness (in Whitaker, *Stories*). Bristow concludes from similar instances of unresolved tension that "male identity is something that can never be fully attained" (226), despite its important role in generating British imperial history. In a similar argument, Martin Green observes "close connections between the love of adventure, the writing of adventures, the progress of democracy, and the expansion of trade, between adventure and, for example, the expansion of the American empire in this modern sense" (*Great American* 8).

These pursuits hold a discourse of mastery in common. Mastery narratives rely on the possibility of dominance in the struggle between man and nature, culminating in the mastery of the hero's internal nature and of the external forces of nature he encounters. In Arctic adventures, heroes persevere through hunger and cold by sheer will, ignoring the immediate needs of the flesh in order to reach their goals. Because needs indicate weakness, masculinity becomes a matter of controlling or mastering the hero's inner nature while also mastering the elements of an external Nature (Seidler, *Rediscovering* 55; Butler 37). As a result, the hero contains the nature-culture binary in his relations to himself and to the world – he cannot exist without them. As Eric Heyne writes, the hero "disputes the middle ground" between nature and culture and "must, of course, ride off into the sunset" (10). In constantly striving for the elusive goal of masculine identity, he is constituted by the binary and cannot transcend it.

Joseph Boone presents a very different view of the frontier, conceptualising it as an outward journey geographically and an inward one psychologically, both journeys allowing for the redefinition of the self (187). Boone rejects the explanation that male readers of frontier literature dream of being rugged masculine individuals (see also Oehlschlaeger 177); instead, he argues, the chance to remove oneself from strictures imposed by society allows the hero to find "an affirming multiform self" that rejects traditional definitions of manhood (188). Whereas most critics writing about the frontier consider it to be a place where the illusion of "free-individuality" can be created through the dominance inherent in the nature-culture binary, Boone supposes that the quest can move into "unknown spheres" where new forms of masculinity await discovery (209). In this way, Boone seems drawn to the metaphor of endless possibility represented in the frontier myth. Unfortunately, Boone's exciting hypothesis, especially the implication that gender identity can be imagined outside social roles and textual conventions (212), finds little support in the realist texts he describes and even less in the Arctic adventure narratives studied here.[6] If Boone is right about the transformative potential of frontier literature, then the Arctic adventure stories set in the Canadian north have not achieved that potential and instead form reactionary representations of masculine identity. Existing codes of masculinity and femininity are reinscribed and reified, not transcended, in northern adventures, so that rather than reconceptualising gender, they ensure that the same boundaries are simply redrawn.[7]

NINETEENTH-CENTURY ADVENTURE BOYS

In the late nineteenth and early twentieth century, magazines such as *Chums* and *The Boy's Own Paper* and books such as R.M. Ballantyne's *Ungava; or, A Tale of Esquimeaux-land* (1857) were part of a popular juvenile literature that "fixed the Canadian north as a great stage for boy's adventures" (Waterston 132), a trend that continues in juvenile literature into the twentieth century in the novels of Farley Mowat and the writers examined later in this chapter. Adventures juxtaposed English or American boys engaged in masculine pursuits against primitive Natives or the brute force of nature in exotic settings. The Canadian north, with its harsh climate and unfamiliar people, became a popular setting. The Inuit are the people most frequently depicted in adventure stories set in the Canadian north; as "Huskies" and "queer little men" inhabiting the scenery, these characters represent a difference that must be claimed or overcome as part of the hero's quest.

The differentiation of racial characteristics structures adventure stories of the period, especially those that attempt to revive the sagas. According to Martin Green, adventures patterned on the sagas reached the height of popularity at the turn of the century, as many agreed with J.F. Hodgetts, a contributor to *The Boy's Own*, that "English boys were too straightforward to like the Greek gods, while the Norse ones would appeal directly to their natural 'Teutonic' impulses" (qtd in Green, "Adventurers" 83). Allen French, author of the Victorian children's novel *The Story of Rolf*, attributes racial origins to the saga form and cites these origins as the reason for their popularity and superiority: "The sagas reveal the characteristics of our branch of the Aryan race, especially the personal courage which is so superior to that of the Greek and Latin races, and which makes the Teutonic epics (whether the Niebelungen Lied, the Morte d'Arthur, or the Njala) much more inspiring than the Iliad, the Odyssey, or the Aeneid" (qtd in Green, "Adventurers" 83).

Arctic settings provide the appropriate backdrop for new sagas in which British characters display revived Viking spirit, drawn from their supposed racial heritage. This spirit inflects national identity with racial attributes that exemplify the kind of independence the nation must have; as Carl Berger concludes, "[t]he northern theme also assumed a racist aspect, holding that the capacity for freedom and progress were inherent in the blood of northern races" (22). Such stories serve didactic purposes: the successful adventurer's independence makes him the model for the pioneer who could go out and claim territory on the nation's behalf. Although the nations that adventure heroes come from may differ, their role in nation-building does not. As Green argues, "It is impossible to account for national competition and national identity as forces without the idea of adventure" (*Adventurous Male* 159).

The Scottish writer R.M. Ballantyne set two of his adventure books in the Canadian north, *Snowflakes and Sunbeams; or, The Young Fur Traders* (1856) and *Ungava; or, A Tale of Esquimeaux-land* (1857). In a comprehensive reading of Ballantyne's adventure stories, R.S. Phillips describes how the "feminine space" of the landscape is enlisted in the formation of "a literary landscape dominated by boys and men" (61). Ballantyne's stories exemplify the "muscular Christian" values boys were to learn in order to become men, including how to triumph in the face of challenge and overcome physical adversity (Phillips 51; Moyles 47). Fearsome inhabitants enhance the danger confronting heroes in Ballantyne's threatening northern landscape. In *Ungava*, the Indians who befriend the adventurers may be "honest" (213) and "good stout, broad-shouldered, thick-set specimens of the race" (88), but the Inuit are depicted in not so sympathetic terms: "... it was known, or at least supposed, that the Esquimaux were fierce and cruel savages, if not cannibals. Their very name implies something of the sort. It signifies *eaters of raw flesh*, and was bestowed on them by their enemies the Muskigons. They call themselves *Innuit* – men, or warriors; and although they certainly do eat raw flesh when necessity compels them – which it often does – they asserted that they never did so from choice" (37–8). In these ethnographic descriptions as well as in the geographical details, the narrator instructs the boys to whom the narrative is addressed with great didactic authority. The heroes can be imagined as even more daring for running the risk of meeting with dangerous races, and the reader is meant to admire and emulate them.

Canadian writers J.M. Oxley and Egerton Ryerson Young also chose the north as a setting for adventure. Oxley, author of the adventure novel *The Wreckers of Sable Island* (1894), used elevated language and a didactic tone in his short pieces glorifying the history of the Hudson's Bay Company in the north. In these pieces, explorers and traders display "self-sacrificing heroism" in their efforts "to pierce the ice-defended mysteries of the Arctic Zone." In "The Romantic Story of a Great Corporation: The Hudson's Bay Trading Company," Oxley openly acknowledges his use of the adventure form to tell the story of the company. By representing these pursuits as adventures, the narrative constructs masculinity as physical, territorial, and economic dominance, the convergence of national and personal interests that Martin Green observes in his analysis of adventure narratives. Boys reading such narratives would be expected to be like such heroes in similar scenarios.

Egerton Ryerson Young drew on accounts such as those written by J.M. Oxley and William Butler for his *Three Boys in the Wild Northland* (1897) and *Winter Adventures of Three Boys in the Great Lone Land* (1899). In fact, Elizabeth Waterston asserts that both novels are based on "an obviously intense reading" of Butler's work (134). Young's *Winter Adventures* shows three young lads, Scottish, English, and Irish respectively, as they learn about the north from a retired Hudson's Bay clerk and his "Indian" wife. The clerk and his wife seem to govern the Native people, overseeing their activities and remarking on everything with great authority.

The Native people, for their part, comply willingly with white dominance and express gratitude to their "kind loving missionary and his family" (126), and the "Christian Indian boys" are described as "[n]oble fellows" glad to have left behind their "pagan," "heathen" ways and "disgusting rites" (119). Conveniently, the Gospel, according to the narrator, has changed the Indian for the better without ruining "his cleverness and skill as a hunter or a guide" (n.p.). In contrast to the laudatory tone in the description of Indians, a horror of miscegenation – the boys themselves are interested only in the white missionary's daughters – shows through the description of the "treacherous halfbreeds" who are depicted attempting to cheat in the dog-sled race.

The three boys distinguish themselves in sporting competitions, of which dog-sled racing is the most thrilling and significant, as well as by becoming well liked by the "dusky Indians" (146). Throughout their adventures, the boys display the "courage, fortitude, cunning, strength, leadership, and persistence" attributed to manliness, and although their Christian beliefs prevent a complete break with the social contract, they display the rugged individualism that characterizes northern heroism, particularly in their dealings with Native people (Demers 18). Native people are helpers or obstacles in the threatening northern environment, and both roles help to define the roles that the young heroes must play as masters in the new territory.

Contemporary adventures featuring girl heroes make strikingly different use of the northern wilderness. Girl heroes in books such as Agnes Maule Machar's *Marjorie's Canadian Winter* (1892), Helen Reed's *Amy in Acadia* (1905), and Anna Chapin Ray's *Janet: Her Winter in Quebec* (1908) rarely get much farther north than Montreal. Their adventures, which involve social outings in the winter setting, emphasize "a love of home, a deference to authority, and a suppression of any personal dreams of success and fame" (Waterston 114) – quite different values from those of their male counterparts. Admirable girls embrace culture rather than nature, and therefore do not need to seek adventure in the northern wilderness. For girls who behave like heroes, one must look to Bessie Marchant's daring girls in novels beginning with *A Daughter of the Ranges* (1905), but Marchant does not create settings in the far north. As Green writes, "the adventure tale was written almost exclusively for a masculine audience. It has been the main literary means by which males have been taught to take initiatives, to run risks, to give orders, to fight, defeat, and dominate; while females have been taught, both by being ignored by the genre and by being reduced to passive roles within it, not to do those things" (*Great American* 1–2).

The didactic nature of literature for children and young adults makes it a reflective surface in which to see the ideas and values permeating a culture in a given historical moment. Certainly, the rugged masculine pursuits of the boys in northern adventures and the glorification of northern racial heritage display the expectations for young men at the end of the nineteenth century. While boys were learning how to be good adult citizens of the empire, grown men were acting on convictions born of the same ideas and values.

THE MEN OF THE NORTH: CHARLES MAIR

In the nineteenth century, the north came to stand for the energetic good health that signified moral virtue, and the south for the effeminacy and disease that were seen to result from moral corruption. Such ideas were expressed by Romantics as diverse as European writer Germaine de Staël and Canada First supporter R.G. Haliburton. Colonial poets believed that Canada's northern climate would engender health and strength in its people, as these lines from Joseph Howe's *Acadia* (1874) suggest:

> Still there is health and vigour in the breeze
> Which bears upon its wings no fell disease
> To taint the balmy freshness of the air
> And steal the bloom thy hardy children wear. (6–7)

Not only were northern people considered to be healthy, strong, vigorous, and brave, but these qualities were associated with manliness in the Victorian period.

Howe's verse exemplifies the conjunction of gender and race evident in political rhetoric of the time whereby the idealized northern race possesses the attributes of the idealized masculine person. When Howe's fellow Nova Scotian R.G. Haliburton refers to "northern races" in *The Men of the North* (1869), he means specifically those descended from the Vikings, and he lists the English, Celts, Saxons, Teutons, Scandinavians, Swedish, and – for the sake of including their descendants in Quebec – Normans. Noticeably absent from Haliburton's list of "northern peoples" are the aboriginal people inhabiting the northern land, and this absence reflects Canada First's dedication to racial dominance. It is important to remember that the ideas shared by the Canada First party members were not the idle bluster of a few young men; in fact, the coincidence of political activity and literary activity in the career of one member, the poet Charles Mair, stands as an example of how imagining a northern nation in literary form and taking actions to create it would have devastating consequences for the races excluded from that vision.

Charles Mair's involvement in the Red River settlement is well known: not only did he publish articles encouraging settlement in the northwest but he settled there himself, and, later, he went so far as to call for military action against Riel. Another Canada First member, George T. Denison, wrote to him in response to Mair's articles in the *Toronto Globe*: "I am very glad to hear such good accounts of the resources and fertility of the great North West. When filled up with a loyal population and a prosperous one, I have every confidence that in time it would prove a great source of strength to the Dominion, and that we, the Men of the North, as Haliburton says, will be able to teach the Yankees that we will be, as our ancestors have always been, the dominant race" (qtd in Matthews 83–4).[8] For his part, Haliburton was encouraged by western settlement and told Mair that he envisioned the northwest as part of a "whole new free nation called Norland instead of Canada" (qtd in Matthews 85). When Mair decided to "light out" for the Northwest Territories, perhaps with the words of his colleagues ringing in his ears, it was in support of territorial expansion and settlement. In his eyes, the end of the Red River Rebellion and the eventual displacement of the Métis would make way for new, loyal Canadians to take possession of the territory.

For Mair, as John Matthews notes, literature served nationalist purposes, for he believed that "the development of a national literature would solve the problem of creating a national sentiment" (81). Although Mair did not represent his western adventures in literary form, some of his poems seem to be shaped by his public life; for example, the speaker in his poem "Wood-Notes" (1868) lays claim to a charming brook with the following lines:

> The Indian sought it year by year,
> And listened to its rippling glee;
> But he is gone, and I am here,
> And all its rippling is for me. (128)

Mair's poetry played to audiences who might share his assumption that Native people were a race on the wane. The ideas of race circulating in political discourse and the depiction of race, particularly in northern adventures of the time, share a historical context as well as a political ideology.

After setting out the history of "sacrifices endured, hardships encountered, and brave deeds done ... when every faculty sprang into earnest, vigourous action" in the settlement of Canada, William Foster asks: "Think you, now, that Canada has no claim to rank with those lands where adventure has had play and romance has had a home ...?" (*Canada First* 6, 13). Writers from Canada and elsewhere certainly thought it did, as the Canadian north, or at least the north adjacent to Canada at the time, became the setting for a proliferation of adventures, and travellers found it an exotic destination and a subject for anthropological investigation. In poetry, this setting was also appropriated to the ends of the national discourse of patriotism.

To look back at Mair as "part of an emergent, distinctive poetic tradition," as Norman Shrive does (xxix), one must consider his choice of content rather than form. His descriptions of nature clearly refer to Canadian landscapes and his inclusion of legendary "Canadian" figures, such as Laura Secord and Tecumseh, show his focus on Canadian subjects. Mair's technique, however, is always derivative and often atrocious, and even such an admirer as Shrive grants "the forced archaisms, the trite epithets, and the evidences of almost snobbish affectation" that Mair tried to expunge from his poetry later in life (xxviii–xxix), and the facile, alternating rhymes, the "jog-trot metre" (xxvii), and the slavish devotion to conventional forms that remained part of his style. Nevertheless, in 1886, Mair's *Tecumseh* "was widely acclaimed as the country's outstanding literary achievement and Mair as its greatest national poet" (Shrive xxiii).

Mair himself described *Tecumseh* as a "labour of love and patriotism," yet despite his apparently Romantic nationalist politics
and exaggerated reputation as the "Canadian Keats," the Canada
portrayed in his poetry is not a nation in the ideal, Romantic
sense. In Mair's poetry, the nation is not a spirit arising from the
people or the land, but a loyal child to Britain, whose freedom
would extend to and enfold the northern territory, and become,
as in his elegy, "In Memory of Thomas D'Arcy McGee" (1868), "A
mighty realm where Liberty/Shall roof the northern climes from
sea to sea" (139). The "northern climes" inspire awe and dread in
many of the poems published in *Dreamland and Other Poems*
(1868). In "Alice," a child longs for the spring rains to come and
fears the "death-flakes" of winter (93–5). In the "North Wind's
Tale," adventurous men succumb as the sadistic personification
of the wind delights in killing everyone in a nautical disaster (27).
Although Mair's nature poetry varies from a Romantic reflection
of the speaker's feelings in "My Love – A Rhapsody" to what
seems to foreshadow the twentieth-century poets in "Midnight"
with its speaker's plaintive "Some ghost had hid me in a wilderness" (145), it is unified by an imperialistic appetite for conquering the wilderness rather than a Romantic desire for a connection
between nation and land.

However, given the stage of settlement and the imperialist sym-
pathies of loyal citizens at the time, it is not surprising that Mair
does not evoke personal connection to the land. To achieve the
imaginative possession analogous to territorial possession, Mair
figuratively kills off the Indians by showing them dying and
disappearing, as in the last stanza of "Night and Morn":

> But, in the ancient woods the Indian old,
>   Unequal to the chase,
> Sighs as he thinks of all the paths untold,
> No longer trodden by his fleeting race.
> And, Westward, on far-stretching prairies damp,
> The savage shout, and mighty bison tramp
>   Roll thunder with the lifting mists of morn. (40)

Unlike the other "exotic" and remote cultures compared in the
poem, such as those of India, Africa, and China, the culture of the
Indians does not survive. In his own life, Charles Mair acted on

the conviction that Native people would disappear by encouraging white settlers to head west, by settling there himself, and by taking an active role in suppressing the Rebellion. Mair does not put forward the notion of Canadians as a "northern race" in a northern land, as his friend Haliburton does, but his poetry envisions racial displacement: the removal of the Indians both physically and imaginatively from the landscape.

Mair's poetry and politics developed in a period of intense national feeling that can be noted in the work of other poets as well. In 1888, after the Red River Rebellion was over, Frederick George Scott's "In Memoriam Those Killed in the North-West, 1885" evoked the fraternity of death in war as a moment of national maturation:

> Growing to full manhood now,
> With the care-lines on our brow,
> We, the youngest of the nations,
> With no childish lamentations,
> Weep, as only strong men weep,
> For the noble hearts that sleep,
> Pillowed where they fought and bled,
> The loved and lost, our glorious dead! (Hardy 53)

It is striking, though not surprising, that Scott should choose to personify Canada as a child initiated into manhood by war. In this poem and other examples of patriotic verse, the conflicts of settlement that help procure the northern territory and bring the nation greater independence are won by exercising the healthy form of Victorian manliness that the north was believed to engender.

Charles Mair's patriotic verse evokes the larger context of literary nationalism that infused patriotic Canadian poetry of the late nineteenth and early twentieth centuries. The enthusiasm poets had for the new dominion can be seen in poems from before and after Confederation that depict the nation as a colony but appeal to the heritage of northern races as a source of its greatness. For example, Helen Johnson's "Our Native Land," published in Edward Hartley Dewart's *Selections from Canadian Poets* (1864) and later reprinted in E.A. Hardy's *Selections from the Canadian Poets* (1920), pictures the American slave who "envies every little bird / That takes its northward flight!" and the "oppressed" who turn to the "Polar star" (Hardy 31, 32). Combining loyalty to Britain with enthusiasm for the new country, patriotic verse exhorted citizens to display cultural pride and national unity, as in James David Edgar's "This Canada of Ours" (1893):

> May our Dominion flourish then,
>   A goodly land and free,
> Where Celt and Saxon, hand in hand,
>   Hold sway from sea to sea. (Hardy 77)

Sir Charles G.D. Roberts called on the "strong hearts of the North" in "An Ode for the Canadian Confederacy," published in William Douw Lighthall's *Songs of the Great Dominion* (1889), and penned the patriotic lines in "Canada" (1889):

> The Saxon force, the Celtic fire,
>   These are thy manhood's heritage!
> Why rest with babes and slaves? Seek higher
>   The place of race and age. (18)

The presumed "race" uniting Canadian subjects was a key rallying cry in patriotic verse, as in Agnes Maule Machar's "A Song for Canada" published in the aptly titled *Lays of the True North* (1899):

> Saxon and Celt and Norman we:
>   Each race its memory keeps;
> Yet o'er us all, from sea to sea,
>   One Red Cross banner sweeps. (43–4)

Like the adventure writers who claimed that the saga made an appropriate genre for the northern races, and the nationalists for whom Canada constituted an environment in which northern races would find their former glory, these poets saw a direct relationship between the north and the new imperialism.

Nathaniel Benson's "Canada" (1930) personifies the nation as a woman, specifically as a dutiful daughter to Britain, who reigns over the landscape: "And the North's green fires at midnight were / her altar-lights austere" (226–7). In Alexander McLachlan's "The Genius of Canada" (1900), the national consciousness is a woman who comes across the "eastern wave" and, hearing the cries of slaves in the south, looks northward for a home:

"I'll seek the northern woods," She cried,
"Tho' bleak the skies may be;
  The maple dells,
  Where freedom dwells,
Have special charms for me;

"For moral worth and manhood there
Have found a fav'ring clime.
  I'll rear a race
  For long to grace
The mighty page of Time."
                                    (*Poetical Works* 194–5)

It is worth noting that the "race," later referred to as a "brood," founded by the "Genius of Canada" issues exclusively from the three British nations represented by the image of the intertwined shamrock, rose, and thistle. In McLachlan's verse, the north brings the health and moral virtue which moulds ideal masculine and racial identity, an image that characterizes other forms used to represent the north at the end of the nineteenth and the beginning of the twentieth century. The personification of the north in these poems cannot be separated from patriotic intentions.

MYTHOLOGIZING THE FRONTIER: ROBERT SERVICE

In the late nineteenth century, at the height of the adventure story's popularity, the Klondike briefly absorbed the rough, rugged men and women who had drifted to the American frontier, and the north was popularized as the new "Wild West" in the ballads of Robert W. Service.[9] Despite his popularity in his day, Service's critical reception has reflected E.K. Brown's assessment of him as a "marginal figure" who had no influence on subsequent generations of poets. In *On Canadian Poetry* (1943), Brown writes that "if it were not for the Canadian themes of so many among the most effective of his pieces, there would be no tendency to regard him as a part of Canadian literature. He caught a noisy, highly coloured moment in our history – the Yukon gold-rush – in his noisy, highly coloured verse" (61). Brown, thinking the appeal of such popular poetry to be on the wane, could not have known that Service would one day be the subject of serious academic attention, including two biographies, nor could he have foreseen the reclamation of popular literature brought about by late twentieth-century cultural studies.

In "The Age of Brass: Drummond, Service, and Canadian 'Local Colour,'" Jay Johnson remarks that popular poetry of the early twentieth century is interesting for "its attempt to mythologize, to imaginatively recreate, specific regions of the country, thus making them, for the first time, accessible to all Canadians" (15). In his biography of Service, Carl Klinck seems to concur by claiming a singular importance for Service's poetry which gave "recreations of life in the Canadian Yukon – vast, cold, hard, savage, magnificent, alluring, beautiful – a frontier of adventure for exiles from cities," in which "[t]he Northern wastes were no more blank: they were given a meaning, an individuality, a language, and symbols of man's restless endeavour" (36).

The image of the poet opening up the imaginative frontier to the north, like a rugged explorer or pioneer, would have no doubt pleased Robert Service who, more than any other poet, mythologized the north as the other side of civilization, the place roamed by "The Men Who Don't Fit In." Service arrived in the Yukon in 1904, and worked as a teller for the Canadian Bank of Commerce in Whitehorse from 1908 to 1910; he also enjoyed a lively social life, giving amateur theatrical recitations of such dramatic ballads as Kipling's "Gunga Din" (Klinck 33). The rhythm of the ballad and the sounds of the music halls that he (like Kipling) had always frequented inspired his "sourdough" poems, while the northern setting provided him with stories and experiences he could write about.

Service's affinity with Kipling, who he mentions by name in "The Nostomaniac" (1912), surfaces in constant references to being driven out to new lands and from empire to empire. Kipling's influential themes of "manly adventure on the frontiers of the world" (Johnson 23) indicate the late Victorian context for Service's work, even though the masculine traits displayed by Service's men of the north correspond only slightly to Victorian ideals of manliness such as self-restraint and duty to one's country. Like the heroes of late nineteenth-century adventure, the men in Service's poems face the challenge set by an unrelenting northern environment, but unlike those heroes, Service's characters do not always possess moral virtue. The north is a place for misfits, those whose "names are writ in hell," as well as for "stalwart knights"; it is the place where the social contract can be broken.

In *Vagabond of Verse: Robert Service, a Biography* (1995), James MacKay presents Service as self-deprecating and shy of the limelight, a travel writer and tourist who admired Robert Louis Stevenson and considered losing his toiletries on the ship to America his first taste of "roughing it" (111). MacKay also notes how Service described himself as a "shrimp" (157) who "energetically cultivated laziness" (123). "The public image of the reckless gold-seeker, the man of action and the rugged outdoor type was only partially true," for although he adopted the life of a wilderness man, acceptance from the masculine, northern men he admired was slow to come (15). In fact, compared to the men whose lives he made into legends, Service, with his love of books and lonely walks, was hardly masculine in the conventional sense. His fascination with the rough men of the north and the vernacular they spoke may have arisen from his own desire to be such a man and the painful realization that he was not.

When addressing the "Men of the High North," Service often positions himself in relation to these men in self-deprecating ways: "Children of Freedom, scornful of frontiers, / We who are weaklings honor your worth" (79). These are the men in "The Rhyme of the Restless Ones" (1907) who "break the hearts of kith and kin" (42), and sing: "But we'll never stay in town and we'll never settle down" (63). In "The Shooting of Dan McGrew" (1907) they are the men who are drawn to the call of the "Great Alone" (30); in "The Call of the Wild" (1907), they hear the "Great White Silence" (17). In these and other poems, Service "reflects an outward bound, centrifugal phase which points toward the frontier and celebrates the tribe of misfits who inhabit the far outposts" (Johnson 16); his is also the poetry of the rugged individual, the particular masculine individual found in other representations of the north.

The counterpart to these restless men is, of course, a beckoning and dangerous female north made even more fearsome by her comparison to the civilized women who make cosy, inviting homes for wayward men. In many of the poems published in *Rhymes of a Rolling Stone* (1912), such as "The Rover," adventure is made more pleasurable by the thought of home, and "Home and Love" even equates its rewards with heavenly bliss. In "The Shooting of Dan McGrew," the music speaks to the lonely men's hunger for a home, while the "lady that's known as Lou" evokes the absence of the ideal woman, for Lou is not "[a] woman dearer than all the world, and true as Heaven is true" (31). By juxtaposing this vision against that of the treacherous Lou, Service makes the contrast explicit: the woman in a domestic setting provides comfort; the woman on the frontier poses a threat.

"The Law of the Yukon" (1907) personifies the Yukon as a terrifying yet maternal woman who, like the whore, is desired and despised and who waits "lonely, shunned as a thing accurst," dreaming of "men with the hearts of vikings, and the simple faith of a child" (12). As I have argued, the allure of the north in this particular period speaks particularly of the racial superiority of northern white races, as Service's idealization of Vikings seems to confirm. Service lets Vikings stand as an ideal of northern masculinity, as other writers of the time do. "Death in the Arctic" (1912) features a cast of Nordic characters, including Olaf, the Blonde, and Big Eric, but even they are no match for the north's merciless climate. As Atwood remarks in her Clarendon lectures, "popular lore, and popular literature, established early that the North was uncanny, awe-inspiring in an almost religious way, hostile to white men, but alluring; that it would lead you on and do you in; that it would drive you crazy, and finally, would claim you for its own" (*Strange Things* 19).

In Service's poetry, the north is primarily a place where rugged individuals thrive rather than a symbol standing for the new nation. As Atwood wittily observes, Service was the "great mother-lode of Northern cliché" who reiterated the images of the north circulating in popular literature before and after the turn of the century (*Strange Things* 17, 80).[10] The strong oral quality of the ballad combined with vernacular language in his work announced a tradition in northern verse which would continue to develop in narrative poetry.

ADVENTURE BOYS AND WILDERNESS MEN IN THE TWENTIETH CENTURY

While the adventure genre was largely shaped and defined in the turn-of-the-century atmosphere of imperial expansion in Britain and in the United States, it was no less popular in former colonies and new nations such as Canada (Waterston 132; Moyles 43). Arctic adventure stories were disseminated throughout the English-speaking world in boys' and girls' magazines, and, just as their audience included Canadian readers, Canadian writers joined those from Britain and America in embracing the form to represent the north.

In her survey of adventures for boys, Elizabeth Waterston remarks the centrality of the Canadian wilderness in the international adventure genre. She sardonically summarizes the quest pattern devised for the boy hero by nineteenth-century adventure writers: "Moving through woods and waters accompanied by an admiring comrade, he pierces the heart of darkness, undergoes ordeals at the hands of animal and human antagonists, and emerges to begin the upward return to his own kingdom" (129). In the twentieth century, certain aspects of the adventure have changed: for example, Native people are no longer adversaries and extensions of the wilderness, the boy's closest companion is usually a Native boy, and the boy's experiences involve symbols of Native culture such as trickster figures. However, despite the appropriation of Native culture in adventure stories, to the point of all-out mimicry in novels such as Ernest Thompson Seton's *Two Little Savages* (1903), the characteristics displayed by the boy hero have not changed considerably. As Waterston notes, in books and magazines for boys, "physical prowess and scorn of sentiment remained the required heroic qualities" well into the twentieth century (137).

Both boys' and girls' stories followed the lead of *The Boy's Own Paper* and *The Girl's Own Paper*, whose stories were usually topical. Exploration adventure in exotic settings, popular during colonial expansion, and boarding school stories reflecting Victorian mores were replaced by war stories in the early twentieth century. Books such as Gordon Stables' *Wild Adventures Around the Pole* (1888) and *Off to Klondike* (1890) reflected the shift from the search for the Northwest Passage to the "race for the Pole." Harris Patten's *Wings of the North* (1932) evokes the north in its title, but satisfied the new interest in aviation, and Stephansson's *Kak the Copper Eskimo* (1924) had more in common with the increasingly popular ethnographic monograph than with the nineteenth-century adventure. Moving away from the *Boy's Own* model, Donald

French turned events in Canadian history into tales of adventure in a history primer entitled *Famous Canadian Stories Re-Told for Boys and Girls* (1931).

What is perhaps most striking about the adventure genre, despite the changeability of its content, is its relative formal integrity to the present day. "In the farthest north," writes Elizabeth Waterston, "... young travellers are presented as still moving along clear paths of heroism, as is apparent in the tragic novels of James Houston" (147). Popular works of fiction written for juvenile audiences today share many characteristics with their late nineteenth- and early twentieth-century counterparts. Heroes continue to display the "personal courage" that Victorian writers looked to the sagas to express, and adventure narratives continue to juxtapose the white protagonist and Inuit although the Inuit are no longer represented as an inferior race.

Even more striking, however, is the continued influence of so-called "Viking" characteristics on the development of the northern hero and the racial content that implies; for example, in Farley Mowat's *The Curse of the Viking Grave* (1966), a Cree boy, a half-Inuit boy, and a blond, blue-eyed boy set out across the barrens in search of a Viking site after becoming "particularly interested" in a book on Viking exploration read to them by a Scottish trapper. Mowat's *Lost in the Barrens* (1956) also centres on the possible discovery of a Viking site by Jamie MacNair, a young Torontonian, and his Cree friend Awasin. *Lost in the Barrens* and *The Curse of the Viking Grave* are both "buddy stories" featuring the initiation of non-Native boys through cross-cultural contact with other boys; however, the features of masculinity boys must attain are represented as the same for all. All the boys become men through feats of daring and through physical trials, by displaying the "Viking spirit" that adventures often attempted to revive.

In literature about the north, the hero must display the attributes of the rugged individual, all of which are classic traits of masculine identity. Like the "idealized Viking" (10) who is the hero of Harold Horwood's *White Eskimo: A Novel of Labrador* (1973), the rugged individual must be "sufficient unto himself" (38).[11] Because the hero must live out the masculine narratives of quest and initiation, adventure stories tend to recreate the frontier context of the late nineteenth century in other periods. At first glance, the north may seem a logical setting for adventures, with its forbidding climate, mysterious peoples, and remote landscapes all providing the circumstances in which the hero can be tested or proven worthy. Certainly, many real adventures have taken place there, but the north as the scene for adventurous exploits is a highly contrived concept.[12] What has been naturalized as the reality of northern adventure serves the ideological content of the stories. Martin Green coins the term "adventure landscape" to describe such imagined settings in which "men seek out danger" (*Adventurous Male* 159). By refusing this naturalization and disrupting the notion that the north produces the adventure story, a study can be made of constructions of gender expectations and ideals. The following symptomatic readings of some popular, contemporary Arctic adventure stories highlight gender differentiation by demonstrating how this structure works through a consistent pattern in the narrative, including the construction of an idealized, all-male community and the identification of ideal masculine characteristics.

James Houston's *Frozen Fire: A Tale of Courage* (1977) provides an example of the narrative which centres on an all-male community. It tells the story of a young white boy, Matthew, and his geologist father, Martin, whose quest for a copper deposit leads the pair north. When Martin, his friends, and the pilot, Charlie, do not return, Matthew sets out to find them with the help of his Inuit friend, Kayak. After losing all the gas for their snowmobile, Matthew and Kayak continue on foot only to find themselves lost. They encounter a "wild man" who takes them in, feeds them, and sends them on their way back to Frobisher. Many more trials await them as they attempt to cross the ice floes, including escaping an attack by a polar bear, but the most significant concerns Matthew's attempt to carry the gold he finds on the way, a mistake that almost costs him his life. Matthew and Kayak are eventually rescued by Charlie in his helicopter, the "Waltzing Matilda," and return to find Matthew's father recuperating in hospital.

The fantasy of male community ends with the boys, their fathers, and Charlie in Martin's hospital room. Although Martin initially seems an inadequate parent who barely acknowledges his son, he recognizes the greed that drove him to search for the copper as his chief flaw, just as Matthew realizes that his attempt to carry the gold was foolish and that the flintstone had been the most valuable thing of all. Martin ends up taking a teaching job, settling down, and promising to stay that way. While the father rehabilitates himself as a parent by the end of the book, the mother continues to be inexplicably absent, and the peripheral position of the Inuit women, as silent providers of food who never leave the igloo, ensures the community's all-male identity. In the end, all the main characters choose the community of men, with Charlie, the tough daredevil from the Australian outback, having the last word.

Gillingham, the hero of Harold Horwood's *White Eskimo: A Novel of Labrador* (1973), becomes the stuff of legend for a group of men travelling north by boat. Horwood's debt to Conrad becomes apparent as stories of an epic hero gradually unfold, representing him as the agent of political change for the Inuit of Labrador. Although *White Eskimo* distinguishes itself from other books discussed in this chapter by its layering of narrative perspectives, the fictional world emerging from these perspectives represents the typical northern hero as rugged individual. Gillingham is identified with a tough, rugged kind of masculinity from his very first description as "shaggy, picturesque, heroic," a man idealized by the other men who speak of his weight and of how "he gave the impression of hugeness rather than height," concluding that "[w]ith his bold, far-seeing eyes, high brow, and blond hair falling to his shoulders, he looked rather like an idealized Viking" (10). Gillingham's self-imposed exile is reminiscent of other heroes of northern adventure, and, like the narrator of Harry Bernard's *Les jours sont longs* (1951), he possesses all the characteristics of the strong, silent type. Faced with a storm, his Inuit companion, Abel, strokes a raven's foot, but, the narrator remarks, "[a]s for Gillingham, he said nothing, no doubt being in his own eyes sufficient unto himself in his living and his dying, and feeling it beneath his dignity ever to call on god or demon or nature spirit in any kind of extremity" (38). Although spirituality appears to be a sign of weakness to Gillingham, he is quite forthcoming on the subject of Inuit spiritual needs, advocating a "return to paganism – tempered, I hope, with rationalism and education, like the paganism of the late classical Greeks" (74). Here, as John Moss comments, Gillingham's quest takes on the form of a search for a truth *for* the aboriginal people (*Reader's* 138). Idolizing Greek civilization is consistent with the construction of the ideal homosocial activities centred on Gillingham, including wife-swapping, which Gillingham defends, saying the women are "exchanged like partners in a dance, in a game played among friends" (97). Despite this, Gillingham is said to find real love with Nasha who, significantly, asks him to beat her, even kill her, for a momentary negligence (216). The "idealized" Inuit woman in Horwood's text resembles the "true woman" found in American Westerns, a woman who is typically either half Indian or half Spanish, close to the earth, and who knows her place (Oehlschlaeger 184). Uniting with Nasha is part of what makes Gillingham a white Eskimo. The same is true of the "white shaman," Richard Tavett, of C.W. Nicol's novel of that name, who has a sexual encounter with the ghost of a revered wise woman in a dream while simultaneously "reaching" the body of his lover many miles away (176–7). By uniting with the idealized Inuit woman, the white hero not only dominates "nature" but also takes over her connection to the land, illustrating how obtaining the indigenous claim to the land is key "from a nationalistic point of view" (Fee, "Romantic Nationalism" 18) and how capturing the "Native" in literature comes to legitimate an ideological colonization of real and imagined territories.[13]

An excerpt from the transcripts of "an emergency meeting of the Inuit Tapirisat" introduces and provides fictional authentication in C.W. Nicol's *The White Shaman* (1979). In the excerpt quoted, Eastern Arctic representative Billy Toby tells a story of a "real white man from England, who became a shaman and then got shot by his own people for it" (xv). The body of the man was said to have been taken to the bottom of the sea where the goddess Luma (or Sedna) "would let the soul out and magic it into the body of a new-born baby, one that was half white, half brown, and that this baby would grow to be a leader for all Northern people" (xvi). Toby uses this story to protest against the "hot-headed talk" (xi) of some young people at the meeting. It is a reminder of traditional means of understanding and communicating as well as an allegory of what political change might entail: a combination of Qallunaat and Inuit ways. By including this introduction, Nicol calls on the authenticating voice of the Inuit leader to support the story that follows, and thereby constrains the reader's interpretation. The hero of *The White Shaman* will live out in fiction what Toby reported as historical, and readers have no choice in the context of Toby's words but to equate the hero with the soul that will eventually become the northern leader.

Although his life comes to take on mythic proportions, the hero, a young Welshman called Richard Tavett but nicknamed Tik after Rikki-Tikki in the Kipling story, shares many characteristics with other heroes in other adventure stories. Like Matthew and like Jonathan, the hero of Houston's *Whiteout* (1988), he is an adolescent, and like Gillingham, he is "a fairly impressive specimen" who is "just short of six feet tall, with a wrestler's chest and arms" (24). He displeases his family by quitting school and saving his money to go to the Canadian Arctic (25). The separation from his own society and initiation into the Arctic world happen under the guidance of two mentor figures: first, the scientist named Philip whom he works for, and then gradually the Inuit hunter Ipeelee. Initiation feats include enduring physical tests like running beside the komatik (28) and learning to succeed at hunting (28, 36, 94 and *passim*).

As the story progresses, Tik does everything he can to become part of the land, including making up his own rituals (160). At first, his body is an ally in his search for a way to connect with the land: "He ran by komatik over the moonscape of sea ice, the day clear and blue overhead, his body functioning true and strong, his face going browner with reflected light, his breath and the breath of the dogs falling behind in clouds... A man became vividly aware of his body here, of movement, of body sounds and body heat for his body marked his existence in a clear, strange land of frozen water and wide sky" (35). Later, however, the connection he desires comes not through the body but through its transcendence and a "metamorphosis" of his spirit. Unlike the typical character on a quest, Tik does not return to his own society after his initiation. Instead, he becomes a sacrifice and a potential saviour when he dies at sea, and his soul remains in the Arctic awaiting resuscitation by Luma. The Christ figure motif figured in the fate of Richard Tavett is reminiscent of Gillingham, especially the "white Eskimo's" function as saviour of the Labradormiut.

In this part of the narrative, there occurs the kind of troubling gap in narrative logic that Joseph Bristow locates in a variety of adventure stories. As Tikkisi, the aspect of his self that has "gone Inuit," Tik finds that he possesses powers which allow him to will things into being. When he threatens to kill Philip, Ipeelee warns him: "Then Tikkisi must take responsibility for his words, so carelessly spat out. Tikkisi must suck them back out of the air and digest them, lest they run and hide and wait to do evil, like the tornait of the windy places" (120). While Ipeelee's warning makes Tik tremble, he does not heed it, and that failure has disastrous consequences for Philip. When Philip dies, Ipeelee does not blame Tik, and Tik never comes to terms with the role he has played in Philip's death. As a white shaman, it seems that Tik transcends the ethical codes of either culture, so despite his rather unheroic actions and his failure to atone for them, he retains his hero status in the story as well as his location in the adventurous place outside the social contract.

In the twentieth century, the Canadian north continues to serve as a setting for adventure stories written in the popular mode, and adventures continue to target young adults, mostly boys, as their audience. As we have seen from these texts, a pattern emerges: the typical Arctic adventure narrative takes place in a predominantly male world and features a white boy, whose father is aloof or dead and whose mother is absent or dead, and a Native boy who befriends and protects him. The hero resembles Robinson Crusoe as a stranger stranded in an exotic land who maintains an exploitive friendship with a Native inhabitant. Whereas Native people were once decorative obstacles for heroes, now they tend to be helpers or mentors, although sometimes, as is the case in James Houston's *Whiteout*, a love triangle develops between the white boy, a Native girl, and the boy to whom she has been promised. The boy's identity develops in opposition to the passive feminine character, whose lack of agency is accentuated by the arrangement of her marriage. The feminine and the Native are brought together to signify what the boy hero must not be. In other adventures, like Fred Bodsworth's *The Strange One* (1959), falling in love with a Native girl parallels initiation into the northern world. The masculine identity achieved by demonstrating self-sufficiency (albeit mediated by the help of aboriginal companions) and accomplishing certain feats earns legitimacy by differentiation from the passive, the feminine, the Native.

In twentieth-century Arctic adventures, erotic triangles are usually interracial, and they often result in the departure of the hero. For example, in the novels of Fred Bodsworth, such as *The Atonement of Ashley Morden* (1964), the feminization of the main character, Ashley, accentuates the importance of traditionally defined masculinity. Ashley's effeminacy defines his actions: "Ash's hand was slender, the handclasp weak and limp" (13). In the erotic triangle that develops between Ashley, Ron Dorkett, and Lilka, Ashley's feminization makes a homosocial connection possible.

Houston's novel *Whiteout* (1988) features a frontier-style hero, community, and friendship. After turning down a music scholarship and being charged with possession, the hero, a white adolescent named Jonathan, finds himself faced with an ultimatum written in the elegant prose and stylish "scrawl" of his mother: either he becomes sensible or he will be disinherited. Reading this, Jonathan "realize[s] that something different in his life was going to have to happen unless he planned to totally self-destruct" (3). His mother, the embodiment of the feminizing impact of civilization and the one who paradoxically advises him to go north in the first place, disappears from the narrative, although she is reported to have given him the copy of *Kabloona* that he takes north with him (5). Jon's quest begins with his separation from his mother's world of dove grey envelopes, Steinway pianos, and expensive scotch, a world which serves as the opposite of the wilderness up north.[14] Significantly, when she reappears, it is again only in the words of a message, this time a radio message acknowledging Jon's intention to stay north another year, regretting that she cannot visit him, and confirming that the sculpture of Sedna, which he has seen in a vision while up north, has not been removed from above the piano (159).

With his father dead and his mother remote, Jonathan's separation from social and parental relations allows him to undertake his quest and to become a man by initiation into the northern world. His paternal uncle, Calvin, a cantankerous Hudson Bay Company trader from Scotland, mediates the initiation by treating his nephew harshly and by forcing him into an ascetic existence of hard work, early mornings, and lumpy porridge. Another trial involves Jon's fight with the principal who refuses to allow him to fulfil his community service by teaching music lessons. The antagonism does not let up until news arrives that a young, single woman will replace the mannish Dorie as the community's schoolteacher, and the principal's mood immediately softens. With the departure of Dorie, Panee becomes the only female character in the community of men and takes her place at the heart of the erotic triangle.

At first, Panee attracts Jon's attention because she is the sister of Pudlo, Jon's best friend, and because "[s]he looked somewhat like Pudlo, but her dark eyes had a softly beautiful curve to them. Her whole smooth face had a bright, intelligent look" (49). Then, despite Pudlo's warning that Panee has an *uingasak* named Edlout and will be married soon (69), Jon and Panee begin to meet in the abandoned whaler's house and to entertain ideas of living in it together (82). The erotic triangle develops around the desire Jon and Edlout share for Panee and is mirrored in the triangular friendship between Jon, Pudlo, and Panee; both triangles are necessary to Jon's initiation as both play an important role in the final test presented by the whiteout.

Although Pudlo seems to endorse Jon's relationship with Panee, he represents a friendly impediment to it during their journey to the fish lakes. At night, when Panee reveals her naked body to Jon, Pudlo, sleeping between them, is the literal impediment to their desire (116). Here and elsewhere, Pudlo acts as a surrogate for Edlout whose presence produces a more direct confrontation, as he and Jon "stood stiff-legged as two strange dogs, their hackles up, deciding whether they should confront each other over Panee now, or later," and Panee gives Edlout "a long look full of uncertainty and sadness before she turned away" (123). As the pivotal figure in the triangle, Panee facilitates both friendship and rivalry. In Sedgwick's terms, Panee has the "kind of ultimate importance in the schema of men's gender constitution" shared by women in all homosocial narratives by "representing an absolute of exchange value" (134). When she disappears in the storm, Pudlo and Jon crawl about blindly calling her name, and when they cannot find her, the two men stick close together to ensure their own survival (134). After the storm, they find her buried in the snow and near death (138); knowing that she must be taken to camp, Jon guides them there by following the instructions given by Pudlo, whose snowblindness incapacitates him. The whole camp rushes to save Panee, but Edlout replaces Jon as the hero by suggesting they send for the nurse. In a moment of reconciliation, Jon pens the note that Edlout will carry.

Jonathan gains self-understanding through these trials. By the end of the novel, he has decided to accept the music scholarship, his uncle has authorized his inheritance, and, with the knowledge that Panee does not want to go south, he has given her up to Edlout. Jon gives Panee what the novel suggests her culture will not: a choice. In a significant gap in narrative logic, all those who seemed to approve of the relationship between Jon and Panee advocate its ending. The narrative of colonization that features white men taking Native women is evoked in the novel but not consummated. As in the nineteenth-century adventure, the boy hero becomes a man through his northern experience, including his differentiation from the feminine and the Native who remain behind. As he flies off, Jon sees the reunited couple, Edlout and Panee, wave to him while the music he composed in the north "rose all around [him] in the plane" (175).

THE NORTH AS WILDERNESS

The narrative patterns of adventure stories set in the Arctic also characterize stories set in other regions of Canada that are represented as northern wilderness; demonstrating the conflation of the Canadian north and the north as Canada, these stories, in some ways, inherit the adventure form. For example, the mountain setting of Howard O'Hagan's *Tay John* (1939) is characterized by the "deep strain of misogyny" (Stouck 217) remarked in wilderness writing. To the mountain men in the novel, acts of rugged individualism, an almost mystical vision of landscape, as well as the firmly entrenched nature-culture opposition, seem to dominate as the characters describe the wilderness in terms of the mysterious feminine.

Discussing the influence of British adventure on Russian writers, Martin Green notes how "making legends out of reality" has been admired as a specifically "Anglo-Saxon" tradition of adventure (*Adventurous Male* 155). In Canadian literature, the attraction to real-life adventure is exemplified in the fascination writers have with the story of Albert Johnson, a story possessing the common elements of the adventure genre within a particular Canadian context. In *Rat River Trapper* (1972), Thomas P. Kelley describes Albert Johnson's story as "an epic of courage almost beyond belief" (141). The novel claims to be the "true story of howling huskies, dangerous trails, and desolate tundra in a frozen world across which a fugitive flees before oncoming posses" (1); however, the same narrator who exhorts readers to remember it as "a true story" asserts the "sheer fiction" of most tales told by the "Eskimos" concerning Johnson later in the narrative (96). In the gap between the truth and the fiction about Johnson, the narrative creates another Albert Johnson who is devoutly religious, abstinent, and romantic, and whose flight allows him to "play his favourite role of a lone Adam in a world devoid of any other human life" (5). Kelley writes in a love interest named Anu, a halfbreed girl who searches all her life for Johnson, knowing "[t]here could be but one man in her life" (43). In his connection with Anu, a version of the "true woman" found in the American Western, and his solitary life on the land, Johnson becomes the typical rugged individual who spurns society in favour of the wilderness. Because society cannot accommodate his individuality, it destroys him. In heroic fashion, he goes down fighting "[w]ith the instinct of the wilderness strong within him – the instinct that decrees you must battle till the last" (134–5).

Rudy Wiebe meticulously assembles the details of the manhunt in "The Naming of Albert Johnson" and *The Mad Trapper* (1980), and again in *Playing Dead* (1989). For Wiebe, the story of Albert Johnson, like that of the Franklin expedition, is one of the Arctic's great mysteries. By "making legend of reality," Wiebe represents and revises the northern hero as it figures in other novels, participating, as Sherrill E. Grace notes, in "both the replication of the dominant discourse and the disruption of its hegemony" ("Gendering" 169). The Albert Johnson depicted in Wiebe's fiction is not the glorious hero he is in Kelley's novel, even though he typifies the flight from civilization across the frontier and the rupture of the social contract. Johnson's survival depends on his flight, and, through most of the story, he is alternately motionless, trying to hide from impending capture, or restless, leaving yet another temporary shelter. He ingloriously kills small prey with his bare hands, cowers over small fires, and dies with a snarl on his face. But while Johnson's escape across the frontier to the north ultimately ends in his death by the representatives of society, the RCMP, his real defeat comes when faced with his identity: "the name come to meet him in his journey north, come out of the north around the bend and against the current of the Peel River, as they name that too, to confront him on a river he thought another and aloud where he would have found after all his years, at long last, only nameless silence" ("The Naming" 277).

The Mad Trapper offers a self-consciously historiographic depiction of events, giving them a linear narrative form. The "red-handed fiend" and "mad trapper" in sensational newspaper stories is set against the mysterious, silent stranger encountered before the shootings who claims: "I never bother anybody … If they don't bother me" (53). In frontiersman fashion, Johnson guards his privacy as fiercely as his identity. In both *The Mad Trapper* and in "The Naming of Albert Johnson," Wiebe, like Kelley, tells the story from the perspective of an omniscient narrator, but he leaves much of the story unresolved. Johnson emerges as a shadowy, strong, and silent character who leaves the men who track him down and kill him asking, "who is he?" (189). If Kelley's Albert Johnson becomes an epic hero fleeing the stultifying effects of civilization into the wilderness, Wiebe's Albert Johnson is a hero whose unknown identity stands for the mystery of the Arctic, the elusive goal of Wiebe's quest in *Playing Dead*.

GOING NORTH, GOING INDIAN

Besides Albert Johnson, perhaps the most commonly known Canadian version of the American frontiersman is Archie Belaney, or Grey Owl, the famous Indian impersonator. The story of Grey Owl has become a symbol of the desire to "go Indian," and Grey Owl has come to symbolize voice appropriation. This racial and cultural imposture is described as a pathology of New World experience in Margaret Atwood's "The Grey Owl Syndrome" which, she notes, is "entwined with a version of the wilderness itself" (*Strange Things* 35), indicating how, in wilderness tales, the perilous north is not necessarily a faraway place. Instead, it is everywhere; it is Canada. Belaney's *The Men of the Last Frontier* (1931) depicts the solitary frontiersman, the American Adam mythologized in stories of Daniel Boone and Davy Crockett: "Dependent entirely on himself, he must be resourceful, ready to change plan at a moment's notice, turning adverse circumstances and reverses to what slight advantage he may" (8). The north, for Belaney, is "the last battle-ground in the long drawn-out, bitter struggle between the primeval and civilization" (29). Although the book concerns men exclusively, it is dedicated to the civilizing influence of Belaney's aunt, for, he writes, the education she provided enabled him "to interpret into words the spirit of the forest, beautiful for all its underlying wildness" (n.p.). This gesture towards the influence of feminine-identified civilization is answered with a text in which the wilderness is a theatre for defining masculinity through conflict, the classic struggle between man, represented by the trapper, and nature, personified as a male deity: "the grim Spirit of the Silent North, who stalks each lonely traveller's footsteps relentless and implacable, whose will is law in the White Silence" (13). As Carl Berger remarks, this is the north Kipling imagined when he wrote: "there is a fine, hard, bracing climate, the climate that puts iron and grit into men's bones" (qtd in Berger, 18). For Belaney, as for many writers who would follow him, the division between civilization and wilderness is inherent in the context imposed on the individual by the frontier, not in the social development of the individual's masculinity. However, history, biography, and fiction, which perpetuate this image of the northern frontier, also represent the hero actively seeking out the context for his exploits and recreating the frontier in order to find it. It is the geographical location of the frontier that changes with the need to find certain conditions and to accommodate the frontier myth, not the individuals who change by arriving in a particular location.

Armand Garnet Ruffo's *Grey Owl: The Mystery of Archie Belaney* (1996) explores the distinction between fiction and reality that is such an important theme in northern studies. Grey Owl's story, told from the perspective of the Anishabek people he lived with, traces his portrait with ambivalence but also tenderness and affection. A bigamist and alcoholic, conservationist and celebrity, Grey Owl emerges from Ruffo's poetic narrative a complex and human figure. The mystery of Belaney's successful transformation lies in the audience's expectations: "Yes, you have met the famous Grey Owl," one of the speakers tells us, "a true wilderness man, an Indian in the flesh who fits every image you have ever had of what an Indian should be" (81). While his Native friends know he "is not born one of us" (145), they accept him. As for the non-Native public, the voice of Grey Owl explains just how he is able to fool them:

> ... it's not me they see at all;
> it's the face in their mind,
> the one they expect (of me),
> born out of themselves,
> in their own image. (84)

In Robert Kroetsch's parody of the Grey Owl story, *Gone Indian* (1973), the hero yields to the wilderness, which is a threatening, feminine presence, by disappearing into it, and accomplishes his desire to "go Indian" by impersonating the impersonator. If, as Sherrill E. Grace argues, the "North does not lend itself to parody; it is too strong, too terrible to be played with" ("Comparing" 251), then in *Gone Indian* Kroetsch must have something other than a parody of northern experience in mind. Indeed, *Gone Indian* has been read as a postmodernist critique of selfhood whereby the hero, Jeremy Sadness, misnamed through a number of intertextual references and assuming the position of "Other" by going Indian, exists at the "meta-level of language" in the interests of "debunking the myth of identity" (Söderlind 192, 194). Sadness assumes his new identity by cultural cross-dressing: a buckskin jacket, moccasins, and Levis; his chest is bare and his hair braided. In some ways, this is the story of Canadian literary history, a constant search for authenticity that plays out Kroetsch's famous gloss on Canadian literature, "the fiction makes us real."

Jeremy Sadness is drawn to the wilderness in an attempt to shake off the grasp of the women who he thinks have cast a spell on his "prick" and who also frustrate his attempts "to flog [his] limp imagination" (52–3). Jeremy's quest for masculine identity, which his professor calls his "great western quest for manhood" (37) takes the form of accomplishing a series of physical feats in an attempt to regain his intellectual and sexual potency. To do this, Jeremy submits to initiation; as Peter Thomas notes, "like any questing hero, he must find his way by a series of ordeals" (73). Even before he "lights out" for the northern wilderness, he practices "obscene little grip exercises" as well as sit-ups, push-ups, and running on the spot (*Gone Indian* 25). In the north, he engages in more challenging and perilous physical tests, and he believes that when his body is "totally spent," he is "free" of it (83). By trying to control his body, he tries to assert his identity: "Combat, goddamnit, that's what it is. Trial by strength. Trial by chance. Trial by wager. Trial by drowning in your own sweat. Trial by freezing your balls off. Trial by falling. Trial by flying" (75). These physical trials constitute what Robert Lecker describes as "a typical Kroetschian conflict between a father figure aligned with the East, the rooted past, narrative definition, and institutionalized learning" and a son who "thrives on inventing himself" and who embraces "the primitive and spontaneous forms of knowledge identified with the 'blank page' of Canada's North" (*Kroetsch* 62).

In the end, Jeremy disappears into the landscape, enacting the fate of the dead or disappearing Indian he has become, but he also makes a symbolic claim to that land by becoming one with it. This ending has been described as a "reconstitution of self" (Thomas 69) of the sort Boone associates with crossing a frontier to find a "multiform self" (Boone 188), and it is regarded as typical of both the challenge Kroetsch poses to "the humanist notion of the self as coherent, unified, and stable" (Hutcheon, *Canadian* 173) and his tendency to show both sides of a duality without choosing between them (Lecker, *Kroetsch* 32; Söderlind 172). Yet, the ending's ambivalence and lack of resolution are in fact witnesses to postmodern narcissism. Far from creating a "multiform self" that takes the multiple constituents of identity, it leaves no self at all, and we are left wondering with George Woodcock if Kroetsch's novels create "an auto-reflexive world that leads reductively to a kind of nihilism of art preying on rather than being sustained by art" (*Introduction* 166).

This creation of a postmodern self, fashioned from the stereotypes of Indian identity and the parody of "shamanistic" practices identified by Peter Thomas, occurs at the expense of Native people. How can one account for Jürgen Schäfer's endorsement of *Gone Indian* as "another attempt to integrate the Indian dimension into Canadian consciousness" (85) if not by the utter failure of parody? When Schäfer refers to Jeremy's "indianization" and to the way the book "grafts" the Indian "past" onto Canadian history, he is not being ironic (87–8). The problem with an account of Jeremy's quest as liberating postmodern narrative of selfhood is that it can distract readers from questions of referentiality in their cultural experience. Once again, by suggesting that there is no such thing as stable subjectivity, or at least not subjectivity that can be trusted, the postmodernist turn silences the "marginalized subjects" articulating themselves in literature. As the feminist critique of postmodern ethnography makes clear, the recuperation of subjectivity in postmodern writing takes place in this kind of marginalization.

If, as Kroetsch has said, "the fiction makes us real," then a fear of "not being real" drives the search for identity. This is the position Margaret Atwood takes in her discussion of what she calls the Grey Owl Syndrome, arguing that the desire to go Indian appeals to those who "can only be real, in their own terms, by turning themselves into something they are 'really' not" (*Strange Things* 57; see also Dawson). Kroetsch may want to push the limits of narrative, but his subversive intent can only be carried through if the stereotypical view of the northern landscape as a destiny for adventurous males is understood. Ultimately, tongue-in-cheek parody of this kind does not alter the stereotypes it plays with, and it does not engage with the racial exclusions that characterize wilderness and adventure writing. By playing with the form, Kroetsch seems to ignore the issues and assumptions of the literary genre he parodies. His parody of the quest as a narrative of conventional masculine identity retraces the conventional narrative by showing the hero's failure to attain the masculine characteristics required, indicating how determined Kroetsch is in his refusal of narrative resolution (Lecker, *Kroetsch* 77, Davidson 139).

NORTHERN ADVENTURE: FEMINIST RESPONSES

Adventure, which has played such a decisive part as a training ground for gender roles, often requires women to either adopt a passive role or take on the same "masculine" characteristics. As Martin Green argues, feminists who might act as "an important source of opposition to adventure" often "disapprove of 'adventure heroes,' in books and in real life, but feel free to claim some truer idea of adventure for their own cause" (*Adventurous Male* 1, 93). The reappropriation of the adventure narrative in the creation of northern heroes and heroines forms the basis of much contemporary writing about the north. The imperialist view of aboriginal people, nature, and women articulated in northern representation, especially in the adventure genre is, as Sherrill E. Grace argues, "a dangerous paradigm that rationalizes racist and sexist behaviour, validates the central authority of the nation state, and facilitates the destruction of the ecosystem of which we are all a part" ("Gendering" 176).

In her perceptive reading of Aritha van Herk's northern fiction, Marlene Goldman asks whether van Herk's experiments in northern fiction "open a potential narrative space for a new feminist genre" (152) or "simply replicate the imperialist projections which gave rise to the western, and account for its pervasive description of an empty, feminine landscape waiting to be conquered" (154). In *The Tent Peg* (1981) and *No Fixed Address* (1987), Goldman remarks, the heroines seek to escape their assigned gender roles by undertaking picaresque adventures. Yet, the heroine of *The Tent Peg*, J.L., is as rugged an individual as any of the men encountered in adventure literature, or at least as rugged as any modern northern tourist.

The initial scene in *The Tent Peg* signals the association of conquering the northern territory with attaining masculinity. The main character, J.L. secures her position as a cook in a northern camp by cross-dressing and assuming a masculine identity. She later reveals her true sex to her employer, MacKenzie, before they go north, and his approval and protection makes possible her perilous negotiations in the northern community of men.

Like Marian Engel's *Bear* (1976), the story of a woman "gone wild," or "gone Indian," *The Tent Peg* begins by subverting the conventional male quest of separation, initiation, and return. At first, J.L., the only female travelling with the crew, expresses the conventional desire for separation, "the promise of aloneness" (23). Already living a "remote, secluded" life before she leaves, J.L. wants "only to get away from the telephone, the bed, the growing chain of men who rattle and clink behind me" (113). Going north, she hopes, will allow her to sever these attachments, or as she describes it, to separate "from all my myriad and tedious connections," to head for nowhere and to "look at everything in my narrow world from a detached distance" (23). The north she wants is the place with "no residue of humans at all" (57), empty, silent. It is the place the character named Hudson sees all around him, the nothingness on the other side of civilization, "the bloody wilderness" (67) that makes him regret his decision to be adventurous.

J.L. goes north for the silence, the emptiness, and the freedom from social constraints, but she soon finds that this north is an illusion. Although in some of her interactions with the men, she can comfort herself in the knowledge that she can find her own solutions because "up here there are no rules, no set responses, everything is new and undefined" (86), at other times, she knows that this too is an illusion. She gradually realizes that she will not find "relief from the cacophony of sound, of confession that surrounded, that always impinged on me" (57). New social constraints are present in the demands the crew places on her as a woman. As the she-bear tells her: "You thought you'd leave all that behind? There isn't a place in the world without it. You can try to escape, but it's better to face it head on" (111). In the end, J.L. faces her role in the camp by giving the men what they need: for MacKenzie, insight into his wife's departure; for Thompson, an understanding of his relationship with Katie; for Cap, a shoulder to cry on. In this way, she becomes her namesake, Jael, who helped the Israelites by driving a tent peg through the skull of their enemy Sisera as he took refuge in her tent. J.L. has also gained her enemy's trust by offering comfort, food, even rest to them. One by one, she provides for them until, on the last night, she dances: "And in their faces I see my transfiguration, themselves transformed, each one with the tent peg through the temple cherishing the knowledge garnered in sleep, in unwitting trust" (226). The idea of the north as a frontier and the narrative of crossing the frontier as a suspension of the social contract have been unsettled as J.L. learns that she cannot be completely liberated from her gender identity, even if she can command its performance.

The openness and contingency of identity is formalised in the structure of the novel. By telling the stories in the first-person from each character's point of view, van Herk creates the impression of a reality made up of various partial perspectives. Reingard M. Nischik calls this the "resonance technique," the narration of the same events from different perspectives achieving an overall mosaic effect (108). While J.L. discovers that social connections and gender roles form and impinge on the individual even when one tries to cast them off, the novel's structure implies that such connections are subordinate to the interests of the individual. Each character is represented in his or her own separate sections with no connecting perspective, so that the "mosaic effect," as Nischik calls it, allows each character a certain amount of autonomy. The events of the plot bind together all these perspectives; however, the form of the novel creates both different perspectives and discrete individuals. These formal considerations underline the plot's subversive quest. The end of the novel revises both the image of the north as a frontier and the narrative of frontier life as a suspension of social contract as J.L. learns that she cannot be completely liberated from her gender identity, even if she has more freedom to perform it than she thought.

Historically, the Arctic has provided "an adventure landscape" in which heroes seek adventure and become men. In that landscape, writers create all-male communities where masculine characteristics are attained through a binary inflected by gender and racial differences in opposition to the feminized other, whether the Inuit, environment, or civilization. The feminine, represented in internal and external nature, provides the central organizing principle and the element that must be mastered in order to fulfil the quest. However, the masculine identity achieved through adventurous exploits requires an endless striving that renders it highly unstable. Constituted in opposition to the feminine, the masculine identity imagined in such narratives cannot transcend the binary and must continually replicate it.

The myths of the north created in adventure literature developed as an articulation of an ideal racial and gender identity and was complicit in the domination of racial others in newly colonized territories. These northern myths form an important part of Canadian literary history and, as such, their revisions and reinterpretations have the potential to re-imagine the history and identity that has emerged from it. Yet, the persistence of this masculine narrative can be witnessed in recent titles such as Graham Rowley's *Cold Comfort: My Love Affair with the Arctic* (1996). Study and critique of these myths must be vigilant in reading the romantic and mystifying views that have their roots in nineteenth-century ideas about race, gender, and nationalism, especially when considering calls to place the north at the centre of future national imagining.

CHAPTER FOUR

Lovers and Strangers:
Reimagining the Mythic North

Here in this white land,
the senses forged in iron silence,
the mind trapped in a snow boot,
I must hold my black tongue.

Rienzi Crusz, "In the Idiom of the Sun"

The erasure of aboriginal people from the literary landscape in patriotic poetry, and their reduction to supporting roles in adventure narratives, signals the will to territorial appropriation at the heart of northern consciousness and its desire for a Romantic nationalism. Northern consciousness, developed as it is out of the imaginations of writers and readers, embodies an intertextual reality that can be read for its general patterns and features such as the gender and racial characteristics possessed by the ideal conquering hero of the imperial narrative. Feminists have rewritten the masculinist narratives, critiquing their gender binarism and addressing racial stereotyping, and thereby enabling new representations of northern inhabitants such as Inuit. In the same way, the implications of northern experience for the nation as a whole can be challenged. Given the literary history of northern representation with its gendered, racist, and nationalistic moments, it is difficult not to view contemporary calls to place northern consciousness and experience at the centre of Canadian national identity as a disavowal of the racial diversity of modern Canada.

What has occurred, however, is an engagement with and revision of works that romanticize and mystify northern experience.

A different nationalist impulse drives contemporary revisions, one associated not with the Romantic view of nationhood but with the Enlightenment view of the nation as separate, independent, and autonomous. Demythologizing the north in Canadian literature with this view becomes an exercise in post-colonial liberation, a way of removing the 'dead hand' of tradition from the throat of the national literature. Writers anxious to find and to depict "true north" turn to personal experience as the stuff of literary imagining. Fiction writers, poets, and journalists travel in the north as ethnographers do, meeting the people, taking field notes, and turning them into polished literary texts when they get back home. What remains to be seen is if reimagining the north by replacing one mythology with another, or by changing the features to reflect new concerns and ideas, actually undermines or reaffirms the north's traditional function as blank page for the nation's narrative.

ROMANTIC REMAINS: THE GROUP OF SEVEN

Nationalistic appreciation for the land expressed itself in the work of the Confederation poets and, later, in the painting of the Group of Seven. As their contemporary critic F.B. Housser wrote: "The message that the Group of Seven art movement gives to this age is the message that here in the North has arisen a young nation with faith in its own creative genius" (215). Emerging as it did from modern dissatisfaction with the effects of industrialization and urbanization and alongside the growing North American conservationist movement, the late Romantic vision of nature in the Group of Seven displays a "vague Transcendentalism" (Altmeyer 32) which was "inspired as the result of a direct contact with Nature herself" (Housser 24). Like the Confederation poets, the Group of Seven participated in the "reinterpretation of nature, not as environment to be transformed," as it had been in the territorial claims of Mair's poetry, for example, "but as a transformative and generative process" (Mandel 20). As Sandra Djwa recounts in her seminal work on this subject, the new view of the north was encouraged by the increased popularity of outdoor pursuits such as canoe trips into the hinterland, voyages that allowed individuals to live out the manly adventures depicted in literature (5). Artists found the ancient geography of the land a fit substitute for

Canada's lack of historical past and developed a romantic nationalist aesthetic from "the fusion of a distinctly Canadian landscape and imported modernist techniques" (3, *passim*).

As remarks by both Housser and Roald Nasgaard indicate, the Group of Seven "conceived of their art as national Romantic" not only in its content but also "because it found its motivation in a mystical bonding with the land, the character of which provided the basis for common experience and, by analogy, national unity" (Nasgaard, *Mystic North* 166). The ideas shared by the Group of Seven were informed by an interest in the theosophical aesthetic of universal spirit, whereby "the artist offers his public a glimpse of universal goodness, beauty, and truth" (Lacombe 111). Indeed, Lismer's article in a 1925 issue of *The Canadian Theosophist* confidently predicted that Canadians would become better artists as they grew more aware of their environment (Housser 13). "Harris too," writes Nasgaard, "spoke of the informing spirit of nature and national expression in the most transcendent and mystical terms, giving the North itself a special place in his ideology" (169).

This sense of the north as mysterious and mystical inspired the Group's Romantic nationalist vision (Grace, "Northern Modernism" 107, "Gendering" 167; Lacombe 115; Hjartarson 70). According to Ramsay Cook, the Group of Seven worked to eliminate European influences in their painting, in order to find a new way of portraying the Canadian wilderness: "For the Group, especially for its most articulate spokesman, Lawren Harris, the natural environment was the North" although "[t]he discovery that Canadian nationality was connected with the north was hardly new" (16–17; see also Hjartarson). The influence that the Group of Seven had on the way the north was and is imagined cannot be overstated. The national focus of the Group's painting contributed to the conflation of "the Canadian north" and "Canada as north," while the imaginary North in Canadian literature owes a great deal to their Romantic nationalism, too. No doubt many Canadians can identify with the experience David Booth describes in *Images of Nature: Canadian Poets and the Group of Seven* (1995): "Throughout my life I have been aware of paintings by the Group of Seven – on bank walls, in school halls and on postage stamps... The Group captured the natural heart of Canada and wrapped me in its vision as if inside the flag" (3). The Group of Seven, as Bruce Hodgins remarks, "rarely put people in their North," romanticizing the north as a landscape rather than a homeland ("The Canadian North" 2; see also Grace, "Comparing" 245, "Gendering" 168). The north is represented as the blank page from which the presence of all people has been erased, presenting the viewer with "a territory to be occupied and possessed, and a symbolic space, a topos being named" (Bordo 102). It is therefore appropriate that David Booth's collection of poetry and painting pairs their work with poems depicting the north as *tabula rasa*, such as Earle Birney's "Ellesmereland I" (1952): "No man is settled on that coast / The harebells are alone" (in Booth 12).

Wherever the north can be found in literature, there can also be found some form of Romanticism, and that Romanticism seems to account for the north's appeal to the idea of national consciousness. Modernist poets also turned to nature, but they turned away from the kind of nature poetry in which "images such as the red maple of autumn and spring's first crocus" flourished (Morley 27). Instead, Canadian modernists F.R. Scott, A.J.M. Smith, A.M. Klein, and Leo Kennedy, in Patricia Morley's words, "rocked these tired native symbols" (27). "The Canadian Modernists," Brian Trehearne argues in *Aestheticism and the Canadian Modernists* (1989), "are set keenly apart from the poetasters of their time by virtue of their recent Aesthetic rather than late Romantic poetic derivation" (13).

The impact of the Group of Seven's aesthetic on modernist poetry is well known. The work of the Group of Seven and the nationalism surrounding it, according to Djwa, exerted considerable influence on modern Canadian poetry, especially the appropriation of imagism and free verse techniques in depicting the landscape (7, 15). The Group's "distinctive visual paradigm of modern Canada" (New 142) is there in F.R. Scott's "North Stream" ("Ice mothers me") or the "Inarticulate, arctic, / Not written on by history" of "Laurentian Shield" (1954). Thus, Sherrill E. Grace and W.J. Keith compare the bold clarity of Imagist verse to the paintings of the Group of Seven ("Northern Expressionism" 111; *Canadian* 58), and Keith argues that "The Lonely Land" is A.J.M. Smith's best-known poem "not because it offers an unforgettable verbal impression of the northern Canadian landscape but because it represents a triumph of subtly controlled vocabulary and carefully modulated rhythms. To call it descriptive would be absurd" (59).

The northern landscapes made famous by the Group became "a resonant symbolic language" in Canadian literature – one need only look to A.M. Klein's submerged poet in "Portrait of the Poet as Landscape" or to the "beauty / of dissonance" in Smith's "The Lonely Land" to appreciate its role. Literary critics stress its importance, too; for example, in *Headwaters of Canadian Literature* (1924), Archibald MacMechan cites "interpretation of the land" as a quality that makes poetry "Canadian" (116). Fifty-five years later, poet Tom Marshall's critical overview of Canadian poetry describes how, in the colonial period, "[t]he eeriness of Canadian space, the apparent emptiness, the silence required another expression" (5).

Finally, D.M.R. Bentley's identification of formal adaptation as the grounds for a distinct Canadian poetry explicates the lasting influence of the Group's depiction of the environment. According to Bentley's ecological theory, form emerges from the experience the poet seeks to articulate; thus, the formal strictures of Imagism are less suitable for poetry inspired by or expressing the vast spaces of the hinterland while the possibilities of free verse give the poet a freedom that is more appropriate to its expression ("New Dimension" 10–15). The poetry of Al Purdy, the Canadian poet who has been most devoted to the expression of northern experience, exemplifies the formal characteristics that Bentley identifies.[1]

DEMYTHOLOGIZING THE NORTH: THE FRANKLIN MYSTERY

As the contemporary poet who, as Lorraine York remarks, has "probably more than any other, set up cultural shop in the Canadian North" (48), Al Purdy waged poetic war on the myths of the north. As is the case with other northern enthusiasts, experience travelling in the north inflects his poetic voice. In his autobiography, significantly entitled *Reaching for the Beaufort Sea* (1993), Purdy describes his excitement as he set off for Baffin Island: "it was virgin territory to me" (190). The Arctic experience was formative for Purdy who credits it with being the place where "I first took my ego in my hands and said to the Canada Council, I can write poems there"; yet he goes on to explain: "When you experience that blindingly white place of sunlight, vivid blue water and solitude that presses on you and surrounds you like air itself – you wonder at your own hubris and insolence in thinking you can write about it" (262). There can be no doubt how important that trip was to Purdy: "That summer on Baffin added new pages to my life, which occasionally return to me in dreams" (195).

Al Purdy was praised by Peter Buitenhuis as one of the writers who "have done their best to pierce the illusions and myths in order to write about the North without attempting to colonize it with the imagination" (6) and who "break through the barriers of perceptions, to reach beyond illusion, myth or utopia to create a convincing image of the North and its people" (4). For Buitenhuis, Purdy's poems are "reminders to us in the south of what is really there behind the myths and illusions" created by representations of the north (12). Purdy's poetry shows us the aestheticized north we see in the travel writing of postmodern writers such as Barry Lopez and Aritha van Herk, but it also constitutes a break with these patterns in representation. Lorraine York sees Purdy "playing with the myth of the north as a blank page, but starting to question it at the same time," so that the north in Purdy's poetry resists the kind of representation in which "the North becomes a huge, white narcissistic playground, passively offering up to us the image of our imposing selves" (48–9).

As John Van Rys argues, Purdy rejects the Romantic national ideal represented in the work of the Group of Seven by criticizing the A.Y. Jackson plates that illustrated his collection *North Of Summer* (1967) in a letter to George Woodcock: "They don't fit," he writes, "not the way I feel or talk. But what the hell, they'll sell books I guess–" (Purdy, *Purdy-Woodcock* 19; qtd in Van Rys 3). Van Rys explains this preference for "the cultural forms and idioms indigenous to Baffin Land" (as Purdy calls it) as part of the carnivalesque inversion that Purdy undergoes by going north and as shaping the poems into "an expression of folk consciousness" (3). But Purdy himself acknowledges that when he went to the Arctic, "I was also fascinated by myself, a navel-watcher, narcissistic as hell" (*Reaching* 189), bent on his own experience and not the experience of others. In the end, the Group of Seven's blank, mystical north that was so closely associated with Canadian nationalism did not resemble the north of his experience or his poetic imagination, let alone his poetic voice.

Initially, Purdy wanted to illustrate *North of Summer* with Inuit drawings (Van Rys 3), and his interest in Inuit culture points away from the aesthetic aspect of his poetry to the ethnographic. In the representative and widely anthologized "Lament for the Dorsets," Purdy takes particular care with ethnographic detail, the tent rings, scrapers, and spearheads that litter the poem. The ivory swan that the speaker imagines a Dorset named Kudluk carving becomes "an analogy" for Purdy's poem (York 50) as the poem is built on the artifact he imagines, or at least on the possibility for reconciliation of past and present it holds. Throughout *North of Summer*, attention to ethnographic details signals the basis on which Purdy builds his poetic vision of the north. As George Woodcock remarks, Purdy shows "the ability to turn intensely felt experience into fine loping poetry without much of Wordsworth's 'recollection in tranquillity'" (*Introduction* 115). Ethnography and travel writing influence Purdy's poetry, and his work shares the ethnographer's emphasis on the authenticating and authorizing role of firsthand experience. In subject matter, Purdy's poetry shows an interest in both the role of experience and the continuation of the past into the present that I have noted in representations of Inuit culture. The young Inuit woman in "Girl," like the Dorset hunter bending over his carving in "Lament for the Dorsets," remains as an emblem of cultural survival and endurance long after the individuals are gone. Cultural survival is assured through art, especially the poet's ability to reconcile the life of the imagination and the real, to make experience meaningful.

Survival is also the theme of Purdy's "Trees at the Arctic Circle," which begins with the speaker's angry reaction to the "Coward trees" as they are mocked by his memories of stately southern trees (29), and ends with the realization "I have been stupid in a poem" (30) when the speaker comes to appreciate the trees as emblems of survival. In "Postscript to 'Trees at the Arctic Circle,'" Purdy further praises their endurance since the ancient time when they appeared "unnoticed by anyone" (31). In *Naked with Summer in Your Mouth* (1994), he continues to seek survivors who might reconcile art and experience, mortality and immortality, as in his elegiac poem for Stan Rogers: "he is not there / but 'driving hard across the plains' / for the Northwest Passage" (63).

In form, as in content, Purdy's poetry depicts the north in terms of lived experience. Purdy's art has been identified as a "poetry of plain talk" that stresses vernacular style, resistance to metric convention, and feeling for the past (Keith *Canadian*, 98–9). This is Purdy the storyteller, whose poetry is "rich in flora and fauna, and rich, too, in anecdotes (full, in fact, of sloughs and ships, and arctic rhododendrons, and cactuses and Sam McGees)" (Bentley, "New Dimension" 15). The element of story in Purdy's poetry accounts in part for the praise it earns as representation of the real north; however, the adaptation of form deals imaginatively with the northern reality. D.M.R. Bentley cites Purdy as one of those poets who adapts the free verse form to the hinterlandscape: "Purdy's well-known response to the 'vast lonely' spaces of the Arctic was to use a short-lined, open-ended free verse and to concentrate, by his own admission, on details and on people" ("New Dimension" 15).

By way of adaptation, *North of Summer* includes what John Van Rys describes as "low and sub-literary genres," such as the diary and the explorer's journal (8), forming an intertextual link with writing by other travellers as well as blurring the boundaries of genre. These formal elements allow Purdy to counter Arctic myths. Purdy takes on the explorer's mystique in "The North West Passage," answering the title with the first line ("is found") that announces the obsolescence of Arctic exploration (20). The speaker, bored, lounges on his bed waiting for dinner. Everything has been named by the time the speaker arrives: Baffin, Boothia, Ungava, Thule, after explorers such as Frobisher and Amundsen and the incongruous Ringnes brothers, the "heroic Norwegian brewers whose names / cling alcoholically to islands up there" (21). Heroes, like myths and illusions, are undone in Purdy's poetry: "The mirror is broken / (glass is fragile anyway) /… all heroes die" ("Heroes," *Naked* 61). The Arctic requires no more exploration, and the speaker's imaginary journey "in search of dead sailors" (20) on the map ends with disappointment:

> but the Terror and Erebus sank long ago
> and it's half an hour before dinner
> and there isn't much to do but write letters
> and I can't think of anything more to say
> about the North West Passage
> but I'll think of something
> maybe
> a break–thru
> to strawberries and ice cream for dinner. (21)

The speaker's unheroic inertia and decadence contrast with the glamour of exploration. In what has been called Purdy's "carnivalized version of epic heroism," the poem creates an epic world in order to turn it upside down so that the reader sees the Arctic world in a new way (Van Rys 6). Al Purdy's work traces the tensions between northern myth and northern reality. Based as they are on his travels in the north, Purdy's poems appeal for the experience at their core, for the stories he tells in poetic form.

When Gwendolyn MacEwen turns to the Franklin expedition as a subject for her verse play, *Terror and Erebus*, written in 1965 and published in *Afterworlds* (1987), she also challenges the myths surrounding the north's history of great men. To do so, she uses ballad form for those passages in which the explorers speak. As Atwood remarks, MacEwen "knows her ballad lore" and its rhythm (*Strange Things* 27). The ballad form, conjuring as it does the legacy of Robert Service, suits the myths of the north, the tales of men prevailing in bleak circumstances, explorers and traders and miners on the margins of the society they flee. Although *Terror and Erebus* is written in free verse form, it also evokes throughout the quatrains of alternating four-stress and three-stress lines and the abcb or abab rhyme scheme:

> How could they know, even stand back and see
> The nature of the place they stood on,
> When no man can, no man knows where he stands
> Until he leaves his place, looks back
>   and knows ...
> As though you created the Passage
> By *willing* it to be.
>   Ah Franklin!
> To follow you one does not need geography. (41–2)

The thematic content of *Terror and Erebus* represents certain myths, including the north as an imaginary space, the north as "the land God gave Cain," and the north as the site of the masculine quest, which Sherrill E. Grace argues "appears to be unironically reproduced" ("Gendering" 167). But MacEwen undermines "masculinist ideology" in her revision of the standard explorer narrative. In its narrative of Rasmussen's search for Franklin, the poem demythologizes the explorer's world-view when Rasmussen confronts Franklin, "You carried all maps within you," and states that Franklin died

Seeking a passage from imagination to
  reality,
Seeking a passage from land to land
  by sea. (42)

In Rasmussen's sections of the play, the clash of knowledges is explicit. As Franklin tries to find the maps in his head by leaving "Cryptic marks" (56), writing and mapping the landscape, and leaving their remains, the Franklin expedition "Like shattered compasses, like sciences / Gone mad" (41) scattered around "cairns / like compasses" and "Marking out all the latitudes / and longitudes / Of men" (56). Throughout the verse play, space is textualized by the movements of the explorers who turn what they imagine into the maps, journals, diaries, and official reports that Rasmussen says "Nobody needs to read" (56). Yet, it is that creation in representation which brings the Northwest Passage into being:

The eye *creates* the horizon
The ear *invents* the wind
The hand reaching out from a parka sleeve
By touch demands that the touched thing
  be. (42)

Like the "hand of Franklin" in Stan Rogers' ballad "The Northwest Passage," "[t]racing one warm line through a land so wide and savage," MacEwen's Franklin wilfully pursues the imaginary passage, leaving Rasmussen asking the question that closes the play:

Or … is it that the way was *invented*,
Franklin?
    That you cracked the passage open
With the forces of your sheer certainty?
    Or is it that you cannot know,
Can never know,
Where the passage lies
Between conjecture and reality … ? (56–7)

MacEwen cuts to the heart of the ideas that supported the search for the Northwest Passage and to the sin of hubris that brought Franklin to tragedy.

Mordecai Richler's *Solomon Gursky Was Here* (1989) is perhaps the most allusive and literate treatment of the Franklin story, and the only one to confront the ideas and values that give the Franklin mystery priority in Canadian historiography. In this satirical history of the Bronfman dynasty, Richler rewrites the legendary history of the Franklin expedition, working "to inscribe Jews into prominent events of Canadian history, spots of time where official Canadian historiography quite obviously does not want them to be" (Korte 495). Richler demonstrates not only the "unreliability" of this heroic tale but the racist attitudes that place it at the centre of national mythology. The main character, Moses, the writer delving into Gursky history, discovers that the Jewish patriarch Ephraim Gursky went to Van Diemen's Land, a significant historical detail that demonstrates Richler's extensive research, for John Franklin would have been colonial governor of Van Diemen's Land at the time. Presumably, the resourceful Ephraim becomes acquainted with Franklin and winds up on board the *Erebus*, disguised as a surgeon. At this point, Richler adds to the impressive stores on board the *Erebus*: "Six coils of stuffed derma, four dozen kosher salamis, a keg of schmaltz herring and uncounted jars of chicken fat, ... garlic cloves" (46). Later, M'Clintock's famous discovery of the life boat on King William Island is given the tantalizing detail that "[t]he only provisions in sight were 40 pounds of tea, a quantity of chocolate, and a small jar of animal fat, probably walrus, that surprisingly enough tasted of chicken and burnt onions" (47). In light of the evidence of lead poisoning described in *Frozen in Time*, a text that Richler acknowledges, it is clear that Ephraim survives the Franklin expedition by eating kosher! If this were not humorous enough irony, as successive expeditions in search of Franklin collect artifacts from the site, objects first assumed to belong to an Inuit shaman are identified as a yarmulke and a talith (51). As the evidence mounts, Moses finds that no one will believe that a Jew was part of the Franklin expedition, and as Barbara Korte argues, the resistance of the WASP professor of history to Moses' findings further exposes the desire to bar Jewish people from Arctic adventure (496). Richler, however, transforms the Franklin mystery into the Gursky mystery. To date, Mordecai Richler is one of the few writers to confront the racial exclusions of northern history, although Rudy Wiebe's ongoing dialogue with anthropology could develop such a critique.

REMYTHOLOGIZING THE NORTH:
CONTEMPORARY TRAVEL WRITING

Robert Kroetsch has declared that "[t]o write is, in some meta-phoric sense, to go North. To go North is, in some metaphoric sense, to write. One goes North at that very point on the page where the word is in the process of extending itself onto the blankness of the page" (*Likely* 14). The history of representing the Arctic as silent, empty space provides the context for its compar-ison with the blank page. Kroetsch's metaphor picks up on the iconography of northern representation that is such an important part of Canadian self-imagining, but it also derives its meaning from the century or more of literature that removed northern inhabitants from the picture, rendering the Arctic landscape par-ticularly welcoming to the white, male hero. In order for the individual to picture himself etching that white space with his presence, this erasure has to occur.

The north as a blank space waiting to be filled in, or a silence waiting to be broken is a stereotype. Shelagh Grant and Ramsay Cook have each noted the use of the term *tabula rasa* to describe the way southerners imagine the northern landscape, and Sherrill E. Grace quotes F.R. Scott's "Laurentian Shield" as "inarticulate, arctic," and the north "empty as paper" ("Comparing" 250–1; see also "Gendering" 171). It is not surprising, given the context they describe, that Kroetsch goes on to depict the north as challenging and beckoning the writer: "The North was a silence that desired as much to be spoken as I desired to speak," writes Kroetsch. "It was the very geography of my desire. It was the landscape of my unspeakable narrative intention" (*Likely* 16).

Robert Kroetsch's radical postmodernist aesthetic, according to which criticism "is really a version of story" (*Likely* 30), leads him to attempt to undo the binary opposition which he identifies at the heart of Canadian experience. But by obsessively representing these oppositions, I would argue, Kroetsch redraws the bound-aries that he seeks to blur or remove.[2] As Robert Lecker remarks, Kroetsch's widely disseminated views on criticism and theory often provide critics with a way of entering his creative writing: for example, in Kroetsch's reading of *Tay John*, his recognition of the "troubled or at least troubling tension between the symbolic and the documentary" (*Kroetsch* 190) in Canadian writing provides a clue to reading his own wilderness stories.³ In a conversation published in *Future Indicative*, Kroetsch makes the statement: "In fact, I think I couldn't be a writer without critical theory" (Kroetsch and Bowering 10). Even as a response to what he calls "the failure of the literary tradition in Canada," this is an interesting claim considering Kroetsch's general suspicion of the very "categories" that constitute critical theory.

While Kroetsch's writing is viewed as exemplary of postmodern irony and parody (Thomas 2; Hutcheon, *Canadian* 161; Kuester 410), Linda Hutcheon also identifies Kroetsch's sexual metaphors with the "male gender-defined version of the procreative urge" (*Canadian* 170), suggesting, however subtly, the masculinist dimension to Kroetsch's work, especially his parodic representation of the north. Sherrill E. Grace situates his work squarely within the tradition of masculine adventure narratives in Canada: "From the nineteenth-century fur-trapping stories of Robert Ballantyne to Robert Kroetsch's *But We Are Exiles* (1965) and *Gone Indian* (1973) and Mordecai Richler's post-modern epic narrative of nation *Solomon Gursky was Here* (1989), the north is figured as the place of male adventure, the space for testing and proving masculine identities, where sissies and wimps will be turned into real men or destroyed, or be sent home/south to the women or the bottle" (166–7). In his early work *But We Are Exiles*, a novel whose debt to Joseph Conrad has been remarked, a fictional community of men run the northern river in an attempt to escape the feminine influence of civilization. While the characters demonstrate some ambivalence, this binary opposition, like the structuring paradox that Robert Lecker identifies as the basis of Kroetsch's fiction, is always held in place, never resolved (*Kroetsch* 148). What Kroetsch's "ongoing attraction to the 'old dualities' defining his bifocal world" (Lecker 61) implies is a form of gender identity defined by mutual opposition. According to Peter Thomas, *But We Are Exiles* announces Kroetsch's later work because it "exposes a powerfully obsessive imaginative core: the problems of the narcissistic self; the ambiguous quest for freedom ... ambivalence towards the past; the central paradox of phallic energy in the quest of death" (36). Yet, while Thomas considers the opposition to the feminine as primarily a defense against the maternal, he does not develop the most valuable and interesting part of his argument, that is, the identification of Kroetsch's narcissism as *specifically* and reductively phallic (37).

Kroetsch chooses going north as a metaphor for the writer's craft because going north has traditionally been equated with flight, with shaking off the constraints of society, breaking the social contract; in so doing, he envisions writing as a masculine pursuit based as it is on the stereotypical masculine quest. The modernist artist-figure is at home in this imaginary landscape far away from the society that threatens his individuality. The writer "goes north" as a means of imaginative self-engendering, and, like the fictional northern-bound individual, society is what he must flee. As a metaphor for writing, going north relies on the specifically defined and gendered quest, not to mention a characteristically modernist view of the artist. If we extend this idea further, it becomes clear why the northern hero must continue to flee further northward by inventing new challenges and then by surviving them. This figure constantly aspires to a perfect solitude, a perfect separation from social bonds, a rupture with the social contract, which, just like an ideal masculine identity, can never really be.

TRAVELLING NORTHWARD:
THE ETHNOGRAPHIC ENCOUNTER

As I argue in "Literary Field Notes," the influence of ethnography on literature can be observed both in its use as source material and in the use of techniques typical of postmodern ethnography. Howard O'Hagan's *Tay John* (1939), though not set in the far north, exemplifies the blurring of boundaries between wilderness storytelling and ethnographic representation. First of all, O'Hagan relied on ethnographic sources, especially *The Indians of Canada* by Diamond Jenness, for the legends he would turn into fiction. In "Ethnographic Notes on Howard O'Hagan's *Tay John*," Ralph Maud attributes the passages that "deal most conspicuously with Indian culture" to the sources as well (95). It is well known that the story of Tay John's birth is based on Jenness's version of a Tsimshian story, "The Dead Woman's Son," which Jenness judged to be one of the rare tales that "stand out like flowers from a tangle of bushes and deserve the brush of a great artist" (*Indians* 195). O'Hagan rose to the challenge of Jenness's evaluation not only by retelling this tale in literary form but also by simulating the Native storytelling voice heard in the translation of Native speech. The novel begins: "The time of this in its beginning, in men's time, is 1880 in the summer, and its place is the Athabaska valley, near its head in the mountains, and along the other waters falling into it, and beyond them a bit, over Yellowhead Pass to the westward, where the Fraser, rising in a lake, flows through wilderness and canyon down to the Pacific" (11). The "aloof historical voice, the mysterious mythic voice" (Keith, *Sense* 35) of the framing narrative echoes the narrative voice adopted in ethnography in order to convey a sense of the drama and ritual of oral performance. O'Hagan would have read of the inverted, passive syntax, the repetition, slow rhythm, and "metaphorical speech" used by Native storytellers in *The Indians of Canada*, as well as Jenness's conclusion that "Indian utterances derived their force largely from the manner of their delivery and lost much of their effect when reduced to print" (200, 201).

The method of representation, the pattern of the subject's construction, shares significant similarities with ethnography. The new or postmodern ethnography that aims to blur boundaries between fiction and non-fiction exerts a certain influence on contemporary travel writing, resulting in a proliferation of postmodern texts that eschew realism yet are grounded in the authority of experience. In first-person accounts of northern travels, the individual's role as a storyteller speaking for the silent north by recording experience in an alien environment occupies the foreground, and this role undermines the independence of the reality it supposedly describes. The influence of social scientific discourses on contemporary travel writing may be attributed to a resistance to the excesses of the adventure genre and exploration narratives. As writers concerned with demythologizing the north attempt to describe their experiences, they turn to those disciplines that have been concerned with issues of truth in representation such as realist anthropology. This interdisciplinary contact is not without perils, but it indicates the general trend of blurring boundaries between genres.

The mutual influence of social scientific and literary forms apparent in the representation of the north begs the question: if literature, or literary theory, can make a significant impact on ethnography, then can the reverse also be true? The Arctic has been visited by a number of Canadian writers, some of whom were funded by southern grants: F.R. Scott in 1956; Al Purdy in

1965 and 1971; Wiebe and van Herk and Paulette Jiles. In Elizabeth Hay's *The Only Snow in Havana* (1992) the tourist role serves the postmodern urge to blend genres and weave together intertextual fragments as the narrator travels intermittently from New York to Cuba to Mexico to Yellowknife. Whether listening to jazz or eating lichee fruit, the narrator freely consumes culture, travelling easily from one country to another, picking up cultures and people and turning them into the book's fragments and clipped phrases: "Serenity: a Chinese woman selling flowers" (89); "Inuktitut has many words with an oriental cast" (141). Such voyages are quests structured as the fieldwork model in which the individual seeks contact with an alien world, but tourists seek to enjoy this contact rather than learn from it.

Rather than developing a scenario for a fictional community of men or an opposition to a feminized landscape or culture, travel writers construct themselves, usually moulding a similar kind of hero figure and encoding some of characteristics of the specific form of masculinity represented in adventure narratives. The choice of personal narrative over fiction, like the postmodernist turn in ethnography, retreats from problems of othering and voice appropriation, but it creates a new and no less dangerous set of problems by excluding northern people from the account, for while appearing to offer an account of first-hand experience, including self-conscious musing on the possibility of such an account, these writers also create an imaginary north.

Arctic Dreams (1987) by Barry Lopez is a postmodern, first-person travel narrative which owes a debt to the new ethnography. The text does not make any explicit claim beyond its expression of the narrator's encounter with the northern environment; in effect, its main concern is the construction of the author's subjectivity within a holistic vision. Yet, in constructing the subject, he recreates the experience of aboriginal people without acknowledging their voices. Instead, Lopez tends to ascribe thoughts and feelings to others. Travelling with some Tununiarusirmiut men, Lopez remarks that his companions "knew beyond a shadow of a doubt, beyond any hesitation, what made them *happy*, what gave them a sense of satisfaction, of wealth. An abundance of animals" (41; emphasis added). Lopez does not report actually conversing with any of the men, and he admits to not knowing their language, yet he admires these hunters and enjoys travelling with them in spite of "a loss of intellectual conversation" and "a consistent lack of formal planning" (202). Throughout, he contrasts the civilized man with his tastes in food, conversation, and lifestyle and the simple *indigène* whose life can only be understood as a grasping survival. With indigenous people, he writes, "one feels the constant presence of people who know something about surviving" (202).

While Lopez acknowledges his dependence on the ideas (his word is wisdom) of his own culture when considering other cultures, his epistemic position finds its basis in an appreciation for the native point of view, which is just the first of many assumptions he shares with some ethnographers. In more than one instance, he attempts to "imagine" what the hunters are thinking as he has imagined the viewpoint of the various animals who are the true subjects of his Arctic quest. It seems that for him (not the "Eskimo" themselves, as he claims) the aboriginal people are "still not quite separate from the animal world" (39). Of course, the suggestion of a superior understanding of the land (equated with a more immediate contact with animals) has an undeniable political utility for aboriginal groups today, but when evoked by Lopez, it also denies the people's voice and fixes them within the romantic ideal of the hunting society currently challenged by feminist anthropologists. As in early ethnography, the hunt occupies the privileged position in this book, thereby satisfying the southern audience's craving for stories of physical survival.

Although he challenges certain stereotypes of Native people, for instance cautioning against the view that aboriginal hunters are "natural" conservationists, Lopez continues the tradition of viewing hunting societies as male-dominated by ignoring the role, even the existence, of women, and when it comes to understanding the hunters, he imagines them as dream people who differ even in cognitive function from non-aboriginal people, a suggestion with no scientific basis: "The mind we know in dreaming, a nonrational, nonlinear comprehension of events in which slips in time and space are normal, is, I believe, the conscious working mind of an aboriginal hunter. It is a frame of mind that redefines patience, endurance, and expectation" (200). As hinted by the titles of three texts considered in this study, *Maps and Dreams, Arctic Dreams,* and *Enduring Dreams,* and brilliantly satirized in Alootook Ipellie's title *Arctic Dreams and Nightmares,* the importance of dreams to aboriginal cultures has created a great deal of interest. At the end of the book, Lopez thinks that he has dreamt the landscape that lies before him and provides a metaphorical rendering of the Indian dream hunt experience: "The edges of the real landscape became one with the edges of something I had dreamed. But what I had dreamed was only a pattern, some beautiful pattern of light. The continuous work of the imagination, I thought, to bring what is actual together with what is dreamed is an expression of human evolution" (414).

As Arun Mukherjee points out in a discussion of Western cinematic treatments of the Third World, dreams can provide a convenient realm for the racial other since "[o]ne can continue with the business of daily living once one has contained the native in this dream space" (*Towards* 104). The dream space fulfils the same fixing function as stereotyping, which Homi K. Bhabha defines as a complete disavowal of difference accommodating a mixed image of its subject, because it offers the same "concept of 'fixity' in the ideological construction of otherness" ("Other Question" 18). Stereotypes of the Inuit, as Hugh Brody shows in his analysis of white attitudes, can portray them as both simple-minded and wise (*People's Land* 78-87). When a text concerning aboriginal peoples such as the one by Lopez collapses different societies into a single "Native perspective," a perspective that centres on the spiritual life of Native people and suggests that they inhabit a mystical or dream-like space, it stereotypes Native people. The effect of such an image is to deny them access to self-representation.[4]

In so doing, Lopez participates in a discourse that mystifies "the Native." In popular culture, aboriginal peoples, communities, and nations have been homogenized within a New Age notion of "aboriginality" that is primarily spiritual. A ubiquitous stereotype that revives the "noble savage" as the new "mystic savage," and like the stereotype that Diana Relke calls the "green Indian," this aboriginality cuts aboriginal peoples off from their own specific cultures – the source of identity and difference – and freezes them in a static, timeless image for the dominant culture, which is so spiritually depleted that it seeks out and consumes others.

Writers who travel north and represent their own individuality obsessively in their travel writing risk denying the same autonomy to members of aboriginal societies. Even though Lopez claims only a space in his own life for his experience, when he vanishes behind the scenes throughout the text, imagining the thoughts and desires of others, he undermines the sincerity of his project and becomes a cultural parasite bleeding another culture for inspiration. His confessional tone draws the reader into a warm conspiratorial relationship, but the narrative shatters the notion of empathy suggested by his attempt to understand "the Native point of view" by simply ignoring the presence of others. At the end of the book, the writer surveys the northern landscape and confides, "When I stood I thought I glimpsed my own desire" (414). At this moment, the dream of empathy fades, for there is no other here, only an adventurous man and a narcissistic text. This final passage reflects the confessional techniques sustaining the postmodern ethnographic mode, while the survival theme places the writer in the context of rugged masculinity attained through the self-denial typical of adventure narratives.

In his book *Enduring Dreams: An Exploration of Arctic Landscape* (1994), John Moss praises the "lyric grace" with which "Lopez writes himself into landscape," and how "the Arctic becomes a flourish on the margin of the chart of the writer's contemplation of himself" (59). Although proposed only as an assessment of Lopez's book, the comment is as true for the narratives of other travellers such as Aritha van Herk, Rudy Wiebe, and Moss himself. At play are the conventions of postmodernism that "call into question the kind of reality that the text claims to represent, the reality of the text itself" (Wilson 57). On the jacket cover, Linda Hutcheon describes *Enduring Dreams* as "[t]he postmodern text we have been waiting for." Postmodern conventions used include a self-reflexive stance evident in the opening of Moss's preface: "The reflection of my face is obscured by the sloping shadow of my hat, so that what I seem is an absence, although I can clearly see the boulders and gravel of the river bottom within my projected shape" (ix).[5] As Al Purdy said, the obliteration of self is also a narcissistic moment. While the text works to bring the absent self into being, it also highlights the nature of the self as an "imaginative creation" (105), and a perilous construction at that: "The danger, of course, is in believing your own account, confusing your own vision of the world with the world itself" (107). Lorrie Graham and Tim Wilson offer a reading of Moss's attempt to find an alternative to the postmodern explanation of being as interpretation, or in the case of Arctic narrative, an attempt to place oneself in the landscape. The strength of the text, they argue, is its "openness to beings that allows them to arise in themselves as themselves, on their own terms," which they call "postmetaphysical" (142).

Understanding the self "on its own terms" can also describe the narcissistic text which is, again, grounded in personal experience.[6] Experience underwrites the authority of Moss's account just as it would an ethnographic monograph, with the narrator referring to the log he keeps and to taking "field notes" (110). Such passages recall the blurred boundaries of postmodern ethnography, and Moss refers to the subjective character of description when he asserts that "every account of the Arctic is also informed by the personal and often confusing desires of each writer to shape history from geography, to attain knowledge or wealth, to escape or discover himself, to be famous" (105), thus acknowledging the centrality of desire to any Arctic adventure. For Moss, escaping and discovering himself involves overcoming the body in typical masculine ways.

Memories of physical endurance dominate the narrator's thoughts. As Moss says in an interview with Christine Hamelin, running in the Arctic gave him a sense of belonging because "[y]ou're acutely conscious that you are an extension of the landscape you are running through" (163). In one passage, the narrator remembers the pain endured as he raced the Iron Man, his heroic finish, and the thought of vindication in the eyes of a male high school gym teacher (81–3); in a passage which bears a striking resemblance to the trials of Jeremy Sadness in Robert Kroetsch's *Gone Indian*, he recalls cross-country skiing from Lachute to Gatineau: "You do these things, extend yourself to limits of what the mind and muscles will endure, because there, while there, boundaries bend, borders blur. This is not a question of transcendence through mortification of the flesh. It is an honouring of the body as landscape, for the endurance athlete becomes the thing being done, becomes the landscape of its doing. It is not denial but affirmation" (64–5). Inscribing the body as an instrument of achievement, performance, and sublimation in this way is, according to Victor Seidler and other theorists of masculinity, a characteristic use of the body as affirmation of masculine identity. Yet, as Moss describes this experience, he is also conscious of the cultural meanings he carries with him, showing that, as Aritha van Herk is reported to have told Rudy Wiebe, one must find "the north in

your own head" (*Playing* 113). The text's complex intertextuality
stands as proof that culture is portable. Going north, the outsider
retains his own cultural background, whatever empathy and
insight the experience may afford.

The Arctic is a place where the masculine individual pushes
himself into being. This is the initiation that the adventurer goes
north to endure: the romance of proving oneself in a rugged
setting. When writing the self into being, the writer chooses to
make the self a certain way, to mirror certain values of the masculine self. As a reader and professor of Canadian literature, Moss
also weaves that self out of literary references and allusions,
describing his method as "drawing from intellectual discourse
and research, adventure and sport, contemplative evasions of
language and thought; from many texts and a critical aptitude,
from travel, teaching, and especially family, from imagination and
a deep desire to know" (x). Yet, the goal of the quest is spiritual,
not intellectual, as he seeks a kind of "secular grace" which will
be found if "the notion of Arctic narrative as a linear quest will
self-destruct; and we, absolved from the structures of grammar
and story, might find among words the power of silence; in the
subversion of imminence" (136). Despite this intention, *Enduring
Dreams* resembles an Arctic adventure narrative in that it follows
the separation, initiation, and return pattern of the quest and risks
encoding masculinist expectations with each self-imposed trial.
The gendering of national identity by this means does not seem
to have been remarked in the reception of the book. For instance,
Robert Kroetsch praises the book for the way it changes "our
sense of what Arctic is; our sense of what we ourselves are,"
suggesting that the north defines "who we are" as Canadians. For
Kroetsch, Moss's text contributes to the definition of Canadian
identity, and the use of "we" refers to the representation of the
north as national heritage. As Moss remarks, the book is "about
Canada" (Hamelin 164).

When Aritha van Herk travels northward, it is, as she puts it
in her characteristically strong way, "beyond the intellectual comprehension or the geographical experience of most of those people
calling themselves Canadians" (*In Visible* 3). *Places Far From Ellesmere* (1990), an autobiographical fiction that the author describes
as a "geografictione," depicts the Arctic landscape as a blank,
white page on which to inscribe her story, "a floating polar desert

for all characters to emulate" (78). It is the abstract landscape in which she can rewrite the story of Anna Karenina: "You are at Ellesmere. You have escaped to Ellesmere. Her island, *tabula rasa*, awayness so thoroughly truant you have cut all connexions to all places far from Ellesmere. This is what you long for. Anna must have too" (77). The heroine regards the place, her self, and the character as the *tabula rasa*, the void stretching before the writer that fills her with desire.[7] While Sherrill E. Grace argues that the book "celebrates its own ability to *imagine* and *construct* woman as Ellesmere" and that both van Herk and Anna "go north to reclaim themselves" ("Gendering" 172), Marlene Goldman wonders if the narrator "is simply putting a playful spin on an old genre, namely, the 'western,'" or if "her fictions open a potential narrative space for a new feminist genre" ("Go North" 153). "The text's subversive casting of a female picaresque character," Goldman continues, "destabilizes certain narrative stereotypes, although this reversal does not prevent the text from maintaining significant links with traditional discourses" (155). Finally, Goldman concludes that *Places Far From Ellesmere* does not address "the political and imperial agendas that continue to determine the fate of the Arctic" (157).[8]

The heroine's relationship to the Arctic seems to replicate those agendas, agendas that characters like MacEwen's Crozier and Franklin carry with them, by thematizing the pursuit of desire. The heroine's desire for this place is both erotic and territorial because she imagines it as a body on which to gratify herself. In an aerial view that recalls F.R. Scott's "Flying to Fort Smith" (1956), she looks down on the island, declaring it a "languid body below you" (87) and a "clean-swept northern desert of desire" (105). Crossing a river, she suddenly feels an urge to sink into the island, and emerges feeling an ecstasy like orgasm. Finally, she satisfies the desire to possess Ellesmere by writing her geografictione on the island, resulting in a postmodern project that rereads and rewrites *Anna Karenina* on the new territory of Ellesmere.

Van Herk again evokes the wordless, white page in her essay "In Visible Ink (1991)" which seeks to invert the encounter between reader and text making the page the so-called agent: "I am reinvented by a great white page" (8); "I am its text" (5). As Goldman notes, in this later work, van Herk engages some of the more difficult issues raised by her representation of the north, yet I would disagree that her discussion of language in this essay makes up for the absences in other works. In fact, the desire for silence and empty possibility remains. Because going north means being "finally freed of words" (2) and aware that "one can be disappeared and re-written in a language beyond one's own" (10), a contrast is established between the wordless north and the south "full of words shouting everywhere to be read" (11), yet, by the end of her journey, she is "given a different text to carry south" (11).

"In Visible Ink" differs from *Places Far From Ellesmere* in that it represents someone other than the narrator (or the good-natured helper) in the northern landscape; it depicts a northern inhabitant, the narrator's guide, Pijamini, who teaches her Inuktitut words. In this passage, Pijamini guides the author as she transcends language, but she refuses to reveal his words' "magic incantations" because, she writes, "They are Pijamini's words, not mine, and if I was able to hear them and to mimic them, it was only through his agency. I will not raid them, or repeat them beyond the Arctic sea, beyond the secret worlds of ice" (10). Pijamini seems to be outside time, which is not measurable in his world (9), and modernity. Significantly, Pijamini receives a mention in the acknowledgments "simply for being Pijamini." In this world of magical language and mystical knowledge, the act of writing becomes radically ahistoric, and the "North," to use Lorraine York's description with reference to poetry, "becomes a huge, white narcissistic playground passively offering up to us the image of our imposing selves" ("Ivory Thought" 48–9). As a result, historically situated issues of cultural exchange are displaced, so the problem of voice appropriation appears to be surmounted.[9]

Paulette Jiles's work is closer to the participatory action-style of anthropological inquiry than the postmodernist style of ethnographic writing. In an interview with Elizabeth Mills, Jiles admits that she considers herself a kind of storyteller in the tradition of her Ozark mountain upbringing, and particularly the legacy of her grandfather (245, 251). Women learn to write stories about their interior lives, says Jiles, so experience is important (247). Northern travels led her to write about the north, turning personal experiences into poetry. While her position with regards to the culture she describes resembles that of an ethnographer, Jiles points out that, unlike the "invading tribe of white experts, the anthropologists and the shaman-groupies and the Indian Affairs advisors," she was invited, hired, and employed by the Ojibwe ("Spontaneously Created People" 269). Jiles was authorized to speak by the people, but she describes her own strangeness as the source of her insight: "When you change cultures you develop antennae that the people whose culture you are entering do not have because they are in it. By virtue of the fact that you are a stranger, you develop very sensitive antennae and maybe my antennae became over-sensitive, but I learned not to take chances and not to make mistakes because they're costly" (Mills 248). Her account of cultural initiation is strikingly similar to the transformation from outsider to insider that is supposed to take place during fieldwork, and it confirms the importance of experience in her work. By virtue of her outsider status, Jiles believes that she can represent other cultures, thus she eschews the self-consciousness of postmodern texts and turns to the memoir style to describe her northern travels.

Susan J. Schenk observes that Jiles finds a distinctly "female" voice in poetry by developing a narrative poetic style that allows her to articulate women's experience (67). Although Schenk bases her remarks on a limited notion of histories as "predominantly male" and uses that definition to assess the subversive nature of Jiles's "Jesse James" poems, her identification of the important role of experience in the feminist focus of Jiles's poetry is valuable. The "female" response, Schenk asserts, is "to transform that experience into story, and in doing so, to reject silence and passivity" (78). On this view, Purdy's work would be "female" too, and the poetry that Jiles writes about the north shows a similar focus on experience, her own and that of others.

In her poems, as in her account of northern travels in *North Spirit* (1995), Jiles "fashions a contemporary female myth of the woman as picaresque hero" (Mansbridge 153). Although the term "male myth" lacks definition, Francis Mansbridge signals the connection between travel and identity in Jiles's work and suggests that it overturns the usual masculine-feminine binary. For example, as if to reaffirm the revision of the myth at the heart of her work, men are associated with the "civilized past," replacing the idealized women who represent southern civilization in the poetry of Robert Service. However, despite Mansbridge's interesting observations, Jiles's work is surprisingly free of the gender opposition it is said to overturn. The narrator in *North Spirit* takes on the masculine characteristics described in quest narratives, but with an interesting difference: the initiation into the northern world does not involve the feminization and subsequent marginalization of the land and the people living on it. Nor is the return that completes the cyclical quest assured. Like the "blending of voices" Robert A. Kelly observes in Jiles's "Jesse James" poems, the absence of binary opposition indicates the difficulty of establishing "firm boundaries between selves, between the external world and the poet's conception of that world" (28).

"Song to the Rising Sun" is the only poem in the collection bearing its name that deals with Jiles's northern experience. As she points out, it was written with "very old devices" in mind, and for that reason, it reads well as a radio drama. The poem's rhythm comes from the repetition of words and phrases, mostly in the form of anaphora. "What did we do all winter while we waited for the sun?" the poem begins as the speaker asks and then answers ironically: "We listened to the radio, we listened to the seductive / and fraudulent voices," following with a long list:

> we drew up plans,
> we cut our losses,
> we re-read our contracts,
> we visited everybody in the village,
> we dreamed,
> we were dreamed ... (13)

Like the storyteller of oral tradition, Jiles's speaker relies on repetition and the rhythms of speech to give the poem its rhythm, and like the work of Inuit writers, these techniques are enlisted to serve political purposes.

As the refrain indicates ("Junk is lethal"), the poem's concern is environmental. From the comment of the pilot, "and he said, you know, / I think Big Stuff will save us" (16) to the imploring statements of the speaker, the poem calls on readers to take notice of what is happening to the world around them:

> I am trying to reach you by radio.
> Listen. Take thought, take thought,
>   think. Listen. Watch.
> I am trying to reach you by radio telephone,
> waiting for the sun to come back. (17)

The speaker's voice is insistent; the language is colloquial:

> because we have torn a hole in the ionosphere,
> because we are pouring out 100 million tons
> of sulphur dioxide a year,
> because we have soaked the Arctic pole in a pollution haze
> that pilots cannot fly through,
> because we have blamed it on everybody else,
> because we have said that poetry will be only
> small lyrics of pastoral love … (24)

In "Song to the Rising Sun," the political content gains force from the influence of oral tradition on the form, and it derives this adaptation of tradition in part from aboriginal writing such as Inuit literature.

This is quite different from Rudy Wiebe's account, at the end of *A Discovery of Strangers*, of how, after tracing Franklin's trek, he and his companions in "established Arctic traveller fashion … raised a cairn" (n.p.). By commemorating the journey with this act and then by choosing to recount the event in his epilogue, Wiebe not only evokes the history of Arctic exploration but symbolically joins the company of explorers. The symbol of the note in the cairn is hardly an innocent one, given its historical association with determining and maintaining territorial sovereignty. It is significant that Wiebe and the others were there as part of the "University of Alberta-Canada Council Research Project," a state-supported excursion.

Why does Canada continue to support (literally) this particular view of our collective identity when the relevance of Arctic travel would seem obscure to most citizens? As I have already argued, this particular view of Canadian identity seems to be a form of political escapism, a view that seeks to overcome regional and cultural differences with a shared experience to which everyone theoretically has access.[10] It exerts an official form of national identity where none exists and comforts us with the idea that we can share an organic relationship to the land. The historical contingency of the ideas at the heart of this identity, especially reactionary ideas about gender and race, should warn us against northern nationalism. These ideas thread their way through the myths of the north from their establishment in the nineteenth century literature of empire to the reimagined north in contemporary literature.

Rienzi Crusz's lines from "In the Idiom of the Sun," which serve as the epigraph to this chapter, contain the striking metaphor of "white land" silencing the "black tongue." As Chelva Kanaganayakam observes in the introduction to Crusz's *Insurgent Rain: Selected Poems 1974–1996*, the images of "elephant" and "ice" in Crusz's poetry "have served as tropes in positioning his 'public' self in a literary climate where ethnicity is a source of endless debate"; with his various poetic personas, these tropes act "as markers for relating the experience of living on the cusp of alienation, racism, identity and nostalgia" (xii). The contemporary writing of "new" or "immigrant" Canadians tends to treat the condition of "northernness" as an undeniable fact of life in the new country. Characters in these texts do not need to go to the Arctic in order to understand that Canada is a northern country, a part of the economically developed north; moreover, they do not see the nation in terms of a shared consciousness that they could attain by going further north. Northernness is not based on the contiguity of the Arctic regions, nor is it limited to wilderness spaces. Instead, northern conditions represent both life in metropolitan centres such as Toronto, settled by the newcomer, and also the new country. It is perhaps not surprising, therefore, that the sense of entitlement with which many contemporary Canadian writers approach the landscape, especially the far north, is absent from the work of newly arrived writers.

Although a complete consideration of contemporary writing in Canada is beyond the scope of this study, the difference in perspective can be presented with the help of a few examples. In works of fiction such as Dionne Brand's *In Another Place Not Here* (1996) and Austin Clarke's *The Origin of Waves* (1997), the northern sky, cold weather, and snow are all part of a setting that is unwelcoming to the main characters, and the whiteness of winter stands as a metaphor for the many ways in which their lives lack colour. In these novels, the stories of the landscape and the characters' relationship to it are stories of exile, loneliness, and longing. In "Dionne Brand's Winter Epigrams," Edward Kamau Brathwaite examines lines from Brand's *Winter Epigrams and Epigrams to Ernest Cardenal in defense of Claudia* (1983) in which "we find her, trying to keep warm heart, warm hope, warm mind, warm friendship," lines in which the persona, in wintry exile, finds strength in herself and the voices of her people (19; 22).

Brand's *In Another Place Not Here*, set in Canada and the Caribbean, depicts the northern environment as another form of oppression endured by the newcomer. Throughout the novel, as Heather Smyth argues, "place, or in particular a sense of belonging to a place, is always deferred" as a response to the exclusion of lesbian and gay men from "Caribbean cultural and national space," but as the characters migrate from place to place, they find that, in Canada, "dispossession and alienation cannot be overcome" (151; 154). The northern sky in November looks "like a bandage over a wound" (Brand 196); the month is "a tragedy of scarred trees and rumpled clothes, of the skin's defensive shrivelling, of huddled shabby bus-stops and a wind ready to ice and crumble the bone" (196). In this waiting for winter, the character Vee feels like she is "shedding and dying" (197). At first, in Toronto, the glare she describes makes her feel like she is "at the centre" of things, like the star of a film she herself is watching. This feeling is fleeting, and her sense of isolation intensifies in the car trip from Toronto to Sudbury. Driving northward, the lonelier and more conspicuous she feels: "In Sudbury all of the people are white except for her aunt and her uncle. She feels a glare, a standing off, a glow around their bodies, her face burns in the grey light" (137). Her aunt and uncle do their best to pretend that they are part of a community whose culture and landscape is as white as its inhabitants; to Vee, "donuts is how Sudbury smells and food wrapped up and frozen" (148). She feels that she is dying there, and her aunt and uncle offer her a place beside them in what she calls "their coffin engraved in ice, ice, ice, in their donut smelling walking dead sepulchral ice" (149).

British immigrant John Metcalf also represents northern Ontario as a cultural wasteland redolent with comic possibility in his novella "Travelling Northward." His character, a self-centred, sarcastic writer, finds those he meets on his reading tour of "North Portage," Ontario, deserving of scorn and condescension. In Metcalf's send-up, the north is a place for white hicks and white trash, granola-munching hippies and obtuse eccentrics. Significantly, neither Metcalf nor Brand sees an aboriginal presence in the north. Both focus on the experiences of alienated individuals. As a black person, Brand's character feels an alienation that is aggravated by the perceived hostility of white people towards her where her racial difference is too visible. Metcalf's protagonist, on the other hand, needs to make social distinctions between himself and the northerners to preserve his fragile ego.

When the reader meets Tim, the main character in Austin Clarke's *The Origin of Waves*, he is walking north on Yonge Street where he accidentally meets his childhood friend, John. Before their encounter, Tim feels a disorientation that has less to do with the direction his walk has taken than it does with his place in the city in the winter: "and I am alone, and I can see nobody, and nobody can see me ... I am walking through a valley with no landmarks on my left side or my right, to give me bearing and remind me of the notice of movement, although I know I am travelling forward, north, since I have set out from the bottom of the street, by the Lake" (21–2).

Tim's difficulty walking on the slippery snow signals his difference in this foreign landscape: "But I try to pretend that I am native to this kind of treachery on ice, that I was born here into this white, cold miserableness, and am not really an obstacle" (25). Tim's experience in winter comes to represent his awareness of his relation to the society he lives in. Others view him as an "obstacle," he thinks, because he is not "native" to the country. What he sees in the winter landscape is a reflection of the society he inhabits, the "treachery of ice" (25), the "white darkness" of the land (231).

Tim does not narrate the events of his alienation in Canadian society; he tells it through the metaphors describing the environment. The slick snow under foot and the disorienting whiteness are signs of his malaise: "I sometimes laugh at myself, as I see my reflection in a store window, as I pass wearing all this clothing, making me walk after all these years with added weight and meaning and cold experience in this new environment, I see how it makes us, at our age, walk with a limp, like huge tamed monkeys, since neither of us has got accustomed to this way of dressing, nor has learned to walk in winter" (29). When he and his friend leave the bar, none of the places he passes know him (231). In the final scenes, the cold, snow, and the night are all equally forbidding (233). While such scenes could be read productively through the ideas of gender convention and performance and "cross-cultural refraction" that Dan Coleman describes in *Masculine Migrations* (1998), what they indicate for the purposes of this study, I think, is the difference in the sense of belonging, and by extension, entitlement to both north and nation felt by Canadian writers. While this brief discussion cannot do justice to their contributions, it is difficult not to notice that many of Canada's most gifted contemporary writers have not joined in the quest northward, and these contemporary writers include a large number of newly arrived or "new" Canadians.

WRITING CULTURE

Like John Moss and Aritha van Herk, Rudy Wiebe's interest in the north has always been embedded in a personal sense of national identity, one that has not altered much since he first publicly lamented the "unfulfilled myth of the north" in the early 1970s ("Western" 29). A more recent book, *River of Stone: Fictions and Memories* (1995), opens with the statement: "North and wilderness. When I consider my country as a place distinct and particular from all the other places I have seen and lived in, that's it: north and wilderness" (ix). Wiebe's writing blurs literary and ethnographic forms, and his writing thematizes the issues of cross-cultural representation that blurring raises.[11]

Rudy Wiebe has contributed to both the mythologizing and the demythologizing of the Canadian north through his fiction: in *The Mad Trapper*, he relies on the myth of the north as a setting for adventure as he destabilizes the figure of the rugged northern individual. He takes these themes further in *Playing Dead: A Contemplation Concerning the Arctic* (1989), a series of lectures whose main project can be described as post-colonial because it rereads Canadian history in order to articulate an independent national identity. In this process, Wiebe deploys the conventions of realist ethnography in order to create an alternative version of Arctic history and myth. Although the methodology constructing his text is not foregrounded, these ethnographic conventions are discernible throughout. Whether describing the events of Franklin's expedition or his own trip north, Wiebe's narrator is an all-seeing presence beside the great men of Arctic exploration or the aboriginal people who witnessed events such as the shooting of the mad trapper Albert Johnson. Although Wiebe inserts himself into the narrative, making it a rather personal contemplation, it is as the "mystical teacher-figure" persona he assumes elsewhere (van Toorn 5).

Speaking in the second person is a common ethnographic technique intended to give the reader the feeling of "being there" as the ethnographer makes his observations and takes his field notes (see Atkinson 100). Walking alone on the tundra, Wiebe remarks: "It seems you can walk wherever you please; there is not a single scattered erratic or even the lowest brush to decide your track" (112); while looking out at the Peel River: "Your hand vanishes when you touch it; it could be bearing a hundred submerged bodies past you and you would know nothing" (43). By shifting to the second person, the author insists on his role as a guide, able to show the reader around on the journey. Ethnographic exposition often relies on this role because the authority of the ethnographer must be grounded in personal experience. In the ensuing remarks, Wiebe returns to his own presence in the scene: "Three ravens on a crossing of driftwood logs tossed up on the muddy river's edge observe me" (44).

The narrator's personal experiences are told in minute detail using the confessional mode that has become popular with ethnographers. This focus on individual "experience" signals its importance in establishing authority on northern subjects. As I have argued, the new ethnographic preoccupation with the ethnographer's role "as a storyteller alive again in the mundane world" responds to the resistance of aboriginal peoples to their continued objectification and usurps the concept underpinning the authority of their claim: experience. While the observer's firsthand experience authorizes his description, it also deflates the experience of his subjects.

The aboriginal people Wiebe describes seem to be beyond mundane experience. When a man offers a version of how Albert Johnson, the mad trapper, was shot, a version that Wiebe seems to consider wild and exaggerated, Wiebe comments: "Something beyond mere facts is being told, a truth only words, not facts, can create" (55–6). In another instance, Wiebe appreciates how William Nerysoo, the trapper who first reported Johnson to the RCMP, teases him with little bits of information that eventually amount to the whole story: "What is it about these strong fierce-eyed old men? They are, in Chekhovian terms, 'insisting so strongly on preserving someone's personal secret.' It seems they are, for that insistence, the most civilized of people" (65). This passage is striking for the hint of surprise in the narrator's voice. At this point, Wiebe seems to be indulging in the cultural relativism practised by the realist ethnographers he has read. For instance, he argues against attaching blame in the case of the Dogrib annihilation of the Yellowknife as retold in Dr John Richardson's journal, noting that, because "savagery" is common to all peoples who engage in war, the actions of the Dogrib do not make them any worse. In this discussion, Wiebe evokes, if he does not actually reconstruct, the dual nature of the noble savage, the uncivilized and sublime.

I do not think that Rudy Wiebe supports such an image or the forms of "plastic shamanism" that usually do, but in trying to forge a spiritual connection between Native and non-Native, he risks comparison of this kind. From studying his other writings, I do not believe that Wiebe is irresponsible in the depiction of cultural others: he often articulates his commitment to the responsible representation of history. His espousal of ethnographic techniques, however, sometimes works against his stated intentions.

Wiebe never denies the cultural contingency of his own position, yet, by assuming a cultural relativist position as he reviews history, he suggests that cultures are constituted by the act of viewing them as cultures; that is, cultures are defined in their interpretation. This is a kind of "framework relativism" or the view that knowledge is culturally relative, a view that will not stand up to its own logic. "If it is true," as Martyn Hammersley succinctly puts it, "then it applies to itself; and therefore it is only true relative to a particular culture or framework, and may be false from the perspectives of other cultures or frameworks" (49).

Cultural relativism protects authors from questions of accuracy or fairness because, locked in our cultural differences, we cannot judge the interpretation offered of a culture that is not ours. The freedom this position affords authors is matched only by the danger it presents for the people being represented in the account. Significantly, the idea of Inuit culture Wiebe articulates in *Playing Dead* is a system of thought based primarily on linguistic evidence, a relationship that has been disputed by anthropological study. In "Legend and Landscape: Convergence of Oral and Scientific Traditions in the Yukon Territory," Julie Cruikshank reevaluates the apparent distinction between "primitive" and "modern" thought by comparing Inuit and "western" forms of knowledge, and concludes that there are no *intrinsic* differences between them.

But Wiebe is fascinated by the cultural differences that he per-
ceives and which he considers to be the essential truth of Inuit
culture because, as he announces: "I desire true NORTH, not PAS-
SAGE to anywhere" (114). What he protests is the desire of those
who sought the Northwest Passage who wanted "nothing except
liquid water" and "a convenient passage to another place altogether" (77). Even though Wiebe insists that "when one person-
ally goes to the Mackenzie Delta, Franklin and Richardson are
amazingly irrelevant," their ghosts haunt his contemplations. In
Wiebe's reconstruction, these heroes – their big dreams, fragile
boats, and cultural blindness – are no match for the superior
enlightenment of the twentieth-century traveller.

Although he protests strongly against those literary tourists
who travel through the Arctic in search of a passage elsewhere,
Wiebe himself is in search of a passage or way to a better consciousness. In practical terms, he desires the experience that would
enrich Canadian national identity and give it meaning. He asks
for "[w]isdom to understand why Canadians have so little comprehension of our own *nordicity,* that we are a northern nation"
(111). With almost evangelical enthusiasm, Wiebe preaches heritage, redeploying one of the northern myths analysed by Shelagh
Grant. By stressing the idea of a common heritage, Wiebe presents
the north as a source of separate and distinct identity. His appropriation of an authentic northern experience indicates a belief in
a national identity based on national consciousness. The suggestion
that all Canadians can easily pick up this "authentic experience"
by travelling northward and thereby raising their consciousness
about their own true identities is made at the expense of northern
inhabitants. As Thomas Berger's report on the impact of the
Mackenzie Pipeline makes clear, the heritage myth contradicts the
interests of the Dene, Inuit, Inuvaluit, Métis, Cree, and other peoples who view the north as their homeland and who are fighting
so hard for self-determination. Despite the relative "cross-cultural
humility" and self-consciousness with which Wiebe approaches
his subject in *Playing Dead*, his vision of Canada's relationship to
northern peoples is inconsistent at this point.

It is important to remember that the text of *Playing Dead* is based
on Wiebe's Larkin-Stuart lectures given at the University of Toronto
and that Wiebe perhaps saves his most national-minded remarks
on the north for such public moments. Indeed, Margaret Atwood

told an Oxford University audience a very similar story about the north in her Clarendon lectures, later published as *Strange Things: The Malevolent North in Canadian Literature* (1995). Or could it be that, as if to prepare the reception for his future work, Wiebe offers the importance of the north to the national psyche as a way of understanding his writing? In *Playing Dead*, the stated goal of Wiebe's quest (for what Arctic traveller does not have one?) is wisdom: "To walk into the true north of my own head between the stones and the ocean" (119). There, he says, perhaps he "will get a new song" and promises "if I do, I will sing it for you" (119). When he did, he called it *A Discovery of Strangers* (1994).

Despite the questionable use of northern voices in some of this work, *A Discovery of Strangers* breaks with the clichéd representation of the Canadian north by engaging with the difficult history of cultural contact and its representation. Most important, while Wiebe may incorporate certain aspects of postmodernist writing in his style, in general he swims against the postmodernist current, offering a bold contrast to the ironic parody of other postmodern writers. While postmodernists hold that language constitutes, at least partly, reality because we know the world through it, Wiebe retains a strong sense of a world outside human interpretation. As Wiebe and Kroetsch make manifestly clear in their interview with Shirley Neuman (1980), their differences run very deep. Both authors admit to sharing a mistrust of "inherited or given history" (230), those "master narratives" that succumb to the scepticism of the postmodern condition. However, Wiebe's incredulity leads him in an ever-expanding world of possibilities while Kroetsch's distrust of authority leads him to the virtual abandonment of meaning, as he complains that "life torments us all the time with the possibility of meaning" (233). Kroetsch's fractured narratives and multiple voices are meant to show the absence of anything unified; Wiebe's "novels deal precisely with the problem of ordering the many voices of the self" (van Toorn 197). In the Neuman interview, Wiebe's earnest desire for the "apprehension of perfection" makes Kroetsch bristle, which in turn provokes Wiebe's witty retort: "Bob, you're always horsing around with language" (Neuman 236).

Wiebe's refusal to "horse around" with language, his insistence on the accountability of history, the accuracy of details, separates him from other Canadian postmodern writers and makes his work all the more compelling. In his novels and essays on the north, the breadth of his sources is impressive, as is the respect with which he treats them. Rather than parody historical records with clever allusions and word play, Wiebe treats his sources as authorities worthy of the respect that is a citation at the end of the text, an acknowledgment in the preface, a reference in the body of the text. These aspects of his writing are all the more important given the subject matter he wrestles with, namely the historical marginalization of aboriginal peoples. Wiebe's nationalism may seem naive, but his cultural critique is not. It has been developing through a lifelong engagement with these issues, and it finds its most subtle articulation in *A Discovery of Strangers*.

A Discovery of Strangers offers an oppositional account of Franklin's first expedition (1819–22). In many respects, the novel's dialogic form seems committed to articulating the "Native's point of view" of the expedition. One critic remarks that, like his other novels, *A Discovery of Strangers* allows Wiebe "to transform the facts into story, giving voice to those who speak only in the gaps of published accounts" (Hoeppner 146). For example, Wiebe constructs a scene from an anecdote taken directly from Hood's journal in which Keskarrah insists on being included in the portrait of his daughter Greenstockings, so that "when the big boss across the stinking water sees her picture, he won't try to send for her" (85). The scene gives voice to Greenstockings' thoughts, in particular her reaction to the first white men she has seen as well as to the stories Keskarrah tells as Hood draws.

Written before the publication of *A Discovery of Strangers*, Penny van Toorn's observation that "Wiebe's novels transmit the Word into an unforeseeable variety of discursive, historical, and cultural contexts, where its meaning and authority become open to negotiation" (8–9) remains apt. *A Discovery of Strangers* creates a dialogue between cultures in a particular historical moment by drawing on Dene and European accounts of the time, by filtering them through Wiebe's imagination, and rendering a fictional account. This technique raises inevitable questions about authenticity and cultural appropriation which Wiebe attempts to answer by laying bare his research.

As the comprehensive list of acknowledgments at the end of the novel indicates, *A Discovery of Strangers* carefully weaves the threads of various texts: transcriptions by George Blondin, Émile

Petitot, Jean Morrisset, Rose-Marie Pelletier, and Richard Slobodin; stories belonging to Angela Sidney, Kitty Smith, Annie Ned, William Ittza; journals kept by John Franklin, Samuel Hearne, Richard King, and C. Stuart Houston; research and editions by Ian MacLaren, Josef-René Bellot, George Calef, Kerry Abel, June Helm, and Timothy C. Losey. I cite this impressive list to indicate the diversity of Wiebe's sources, a diversity that he translates into the forms used in the novel: letters, journal entries and quotations, narration that varies from stream-of-consciousness to first-person and third-person perspectives.

Much has been made of Wiebe's "moral vision" by his critics. Starting from Penny van Toorn's observation that Wiebe shows "a lingering nostalgia for absolute truth" (145), Kenneth Hoeppner argues that *A Discovery of Strangers* is a departure that "accepts the postmodernist challenge" (145). While Wiebe's other novels translate "the Word" into the "language of men," Hoeppner argues, this novel emphasizes the untranslatability of the Word. The dialogic, which is given precedence in the novel, serves to represent the transcendent, according to Hoeppner, and the inter-action of a community rooted in a sense of place and spirituality with the transcendent amounts to truth.

The form of the book evokes the lessons of the postmodernist turn, if not its politics. The absence of irony signals the distance Wiebe places between his writing and that of postmodernists. In *Playing Dead*, Wiebe refers to "the present dark age of irony" that makes an "ancient, old-fashioned" word like "wisdom" seem almost embarrassing (111). Wiebe may have incorporated some of the stylistic elements that postmodernist writers claim as their own: "contingency, multiplicity, fragmentation, discontinuity" (Hutcheon, *Canadian* 19), but he remains dedicated to the moral vision associated with realist novelists. For Wiebe, the novel is a moral as well as a political form.

The attempts to claim Wiebe within a postmodernist canon con-tinue. In his review of *A Discovery of Strangers*, John Moss offers a reading steeped in the language of postmodernist ethnography: "*A Discovery of Strangers* is a confessional exposition, a confabula-tion of private dreams" (43). To read the novel as "a sort of spiritual and moral autobiography" (44) defends against an appropriation charge, a defense which Moss bolsters with further attention to Wiebe's "kind of solemn playfulness that alerts the reader to his narrative presence as metaphysician within his own text" (43). Allowing Wiebe's figure to overshadow those of the historical characters portrayed in the novel circumvents the question of representation, and while Moss sees that Wiebe presents us with "a dialectically alternative reality" (44), he also suggests that the novel falls short of an "articulation of its philosophical argument" (44), perhaps because it presents a challenge to ethnographic representation and to the postmodernist style.

Rather than see the dialogism as a sign of a new spirituality akin to the original Native spirituality, I consider the book's dialogic form important for the way it highlights the cultural differences that make cultural encounter perilous. For example, Wiebe develops storytelling among the Tetsot'ine in a way that indicates both its profound meaning and its adaptability. The whites appear to have "no stories in them" (39) to the Tetsot'ine, for whom stories bind the people together and bring events into being. Thus Keskarrah's way of telling the story of the "Stolen Woman" leads as inevitably to Greenstockings' abduction as its many previous tellings could never have. Besides representing this cultural difference, the novel offers an enriched treatment of the historical events that have gained mythic status in the national imagination. Fiction such as Wiebe's *The Temptations of Big Bear* creates, in the words of Diana Brydon, "the cultural dialogue that history itself never allowed" ("Troppo" 21), a quality in his writing that has been linked to his fundamental humanism (Bailey 78). In his characteristic fashion, Wiebe takes historical artifact and tries to give it living dimensions, what Brydon calls "writing the muddiness of mud back in," the messy details that fiction generally suppresses in favour of an ordered form ("Troppo" 28).

By having the story told from the point of view of several of the characters, with the significant exception of Franklin, Wiebe lets different methods of storytelling raise the issue of how language articulates culture without making it "carry" or "stand for" culture. In chapter 1, the narrator speaks on behalf of the natural world through the thoughts of the animals. This section announces an important issue raised in the novel: the devastation caused by exploration. Keskarrah describes the economic and environmental devastation brought about by the expansion of the hunt to feed Franklin's men who "require almost a full ton of meat a week;

that is, a minimum of twenty large dressed deer" and "at least twice" that many deer to supply the trip along the barren coast (48–9).

In a prophetic discussion with the other women, Greenstockings becomes indignant at the suggestion that her people will accommodate the voracious English appetite: "Yes! All our mighty men agree, listen to Thick English and they pile things on us to carry. And they'll kill all the animals, so many they'll go away to avoid being killed, and we'll have to drag what they kill here to our fires and skin them for These English and cut the meat into strips and smoke it and cook it and sew their winter clothes so they won't freeze after we scrape and tan all those hides, these mighty English! Let them freeze stiff as cocks in their cloth!" (36) Only Hood, in Wiebe's imagination, realizes the burden their presence places on the women when he points out to Back that the three voyageur women they have brought with them will not be able to keep up with skinning, cutting, and drying all the meat they have required and that the Tetsot'ine women will be called upon to help (49).

Wiebe demonstrates both his extensive research into the documents surrounding these events and his desire to take the documentary aspect of his style further into critique. The fictionalized narration provided by George Back, for instance, closely resembles the prose of his journal from a later expedition, yet it is also emblematic of the prose written by ethnologists who were roughly his contemporaries. Back seems certain that the Yellowknife culture is distinct from his own, a separate object he can observe, and he imagines it to be stable, unchanging for all time. Back speaks not only for the nineteenth-century man and explorer but for any discourse on cultural others that is characterized by Eurocentrism, as when he describes the women: "The women, as saggy and wrinkled as native females invariably are – their breasts undergo great distention from an early age from long feeding of their infants, the sight of which can only be repugnant – took up the chief's lament, whereupon Lieutenant Franklin quickly had our extra flag unrolled" (45). Back takes everything he sees at face value and the validity of his interpretation of events for granted, throwing off phrases such as "the Indian mind being as superstitious as it is" (41) and "we are not proof against the possible treachery of a native" (47).

While Back seems to voice the view of culture later expounded by some realist ethnographers, the Tetsot'ine women seem to represent a dialogic view of culture. It is a one-sided dialogue, with the English hearing nothing of what they are being told. As Keskarrah warns: "When you come to our land, ... you cannot continue to be what you've always been" (202). Yet, Wiebe represents the possibility of an inquiry into culture that is not guided by presupposition. The women take a humorous and querying approach to the white men, trading stories and speculation concerning their strange bodies and habits. While they joke and tell stories about the men, especially their ridiculous ideas and bodies, the narrator remarks that "[i]nto their play of words about Whites has crept the simple and continually unfathomable burden women must carry – all men" (32). While Wiebe is falling back on a notion of a strictly defined division of labour for the double meaning of that burden, he is also further emphasizing the strain on the economy by drawing attention to the women's labour. The women realize that these strangers, as strange as they may be, are as demanding as any men, as Greenstockings will later realize "they are all men, and there are too many of them" (207).

Through the fictional women, Greenstockings in particular, the narrator shows that the culture is not as stable and fixed as Back and the other English suppose. The change is observed first in the men who, eager to accommodate their guests, begin to act like the English: "Greenstockings passed them with the other carrying People. It was all so undignified, scrabbling into deliberate council as soon as they stepped ashore. Ludicrous, her father and the men behaving without calmness like Whites; the hideous, burned land must be affecting them" (72). The men's behaviour is so strange to Greenstockings that she must account for it somehow. Wiebe imagines Greenstockings, a historical person about whom very little is known, to be a feisty, intelligent, and outspoken young woman. However, he also imagines her submitting to her fate passively, especially during her abduction by Michel and in her resignation to the existence of "men always above her" (85). In this case, Wiebe represents the women according to the assumptions arising from ethnographic accounts of an enforced and gendered division of labour. Having accepted this view of Native culture, Wiebe shows the women to play a subordinate role in the group.

When he does permit Greenstockings the sort of agency that her characterization as a strong, independent woman seems to call for, it is so that she can fall in love with Robert Hood. By imagining the encounter between Greenstockings and Hood as a love story, Wiebe creates an occasion for human relations outside language and culture. As Hood sketches her famous portrait, he realizes that "he does not want to understand any word she ever speaks. None. The freedom of watching, of listening with incomprehension, fills him with staggering happiness" (158). The scenes between them are filled with the tenderness of tragic, ill-fated love. Greenstockings resigns herself to the fragility of this alliance: "In the fixed conjunction of her mother's and father's power, they two have lived this strange – almost as if they were hidden, sweetly, under furs in the long darkness – lived this strange, short moment of profound difference" (207).

The love between Hood and Greenstockings becomes the embodiment of Wiebe's humanism, a harmonious accommodation of difference without violence. However, sex between white men and brown women is a fact of colonization, and as such, is as much a story of loss and dispossession as of contact and communication. By imagining the relationship between Greenstockings and Robert Hood as a love story in which Greenstockings chooses to give herself to the white man, Wiebe retells this story as if it is not part of the history of territorial possession, power, and violence that surrounds it. Instead, Michel Terohaute, the treacherous halfbreed figure so well-known in Arctic adventure, is represented as the violent one who takes what he wants. That Michel was considered a murderer and cannibal by the explorers is part of historical record, yet his brutal attack on Greenstockings is a fictional account. In comparison to this rape, Hood's sexual relationship with Greenstockings is innocent. Here, Wiebe allows conventional images of northern representation – the erotic triangle, the treacherous halfbreed, the acquiescent female – to inform his historical representation.

If the North has any meaning in the modern Canadian imagination, or in Canadian literary history generally, it has greatest meaning for the writers who have travelled to the Arctic. Canadian writers who equate travelling northward with entering a blank, white world and filling a blank, white page attempt to "make us real" by imagining Canadians as northern. In fact, the diversity of existing representations of the north points to the impossibility of defining a northern "character" or "consciousness" on which to base a unified Canadian identity.

While the turn to storytelling and postmodern representation suggests that the Romantic nationalist vision of the Group of Seven has been left behind as authors de- and remythologize the north, the shift from realist representation in traditional Arctic adventure narratives and novels to postmodern representation in first-person travel narratives has not achieved a complete break with the past ideology. For example, the hero's masculine initiation through the quest has been appropriated to ends as diverse as parody and patriotism, or invoked as a way of avoiding the problem of speaking for others. In this sense, the shift in representation resembles the movement in ethnography from realism to postmodernism.

Throughout Canadian literary history, two narrative modes have dominated representations of the north: one is the strong, almost naturalistic form of realism; the other is a slightly realistic form of postmodernism. Contemporary postmodern texts involve tensions between the writer's stated concern for authenticity in representation – for the true north understood through experience – and the investment in a postmodern narrative style. The former indicates an investment in a sort of mind-independent reality; the latter seeks to destabilize just such a reality. Despite these tensions, northern experience remains the authenticating component of northern representation.

Unsettling the Northern Nation

Canadians are surrounded by imagery presenting northern experience as national symbol. On Saturday, 24 March 2001, for example, the *Globe and Mail* featured an article about the Governor
General's seven-day tour of Nunavik, the Arctic region of Quebec
adjacent to Labrador. It was the first official visit since Governor
General Vincent Massey's in 1956, the same year that F.R. Scott
contemplated the Mackenzie Delta. When the figurehead of the
Canadian government visits a region, the trip marks the place as
Canadian sovereign territory. Rather than interpreting the visit as
another assertion of Canadian sovereignty, however, the article
reports that Governor General Adrienne Clarkson and her husband John Ralston Saul "wanted to show that the north is not all
negative." In the article, which was accompanied by photos that
included one of the couple on a dog sled, reporter Tibor Kolley
emphasizes the couple's experiences in contact with Inuit culture.
"Like many Canadians," Kolley speculates, "the Governor General
has often wondered what it would be like to sleep in an igloo,"
and Clarkson describes to him how the people of Puvirnituq
made it possible:

They built seven little igloos for us just outside the village, and they lit
a candle in each one. As we travelled from our hotel on snowmobiles
they glowed, blue domes in the dark. It was absolutely magical ... You
climb down into it and then come up again into a chamber. There's a
willow mat covered with caribou skins and Arctic sleeping bags. We slept
in our long underwear and a toque. An aide rolled an ice block over the

entrance, but there was [a] hole in the ceiling to allow carbon dioxide to escape, otherwise you'd die ... I don't think we will ever forget it. (R10)

In this interview, Clarkson adopts an authoritative scientific tone, and in what seems to be unselfconscious narration, uses a number of the strategies of realist ethnography, including the description of material culture, the friendly second-person voice, and the sense of the strange and exotic, the north as "remote and beautiful land."

Northern experience was not new to John Ralston Saul who, accompanied by fellow PEN members Chinua Achebe, Blanche d'Alpuget, Duo Duo, Édouard Glissant, Betty Friedan, and Wendy Law-Yone, went to Baffin Island to meet participants in the Baffin Writer's Project in 1989. Like so many Canadian writers, he wrote about his travels; his piece was entitled "Subversion in the North." He describes the kind of sublime moment recorded by many contemporary travellers to the far north, the moment when the "marginality of life could be felt like a great broom sweeping away any sense of self" (266). As the title indicates, Saul claims that making such a journey and having such an experience "subverts" Canadian ideas, for Baffin Island, he argues, "is simple proof that Canada is not what its urban élites pretend." According to Saul, those élites "can live along the border and resolutely face themselves south, but any fool can see that this involves turning their backs on their own reality" (263–4). By emphasizing the fact that most Canadians have not had the opportunity to make a similar trip, and therefore lack first-hand experience of the north, Saul supports his cautionary message concerning northern development by greedy southern interests. Now, as consort to the individual occupying arguably the most "élite" position in Canada, he continues to try to "subvert" Canadians' ideas about who they are.

For a nation of settlers amid indigenous people, occupying real territory means imagining it too, raising problems and anxieties of authenticity. Therefore, the argument that northern experience unites Canadians and makes the Canadian nation distinct from others refers to relations between inhabitant and settler, Native and non-Native, because it assumes that those geographical regions called 'north,' and the territory that 'north' represents, belong to all Canadians whether they live there or not, whether they are settlers or indigenous. But, the fact that most Canadians have not *been to* the north does not account for lack of interest in northern affairs. It is the fact that they do not *live there* that makes the difference, the difference between travel destination and homeland that underlies the contrast of "real" and "imagined" north. As Justice Thomas Berger stressed when he identified it, this difference between "heritage" and "homeland" describes both a reality and a way of seeing that reality.

The cult of nordicity creates distinctions between outsiders on the basis of first-hand experience, but it does not eliminate the distinction between insider and outsider. For outsiders, like Clarkson and Saul, even first-hand experience in the north is imagined and reinterpreted through representation. As John Moss observes in *Enduring Dreams* (1994), "When you enter Arctic narrative, you enter every narrative of the Arctic ever written. When you enter the Arctic in person, you become part of the extended text. When you write the Arctic to affirm your presence in the world, you become in writing an imaginative creation. You could imagine anything and write it down and it would seem real for ever" (105).

Yet, despite the tension between real and imagined even as experience is being lived, first-hand experience continues to authorize such "imaginative creations" and to spatialize difference in a way that gives outsiders access to real and imagined territory. It turns the difference between inhabitants of northern and southern regions into a matter of geography so that going to the geographical north entitles the study and description of the discursive or imagined north. Returning to James Clifford's insight, personal experience is difficult to argue with and "its invocation often smacks of mystification" ("On Ethnographic" 128). Because geographical boundaries can be crossed whereas the boundaries between cultures or identities are not so well defined, reimagining difference in terms of geography may even be nostalgia for the separate, stable cultures of the ethnographic past.

In contemporary writing, crossing the shifting border between north and south is analogous to the initiation anthropologists must achieve before writing about a subject culture. Writing that is authorized in this manner rests on the idea that outsiders, usually southern Canadians, gain special insight by the experience of going north – or spending a night in an igloo. But the literary representation of northern issues in the south will not subvert Canadian power relations if it continues to replicate the fieldwork model of the outsider who gains inside knowledge. The anthropological distinction between "insider" and "outsider" in cultural terms becomes a spatial distinction between "inside" and "outside" the geographical region known as north. That the first-person accounts by privileged outsiders proliferate at the moment when the voices of dispossessed peoples, First Nations and aboriginal peoples in particular, are not only emerging but gaining strength is suggestive.

When John Moss calls anthropology "the bastard offspring of colonialism" (*Enduring* 75), he locates the roots of ethnography in unequal power relations between colonized subject culture and the colonizing gaze of the observer. In the post-colonial age of globalization, the search for an intense, authentic experience perceived in the persistence of the ethnographic impulse reflects the malaise of modernity, to use Charles Taylor's paradigm. Rejuvenating the moral and creative exhaustion associated with this malaise creates an appetite for tradition. With globalization, this appetite can be satisfied by consuming goods such as traditional music and art, or by contact with traditional ways of life through tourism. For the global citizen, the north becomes another consumable item in a world of choice. This commodification of the north is extended in representation of northern experience. Moreover, a "participation mystique," that feeling of sympathy and understanding obtained from the representation of otherness, masks the unequal power relations that exist and that globalization exacerbates (see Taussig). As writers head north in search of an intense experience that will assuage cultural malaise by mimicking the initiation model, their writing risks becoming, to rewrite Moss's phrase, the bastard offspring of globalization.

First Nations and aboriginal people speak of personal experience in autobiography and life writing as well as in media, and sharing experience has been a powerful tool in developing a pan-Native identity and political voice. When First Nations and aboriginal people are heard explaining the issues – and I stress "when they are heard," since they have been explaining for hundreds of years – often it is the story of a life or lives that is told. The articulation of experience as aboriginal people has undeniable political importance. Thus, to hear the "experience as" a northern inhabitant, and most northern inhabitants are aboriginal, has great epistemic value. The understanding of "experience as" an inhabitant, however, collapses into experience of and in the north regardless of the observer's identity. "Experience of" or "in" the north claims epistemic privilege in the same way that fieldwork experience authorizes ethnographic representation and drowns out the emerging voices of colonized peoples, as reflected in the reception of work by Inuit authors.

The blurring of literary and anthropological discourse observed in the importance of ethnography both as an authoritative source and as a method of understanding cultures in imagining the north necessitates the "interdisciplinary mix of anthropology, history, and critical theory" that Arnold Krupat calls "ethnocriticism" or "ethnohistorical literary criticism" (*Ethnocriticism* 4). While reject-ing relativist claims that "metadiscourse ruled by reason and logic is always trapped in the prisonhouse of rhetoric and ideology" or that "any would-be explanatory account in the interest of truth or knowledge is inevitably just another occasion-bound story (rhetoric)" (9), Krupat describes the sort of methodological syn-thesis that characterizes cultural studies. This method recalls Northrop Frye's view that the task of the Canadian literary critic is "to settle uneasily somewhere between the Canadian historian or social scientist, who has no comparative value-judgments to worry about, and the ordinary literary critic, who has nothing else" (*Bush Garden* 163). Because it engages with the many aspects of Canadian history, politics, and society that bear on literary representation, Canadian literary history and criticism has always been interdisciplinary, as well as thematic, even ethnocritical.

Reading representations of the north ethnocritically reveals how the nation is imagined in particular contexts even as those repre-sentations submit to pressures of genre, history, and individual sensibility, as well as to national and international movements, ideas, and history. In the nineteenth century, representations of the north were characterized by ideas of racial superiority; in the twentieth century, they fragment and reflect the diversity of a mosaic as late nineteenth-century patriotism and imperialism gives way to twentieth-century self-consciousness, even narcis-sism. Throughout, the definitions of gender fluctuate too: while they retain an oppositional structure, the mastery of other races in the nineteenth century is replaced by the mastery of the body in the twentieth; the restraint and moral virtue of rugged individ-uals in the Victorian period gives way to the lawlessness of the

Gold Rush days followed by the pursuit of personal desire by the tourists of the contemporary period. Characteristics of gender identity, which can be described at particular moments, change with the times and with the pressures asserted by conventions of form and genre, but they also retain certain important general attributes which are represented repeatedly.

As the preceding chapters show, stabilizing masculine identity through reiteration of binary opposition or exclusion can lead to misrepresentations; this becomes clear in the depiction of aboriginal people who become a feminized term in the masculine constructions of various texts. When specific characteristics are attributed to one gender in this structure, the opposite characteristics tend to be attributed to the other; thus, whenever masculinity means strength, self-sufficiency, and activity, then weakness, dependence, and passivity are attributed to femininity. The definition of masculinity by opposition and exclusion, which must be constantly reiterated, signals its own instability.

The historically specific manifestations of gender, racial, and national identities in the representation of the north point to the necessarily contingent nature of identity. Feminists first brought these issues to light by suggesting that gender identity could be constructed, and although many critics of masculinity acknowledge the insights of feminist methods, the importance of feminist challenges to representational authority is made all the more clear by efforts to deny them. Race, a category once believed to have an empirical basis that is now rejected, is similarly contingent and often bound up with gender. Uncovering the ways in which ideas about gender and race inflect the representation of the north further exposes the way the shared consciousness said to emerge from northern experience is an imaginary one constructed from literary images and ideas. The notion that Canadians inherit a national consciousness from "northern races," an idea that should have vanished along with nineteenth-century notions of racial superiority, cannot speak to Canada's population today.

Critical arguments for a distinct Canadian literature and culture are usually grounded in ideas about collective experience and in an idea of cultures as separate, distinct entities, an assumption challenged by new anthropological theories and practices. Yet claims for a distinct culture persist. The Canadian national identity emerging teleologically from a national consciousness defined by its relationship to the north is an argument for a distinct Canadian culture. Writers create characters who earn their individuality through feats of survival in harsh circumstances, creating narratives based on mastery. The hero's mastery of internal and external forces signals the correspondence between the body as the site of gender identity formation and the land as site of national identity formation so that the northern hero's quest performs the masculinization and nationalization of the space he seeks to inhabit. In these narratives, the hero's relation to his own body serves as a metaphor for quest and conquest, reflecting the argument made by Victor Seidler and others that masculinity based on a purely instrumental relationship to the body reflects the representation of male sexuality as performance and conquest.

By representing the north as a setting for the quest, for feats of endurance and survival, writers thematize the development of a traditionally defined masculine identity, thereby constituting what some call "the spirit of the north" as a set of qualities the rugged individual possesses. Rugged, individualistic characters populate Canadian literature set in the north. The Romantic national consciousness associated with this set of qualities implies that the Canadian nation is similarly rugged and individualistic or, negatively, lacking and needing an understanding of its true nature as rugged and individualistic. But the nation so conceived is a theoretical entity that shares the "situationless freedom" with the liberal individual (Di Stefano 21), an autonomous self who is rootless, homeless, alive in theory only (Butler 3). One of the insights of feminism has been to demonstrate that this particular theoretical individual is gendered. However, the mutually dependent meanings of gender, national, and racial traits render them unstable; like masculine identity, other forms of identity require constant striving for attainment and seem elusive.

While feminist critics and some critics in the men's movement continue to expose the traditional and ubiquitous markers of masculine identity, the destabilization of these markers in North America leads to a nostalgic desire for a place where the traditional forms of masculine identity once thrived. The renewed popularity of adventure stories set in the Arctic, such as the Hollywood films *White Fang* and *Iron Will*, and the proliferation of first-person travel writing indicate that the north remains a setting for narratives of rugged individualism. But the engendering of the north goes further than the simple creation of all-male communities, heroic adventures, or epic conflict in northern settings, and the Canadian identity implied in the representation of the north takes on the characteristics of the rugged individual in more than a thematic context. Writers who call on Canadians to grasp their northern heritage conflate the characteristics of the northern hero with those of the theoretical national identity. This conflation is an effect of blurring the boundaries between forms of literary and social scientific discourses. If we understand nordicity, northern enthusiasts tell us, Canada will be the kind of nation it needs to be, in the words of W.L. Morton, "firm, decisive, and different from the south" (231). But embracing such a national identity is not possible without giving credibility to the ideas by which it has been defined historically.

In Canadian literary history, literature continues to portray a "national-referential aesthetic" (Lecker, *Making It Real* 4) whereby it is read in terms of its relationship to society and culture. Within this framework, the idea of a national culture emerges from the need to define the state as a nation for purposes of legitimation, rather than from the existence of a shared consciousness or experience. While the association of attributes such as self-sufficiency, independence, and endurance with Canadian identity helps to give Canada the characteristics of modern nationhood, this definition arises as an official national identity whose accuracy and authenticity can be disputed on the grounds that it does not account sufficiently for regional, historical, racial, and gender differences. It is worth asking whether any single definition of an authentic national identity, especially one whose representation is inflected significantly by unstable categories of gender and race, is possible. If national identity cannot be defined once and for all, can it ever be anything other than an official form imposed on the many by the few?

This study has sought to unsettle the idea of the north as evoked by some of our writers by disputing the notion of a central, unifying national experience. Rather than a mimetic account of Canadian experience, "Canada as north" is a way of imagining a nation through the Romantic notion of consciousness. If we consider Romantic nationalism to be a "metanarrative" in Lyotard's sense, then my incredulity, which is as historically contingent as any of the ideas discussed, could be called postmodern. Contemporary national commentary, such as Richard Gwyn's *Nationalism Without Walls* (1995) or John Ralston Saul's *The Unconscious Civilization* (1995), suggest that Canada could be the first postmodern nation: the first nation in which incredulity toward national identity actually comes to define and to legitimate the state. However, as we see in northern representation, postmodernist writing can also mask a will-to-power and redraw the boundaries it is supposed to blur. That identity is complex and contingent means not that it defies description but that limiting national identity to consciousness of experiences that all Canadians supposedly share is insufficient, if not specious.

Individual identities can be formed in relation to the development of traditions imported from elsewhere, preserved from the past, or created in the present. Ideas of gender, race, and nation too have been imported and adapted; they do not develop in context-free experience. While environments, social, natural, economic, affect the way writers work and the things that they write about, their ideas are also shaped by personal, literary, and national histories. Therefore, topocentric and ecological accounts, which suggest the existence of a collective, national consciousness, only describe the impact environment has on the process of adaptation.

While Canada possesses a set of institutions in which, ideally, all citizens are said to participate, while these institutions are important, and while they may identify what it means to be Canadian, they do not assimilate all citizens to one uniform culture. "Canadian culture" is a collection of myths. Historically, the people living in Canada have preserved the cultural identities that existed before Canada – whether indigenous or imported – while adapting them to the changing conditions of time and place. These cultures and traditions – one might call them "local" – have more meaning for people than the official forms proposed as belonging to each and every one of us. This is not to deny that there is a dominant culture in Canada, one constructed through representation in the interest of maintaining power. The idea of Canada as a northern nation is one of these representations, a myth that seems to transcend local and individual identities and unify Canadians, though the potential of such myths to transcend differences in order to deny, constrain, or even erase them remains.

Notes

1 In the introduction to the special issue of *Essays on Canadian Writing* on "Representing North," Sherrill E. Grace paraphrases Grant's observation: "there has long been a deeply held belief among southern Canadians that 'North' defines us as Canadians" (1), and in "Canadian Art: Northern Land, Northern Vision," Patricia Morley phrases it thus: "The experience of wrestling with a rigorous northern climate and wilderness conditions has shaped our people and, of course, their art" (22).

2 See, for example, Justice Thomas R. Berger's *Northern Frontier, Northern Homeland* (1977).

3 For example, John Moss concludes his essay "Imagining the Arctic: From Frankenstein to Farley Mowat, Words Turn the Arctic Landscape into Unreality" (1990) with the assertion that, for many, the north is what writers imagine it to be.

4 This imaginary North created by and for southern Canadian audiences by writers in southern Canada has been analysed in the work of Peter Buitenhuis, David Heinimann, Aron Senkpiel, Bruce Hodgins, John Moss, and Linda Roth. For a quick genealogy of the word "north" in Canadian studies, see David Heinimann's "Latitude Rising: Historical Continuity in Canadian Nordicity." Although Heinimann maps the changing definitions of North, noting that in "the last 10 years, the association of North with Native has intensified" (136), he does not cover the north's history as a discursive concept.

5 Significantly, in *Margin/Alias: Language and Colonization in Canadian and Québécois Fiction* (1991), Sylvia Söderlind notes that, because

Canada does not have a Wild West tradition, the frontier in Canada does not have the same significance it does for America (173). In "Comparing Mythologies," Sherrill E. Grace offers a reading of west and north that is not derivative but comparative.

6 Writers including Margaret Atwood, Lisa Bloom, Sherrill E. Grace, and Elizabeth Waterston, among others, acknowledge the masculine language used in depictions of the north. In *Places on the Margin*, Rob Shields recognizes that the north is "masculine-gendered" (163) but does not explore the idea further. Lisa Bloom's *Gender on Ice: American Ideologies of Polar Expeditions* (1993) describes the "race for the Pole" as a "spectacle of male rivalry." As Sherrill Grace notes, Bloom equates masculinity with a conjunction of scientific and imperial interests ("Gendering" 166).

7 In contrast, Leon Surette argues that "even if Herderian nationalism had not acquired an odour of evil, it could hardly serve the interests of English-Canadian nationalists as it does French Canadians" ("Creating" 22). Québécois nationalism is not addressed specifically in this discussion, although three popular novels depicting the Inuit by francophone writers and available in translation are included. To the extent that the definition of Canada as a northern nation purportedly includes Quebec and acts as a unifying discourse, however, it may be a response to the threat that Québécois nationalism poses to the official national identity. But it is important to note that the Canadian identity based on a northern consciousness, while theoretically inclusive of Quebec, is generally applied specifically to Canadian literature written in English.

8 In "Here is Us: The Topocentrism of Canadian Literary Criticism" (1982), Leon Surette uses the term "topocentrism" to describe the "belief that human cultures are in some not clearly specific sense the product of the physical environment" (22), in effect offering the sort of spiritual connection between the people and the nation identified by the German Romantics in the nineteenth century. Dermot McCarthy's study of the nationalistic impulse in Canadian literary history similarly identifies the teleology (and tautology) of canon-formation (41), and uses Surette's term to note a "topocentric fusion of place, identity, authenticity, and authority in the process of Canadian canon-formation" (35). "Canadian literature," writes Leon Surette, "must be literature that is proper to Canada," and, consequently, criticism on Canadian literature has

been dedicated to the "discovery and identification of its subject of study" ("Here is Us" 45).

9 For an original reevaluation of Frye's "garrison mentality" and its impact on thematic criticism, see Susan Glickman's *The Picturesque and the Sublime: A Poetics of the Canadian Landscape* (1998).

10 Shelagh Grant explores the correlation between interest in the north and fear of losing it as a territorial possession in *Sovereignty or Security?* (1998). Other studies of the north and the Canadian state include Franklyn Griffiths' *The Politics of the Northwest Passage* (1987) and Edgar J. Dosman's *The Northern Interest: The Politics of Northern Development, 1968–1975* (1975).

11 As W.H. New observes in his analysis of this poem: "The nationalism of the Arctic metaphor, the resistance to American intervention in Canadian affairs, the indeterminate certainties of the northern landscape: these are familiar political and literary paradigms" (*Land* 120).

12 Jonathan Kertzer investigates this connection in *Worrying the Nation* (1998), highlighting the "puzzling inconsistency" of nationalist discourse which "promises to unify a people and/with/ through their literature, but … speaks simultaneously of their irreducible plurality" (35).

13 I develop this argument further in "Blurred Visions: The Interdisciplinarity of Canadian Literary Criticism."

14 It is illustrated, I think, in the tendency to indicate different perspectives by pluralizing words like "north," as in the closing sentence of the introduction to the special issue of *Essays on Canadian Writing* devoted to the north: "If we value the images and stories, we must also learn to value, to understand, and represent the real norths" (Grace 4). The plural form undercuts the possibility of "real," seems to make it indistinguishable from "images and stories," and begs the question: will all "real norths" be equally true? This is also a dilemma for the postmodern ethnographer: how to highlight one's own role in generating reality without abandoning the independent reality that one seeks to describe.

15 The value of philosophical realism is eloquently defended in Paisley Livingston's essay "Why Realism Matters": "In a very broad sense, realism is the notion that there is a reality that exists independently of our minds, and that we can know aspects of this reality. The epistemic value of this notion resides in the cognitive achievements it makes possible, and some endeavors

indeed require the belief that inquiry can sometimes result in our discovering something about what is actually the case" (150).

16 R. Radhakrishnan raises the same point and criticizes post-colonial subjects for embracing nationalism as a concept while ignoring the fact that nationalism developed under specific historical circumstances in Europe (87). Timothy Brennan also demonstrates how imperialism contributes to the development of national ideology (58).

17 This phrase, "the Idea of North," is the title of Glenn Gould's 1967 radio documentary. It has proven to be a useful phrase for the subject of northern studies: for example, Sherrill E. Grace uses the term widely in her research. Interest in Gould's composition continues to be strong. See Paul Hjartarson, "Of Inward Journeys and Interior Landscapes: Glenn Gould, Lawren Harris, and 'The Idea of North'"; Kevin McNeilly, "Listening, Nordicity, Community: Glenn Gould's 'The Idea of North'"; and Peter Dickinson, "Documenting North in Canadian Poetry and Music."

18 The term "northern hero" is used by Peter Buitenhuis in "Born Out of Fantasy and Cauled in Myth: The Writer and the Canadian North" (4).

19 Such studies include I.S. MacLaren's "The Aesthetic Map of the North, 1845–59"; "The Aesthetic Mapping of Nature in the Second Franklin Expedition"; "Retaining Captaincy of the Soul: A Response to Nature in the First Franklin Expedition"; and "Samuel Hearne and the Landscapes of Discovery;" Barbara Belyea's "Captain Franklin in Search of the Picturesque"; Robert Stacey's "From 'Icy Picture' to 'Extensive Prospect': The Panorama of Rupert's Land and the Far North in the Artist's Eye, 1770–1830"; and Sherrill E. Grace's "'Mapping Inner Space': Canada's Northern Expressionism." See also Sherrill E. Grace's forthcoming study *Canada and the Idea of North*.

20 I make this argument in "Literary Field Notes: The Influence of Ethnography on Representations of the North," an article based largely on chapter 1 of this study.

21 As Eric Hobsbawm observes, to insist on national consciousness is "to subordinate the complex and multiple ways in which human beings define and redefine themselves as members of groups, to a single option: the choice of belonging to a 'nation' or 'nationality'" (8). Hobsbawm signals the impossibility of establishing identity once and for all, an impossibility which is particularly true in the case of Canada.

CHAPTER ONE

1 In his "Realism and Reification," Steven Webster provides a useful summary of the definitions Marcus and Cushman give (51).

2 Steven Webster writes that Geertz's "renewed hermeneutic restored the social scientist's narrative role, an ordinary story-teller alive again in the mundane world, telling a story about a past experience" ("Ethnography as Storytelling" 191). The ironic use of "ordinary" is unmistakable here, for Geertz suggests that the ethnographer must possess special empathetic powers, summarized in the troubling notion that the ethnographer's aim should be "putting one's self into someone else's skin" (in Basso and Selby 224).

3 Henrietta Moore takes this further in her critique of the postmodernist turn, writing: "Informants are hybrid, but anthropologists are not" ("Interior" 134). Moore exposes the oppressive effects of retracing the self/other distinction this way, and relates it to the trend towards particularism produced by the "problematic status of theory in the wake of the postmodernist critique."

4 For an extensive study of the contributions made by Schoolcraft, Morgan, and Boas and of the historical relationship of literature and anthropology, see Arnold Krupat, "Ethnography and Literature: A History of a Convergence" in *Ethnocriticism* (49–80).

5 Here I am referring to the aim of ethnographic realism "to discover and represent faithfully the true nature of social phenomena" (Marcus and Cushman 44). Sally Cole describes this type of ethnography, the type she was trained to write as a student of anthropology, as "ethnographic naturalism," that is, a style which creates a "taken-for-granted representation of reality" (117).

6 Van Maanen offers examples of these conventions and explanation in *Tales of the Field* (45–54). Paul Atkinson concurs with Van Maanen's description of ethnographic realism as "conveyed through textual representations of the concrete, the local, the detailed" (33).

7 It is important to note, however, that the term "dialogic" was introduced to anthropological discourse before Bakhtin was widely known in the West. Kevin Dwyer's "On the Dialogic of Fieldwork" and "The Dialogic of Ethnology," published in the 1970s, advocate an exploration of the "Self" in dialectical relation with the "Other," an argument made without reference to Bakhtin.

8 The blurring of boundaries between the discursive practices of anthropology and those of fiction has been noted by Graham Huggan ("Maps, Dreams, and the Presentation of Ethnographic Narrative" 57).

9 Some ethnographers and theorists, such as John Van Maanen, recognize how cultivating a literary style has become an attractive option that does not change the methodology upon which the ethnographer's work is founded (34). Mascia-Lees, Sharpe, and Cohen also voice the concern that postmodern innovations may be nothing but a matter of style (31).

10 See Arnold Krupat's extended study of the relationship between literature and ethnography in *Ethnocriticism: Ethnography, History, Literature*. John Van Maanen's *Tales from the Field* includes a description of how early ethnographers tried to distinguish their writing from travel writing by providing an exhaustive treatment of the culture (14).

11 An earlier version of my argument concerning the apolitical nature of ethnography that takes the postmodernist turn can be found in *Representing the Canadian North* (1996).

12 While the list of essays describing the general proliferation of quest pattern motifs in Canadian literature about the north is too long to reproduce here, Maurice Hodgson's "Initiation and Quest: Early Canadian Journals" is representative.

13 Stephen Slemon and Helen Tiffen take an even stronger position by claiming that the "crisis in representation" at the heart of poststructuralist inquiry "functions as a technology of containment and control within the cross-cultural theatre of neo-colonial relations" (*After Europe* xi).

14 For Clifford Geertz's explanation of his use of exemplars, see "'From the Native's Point of View': On the Nature of Anthropological Understanding." Lynnette Turner notes the vital importance of the exemplary informant in nineteenth-century ethnography ("Feminism and Ethnographic Authority" 246). Neither author recognizes the practice as synecdoche.

15 Judith Stacey's recognition of this strategy has been discussed in Mascia-Lees et al. (21).

16 Although *Maps and Dreams* displays an awareness of the literary conventions used, its inadequate exploration of the author's subjectivity leaves the perspective of a realist monograph intact, a point also made by Graham Huggan in his review essay "Maps, Dreams, and the Presentation of Ethnographic Narrative."

17 Farley Mowat, an amateur and unreliable ethnographer, criticizes
    the way "we smugly assume that because these people live unar-
    moured by our ornate technology, they must lead the most mar-
    ginal kind of existence, faced with so fierce a battle to survive
    that they have no chance to realize the 'human potential'" (*The
    Snow Walker* 15).

CHAPTER TWO

1 That colonialism characterizes the relationship between the Canadian state and the north is a commonplace of northern studies
   reiterated in, among others, *Canada's Colonies: A History of the
   Yukon and Northwest Territories* by Kenneth Coates, *The Modern
   North: People, Politics and the Rejection of Colonialism* by Coates
   and Judith Powell, and *The Canadian North: Source of Wealth or
   Vanishing Heritage?* edited by B.W. Hodgins, J. Benidickson, and
   R.P. Bowles.
2 In "Samuel Hearne and the Inuit Oral Tradition," Robin McGrath
   uses Inuit accounts to dispute the likelihood that such a battle
   actually took place. McGrath identifies this passage as key to the
   stereotype of the savage Indian and the peaceful Inuit, a version
   of the "howling" versus the "noble" savage described by Paula
   Gunn Allen (5).
3 Europeans often named one aboriginal group using their name in
   the language of another aboriginal group: this is the purported
   origin of the word "Eskimo."
4 As discussed in chapter 1, Ann Fienup-Riordan identifies the
   emphasis on survival as a bias in ethnography about the Inuit in
   her book *The Nelson Island Eskimo.*
5 Many critics, including LaVonne Brown Ruoff, Thomas King, and
   Louis Owens, acknowledge this "dying Indian" motif as pervasive
   in North American culture.
6 It has come to my attention since writing this that Arnold Krupat
   uses the same image, quoting David Hollinger's theory on how
   cultures (and something called "sub-cultures") can be used as
   "repositories" available to humanistic studies or "that can be
   drawn upon in the interests of a more comprehensive outlook on
   the world" (*Ethnocriticism* 242).
7 Here we see a convergence of anthropological interest in physical
   survival with a similar preoccupation in literary criticism, as witnessed in Atwood's thematic study in particular. Sherrill E. Grace

also notes that Canadians, in inventing themselves, "insist upon surviving" ("Comparing" 247).

8 Peter Buitenhuis takes issue with the representation of the north by southern Canadians and warns against the "colonization of the imagination" (4). Buitenhuis does not refer explicitly to the colonization of aboriginal people but distinguishes between those who "imagine the north" and those who have a "true" understanding.

9 In the course of correspondence with Dale Blake, I have come to consider the distance that Campbell creates between herself and other Natives to be part of her assertion of an independent, "authentic" self, and not necessarily a sign of self-loathing. In her essay "Women of Labrador: Realigning North from the Site(s) of Métissage," Blake shows how Campbell and Baikie celebrate mixed blood heritage specifically, and this celebration accounts for the differentiation from other groups.

10 Comparisons can be made between Goudie's experiences as a trapper's wife and those recorded in Olive A. Fredrickson's *The Silence of the North* (1972): Fredrickson, a white woman living in northern British Columbia, focuses on hardships too, but does so in order to glorify the pioneer lifestyle.

11 At the same time, ethnography was proliferating. Writers such as Richard K. Nelson, whose *Shadow of the Hunter* appeared in 1980 along with Michael Mitchell's *Singing Songs to the Spirit: The History and Culture of the Inuit*, and Fred Bruemmer, whose *Arctic Memories: Living with the Inuit* appeared in 1993, based their texts on brief time spent with the hospitable Inuit, while children's writer Carolyn Meyer collaborated with Bernadine Larsen on a fictional account entitled *Eskimos: Growing Up in a Changing Culture* (1977).

12 Robin McGrath outlines these problems with specific reference to the transcription and translation of the oral in "Editing Inuit Literature Leaving the Teeth in the Gently Smiling Jaws."

CHAPTER THREE

1 For example, Stephansson's *Unsolved Mysteries of the Arctic* (1938) devotes itself to the stories of Franklin, Simpson, and Andrée the Swedish balloonist – rugged individuals all.

2 The term "northern hero" is used by Peter Buitenhuis in "'Born Out of Fantasy and Cauled in Myth': The Writer and the

Canadian North" to describe the typical rugged hero of northern adventures (4).

3 Ironically, the term "Northern," coined by Leslie Fiedler as a counterpart to the Western, does not describe the representation of a northern frontier. As T.D. MacLulich notes, the main conflict in a "Northern" involves the encounter of a sensitive individual and a closed society in which "environmental and social oppression reinforce each other," as in *The Mountain and the Valley* or *As For Me and My House* (*Between Europe and America* 127). Most stories about the far north do not belong to this classification, because, in them, the individual generally "lights out" for the northern regions in order to escape the scenario described in the typical Northern. See Sherrill E. Grace, "Comparing Mythologies."

4 Martin Green also observes how the experience of adventure has been a rite of passage from boyhood to manhood as exemplified in the Boy Scout movement (*Great American* 6).

5 Some recent accounts of the quest, such as Dana A. Heller's *The Feminization of the Quest-Romance* (1990), claim that the quest is being transformed by women writers to articulate feminine identity (15). Heller's account of how women writers are taking on the role of the hero does not provide any evidence to suggest that this feminization is anything more than derivative of and dependent on the patterns associated with the development of masculine identity.

6 One variation to the triumphant masculine quest narrative is John Buchan's *Sick Heart River* (1941), a novel in which, as W.H. New observes, the north is "a place of death, decay, corruption and despair" (*Land* 14) equated with the hero's dying body.

7 In "Gendering Northern Narrative," Sherrill E. Grace warns against the danger of discussing "masculine" and "feminine" in opposition to each other and "the risk of merely replicating the old binaries, of lapsing back into essentialism that classifies masculinist as essentially bad and feminist as essentially good" (175). This is the difficulty with narratives that attempt to revise the existing division of gender.

8 In "Encompassing the North," her fascinating study of the role of nineteenth-century science in Canadian nation-building, Suzanne Zeller demonstrates how "developments in the science of meteorology bestowed legitimacy upon a growing Canadian expansionist

movement" and "challenged Canadians' views of themselves as a mere colonial people" (176).

9 Melody Webb's history of Alaska, *The Last Frontier* (1985), appropriates the rugged individualism celebrated by Service in the Canadian north as a specific feature of American identity. Webb depicts the "red-blooded Americans" of the era as more manly than the heavily taxed and bureaucratic Canadians in the north (129).

10 As Rob Shields argues, the cliché bears a cultural significance, and "the entry of many metaphors into the realm of cliché is partial evidence of the diffusion of Northern images" (*Places* 172). Ken Coates and William Morrison point out that even the "True North, Strong and Free of our national anthem is a cliché worn smooth by generations of repetition" (*Purposes of Dominion* 1).

11 Viking exploits have a particular resonance in stories from Newfoundland and Labrador. For example, Labrador explorer Sir Wilfred Grenfell is dubbed a "Christian Viking" in William Byron Forbush's dedication to *Pomiuk* (1903).

12 Consider, for example, the contrived quest motif in Thomas York's *The Musk Ox Passion* (1978): a draft dodger who describes his life as a religious quest travels north to the Mackenzie Highway lured by an ad in *Macho*, a fictional feminist magazine.

13 The Native woman represents the nature side of this opposition in many books about the north. For example, in Thomas York's *Snowman* (1976), the local Native women are called "wildees" (14 and *passim*). While the Priests expound against the dangers of the wilderness, including the Native people, the character called Bard procures Native women for sex with the workers at Giant Mines.

14 It is significant that Thomas P. Kelley's Albert Johnson also describes his mother as the epitome of civilization, "an aristocrat to her fingertips": "She was wealthy, she was intelligent, and she was an outstanding beauty" (*Rat River Trapper* 114). Although he provides few details, her demise causes him to forsake human society and go north.

CHAPTER FOUR

1 Susan Glickman's *The Picturesque and the Sublime: A Poetics of the Canadian Landscape* (1998) extends Bentley's critique in an original manner.

2 Here I am in total agreement with Rita Felski that "the espousal of linguistic free play and a rejection of critical reason can have strongly conservative political consequences by encouraging a relativism which lacks any evaluative, critical, or oppositional edge" (70).

3 T.D. MacLulich makes a similar point in *Between Europe and America*, identifying the "documentary" and the "literary" as the two dominating impulses in Canadian literature (11–16).

4 Discussing the historical and cultural contingency of stereotypes, Sander Gilman indicates that, although stereotypes work by analogy, often as metaphors, those who hold them also believe them to be real (21). With reference to Native North Americans, Gilman's insight can be applied to the way non-Natives believe that dreams *really* define Native spirituality.

5 As Robert Lecker remarked to me, this passage makes a strong allusion to Lampman's "Heat."

6 As Joanne Saul argues, postmodern texts like *Enduring Dreams* risk erasing the landscape completely because it "destabilizes by deconstructing without offering any grounds from which to reconstruct" (104).

7 For my original arguments concerning the narrator's view in *Places Far from Ellesmere* of the land as a blank space on which to write her own story, and my original reading of *Enduring Dreams*, see *Representing the Canadian North* (1996).

8 In "Aritha van Herk's *Places Far from Ellesmere*: The Wild and Adventurous North?," Asta Mott takes Goldman's critique further, concluding that the book constructs "a blank space ready to be inscribed with southern narratives – in other words, ready to be colonized by the southern Euro-Canadian imagination" (110).

9 Joanne Saul has made a similar observation about John Moss's representation of the north as "beyond words": "What we are left with then is silence, and it is this kind of silence that has arguably allowed for the hyper-textualization of the north in the first place" (104).

10 Perhaps this is not surprising, for, as Eve Kosofsky Sedgwick suggests, the function of any ideology, such as the idea of northern identity, is "to negotiate invisibly between contradictory elements in the status quo, concealing the very existence of contradictions in the present by, for instance, recasting them in diachronic terms as a historical narrative of origins" (119).

11 In "Imaginative and Historical Truth in Wiebe's *The Mad Trapper*,"
Nancy Bailey recognizes the binary groupings on which the representation of the north has been based: "Wiebe uses the Indian to
stress both the potential unfulfilled union of Indian, white, and
Arctic world, and the breaking of this triad. This would be a
union based on ways of knowing that would unite reason, science
and language with what are thought by the white Western culture to be feminine inarticulate traits of sensation, intuition and
feeling" (73).

References

Alcoff, Linda. "The Problem of Speaking for Others." *Cultural Critique* 20 (1991–92): 5–32.

Alcoff, Linda, and Elizabeth Potter, eds. *Feminist Epistemologies.* New York: Routledge, 1992.

Allen, Paula Gunn. *The Sacred Hoop: Recovering the Feminine in American Indian Traditions.* Boston: Beacon, 1986.

Altmeyer, George. "Three Ideas of Nature in Canada, 1893–1914." *Journal of Canadian Studies* 11.3 (1976): 21–36.

Anderson, Benedict. *Imagined Communities: Reflections on the Origin and Spread of Nationalism.* London: Verso, 1983.

Angus, Ian H., and Sut Jhally, eds. *Cultural Politics in Contemporary America.* New York: Routledge, 1989.

Armstrong, John Alexander. *Nations Before Nationalism.* Chapel Hill: University of North Carolina Press, 1982.

Ashcroft, Bill, Gareth Griffiths, and Helen Tiffin. *The Empire Writes Back: Theory and Practice in Post-Colonial Literature.* London: Routledge, 1989.

Atkinson, Paul. *The Ethnographic Imagination: Textual Constructions of Reality.* London: Routledge, 1990.

Atkinson, Paul, and Amanda Coffey. "Realism and Its Discontents: On the Crisis of Cultural Representation in Ethnographic Texts." In *Theorizing Culture: An Interdisciplinary Critique after Postmodernism.* Eds. Barbara Adam and Stuart Allan. 41–57. New York: New York University Press, 1995.

Atwood, Margaret. *Second Words.* Toronto: Anansi, 1982.

– *Strange Things: The Malevolent North in Canadian Literature.* Oxford: Clarendon, 1995.

– *Survival: A Thematic Guide to Canadian Literature.* Toronto: Anansi, 1972.

Austin-Broos, Diane J. "Falling Through the 'savage slot': Postcolonial Critique and the Ethnographic Task." *Australian Journal of Anthropology* 9 (1998): 295–309.

Baikie, Margaret. *Labrador Memories*. Happy Valley, NF: Them Days, 1983.

Bailey, Nancy. "Imaginative and Historical Truth in Wiebe's *The Mad Trapper*." *Journal of Canadian Studies* 20.2 (1985): 70–9.

Ballantyne, R.M. *Snowflakes and Sunbeams, or, The Young Fur Traders: A Tale of the Far North*. Boston: Phillips, 1859.

– *Ungava; or, A Tale of Esquimeaux-land*. London: Ward, Locke, 1857.

Bartky, Sandra Lee. *Femininity and Domination: Studies in the Phenomenology of Oppression*. New York: Routledge, 1990.

Basso, K.H., and H.A. Selby, eds. *Meaning in Anthropology*. Albuquerque: University of Mexico Press, 1976.

Beattie, Owen, and John Geiger. *Frozen in Time: Unlocking the Secrets of the Franklin Expedition*. New York: Dutton, 1987.

Beissel, Henry. *Inook and the Sun*. Toronto: Playwrights, 1974.

Belaney, Archie. (Grey Owl). *The Men of the Last Frontier*. London: Country Life, 1931.

Belyea, Barbara. "Captain Franklin in Search of the Picturesque." *Essays on Canadian Writing* 40 (1990): 1–24.

Benhabib, Seyla, and Drucilla Cornell, eds. *Feminism as Critique*. Minneapolis: University of Minnesota Press, 1987.

Benjamin, Jessica. *The Bonds of Love: Psychoanalysis, Feminism, and the Problem of Domination*. New York: Pantheon, 1988.

Benson, Nathaniel A., ed. *Modern Canadian Poetry*. Ottawa: Graphic, 1930.

Bentley, D.M.R. *The Gay]Grey Moose: Essays on the Ecologies and Mythologies of Canadian Poetry, 1690–1990*. Ottawa: University of Ottawa Press, 1992.

– "The Mower and the Boneless Acrobat: Notes on the Stances of Baseland and Hinterland in Canadian Poetry." *Studies in Canadian Literature* 8.1 (1983): 5–48.

– "A New Dimension: Notes on the Ecology of Canadian Poetry." *Canadian Poetry* 7 (1980): 1–20.

Ben-Zvi, Linda. "'Home Sweet Home': Deconstructing the Masculine Myth of the Frontier in Modern American Drama." In *The Frontier Experience and the American Dream*. Ed. David Mogen, Mark Busby, and Paul Bryant. 217–25. College Station: Texas A & M University Press, 1989.

Berger, Carl. "The True North Strong and Free." In *Nationalism in Canada*. Ed. Peter Russell. 3–26. Toronto: McGraw-Hill, 1966.

Berger, Thomas R. *Northern Frontier, Northern Homeland*. Rev. ed. 2 vols. Toronto: Douglas and McIntyre, 1988.

Bernard, Harry. *Les jours sont longs*. Ottawa: Le Cercle du livre de France, 1951.

Berton, Laura Beatrice. *I Married the Klondike*. Preface by Robert Service. Toronto: McClelland and Stewart, 1954.

Bevis, William. "Native American Novels: Homing In." In *Recovering the Word: Essays on Native Literature*. Ed. Brian Swann and Arnold Krupat. 580–620. Berkeley: University of California Press, 1987.

Bhabha, Homi K., ed. *Nation and Narration*. London: Routledge, 1990.

– "The Other Question – the Stereotype and Colonial Discourse." *Screen* 24.6 (1983): 18–36.

Blake, Dale. "Women of Labrador: Realigning North from the Site(s) of Métissage." *Essays on Canadian Writing*. Special issue edited by Sherrill Grace. 59 (1996): 164–81.

Blodgett, Jean. *The Coming and Going of the Shaman: Eskimo Shamanism and Art*. Winnipeg: The Winnipeg Art Gallery, 1978.

Bloom, Lisa. *Gender on Ice: American Ideologies of Polar Expeditions*. Minneapolis: University of Minnesota Press, 1993.

Boas, Franz. *The Eskimo of Baffin Land and Hudson Bay. Bulletin of the American Museum of Natural History*. Vol. xv. New York: AMS, 1901.

– *The Ethnography of Franz Boas*. Ed. Ronald P. Rohner and Evelyn C. Rohner. Chicago: University of Chicago Press, 1969.

Bodenhorn, Barbara. "'I'm Not the Great Hunter, My Wife Is': Inupiat and the Anthropological Models of Gender." *Inuit Studies* 14.1–2 (1990): 55–74.

Bodsworth, Fred. *The Atonement of Ashley Morden*. New Canadian Library 140. Ed. Malcolm Ross. Toronto: McClelland and Stewart, 1964.

– *Last of the Curlews*. New York: Dodd, Mead, 1954.

– *The Sparrow's Fall*. New York: New American Library, 1966.

– *The Strange One (of Barra)*. New York: Dodd, Mead, 1959.

Boone, Joseph. "Male Independence and the American Quest Genre: Hidden Sexual Politics in the All-Male Worlds of Melville, Twain, and London." In *Gender Studies: New Directions in Feminist Criticism*. 187–217. Bowling Green, OH: Bowling Green University Press, 1986.

Boone, Joseph A., and Michael Cadden, eds. *Engendering Men: The Question of Male Feminist Criticism*. New York: Routledge, 1990.

Booth, David. *Images of Nature: Canadian Poets and the Group of Seven*. Toronto: Kids Can, 1995.

Bordo, Jonathan. "Jack Pine – Wilderness Sublime or The Erasure of the Aboriginal Presence from the Landscape." *Journal of Canadian Studies* 27.4 (1992): 98–128.

Brand, Dionne. *In Another Place Not Here*. Toronto: Vintage, 1996.

Brant, Beth. *A Gathering of Spirit: Writing and Art by North American Indian Women*. Rockland, ME: Sinister Wisdom, 1984.

Brathwaite, Edward Kamau. "Dionne Brand's Winter Epigrams." *Canadian Literature* 105 (1985): 18–30.

Bratton, J.S. *The Impact of Victorian Children's Fiction*. London: Croom Helm, 1981.

Brennan, Timothy. "The National Longing for Form." In *Nation and Narration*. Ed. Homi K. Bhabha. 44–70. London: Routledge, 1990.

Breuilly, John. *Nationalism and the State*. Chicago: University of Chicago Press, 1982.

Breummer, Fred. *Arctic Memories: Living with the Inuit*. Toronto: Key Porter, 1993.

Brewster, Benjamin. *The First Book of Eskimos*. Illus. Ursula Koering. New York: Franklin Watts, 1952.

Briggs, Jean. "Eskimo Women: Makers of Men." In *Many Sisters: Women in Cross-Cultural Perspective*. Ed. Carolyn J. Matthiasson. New York: Free, 1974.

Bristow, Joseph. *Empire Boys: Adventures in a Man's World*. London: HarperCollins Academic, 1991.

Brizinski, Peggy. *Knots in a String: An Introduction to Native Studies in Canada*. Saskatoon: University of Saskatchewan Press, 1989.

Brod, Harry. *The Making of Masculinities: The New Men's Studies*. Boston: Allen and Unwin, 1987.

Brody, Hugh. *Living Arctic*. London: Faber & Faber, 1987.

– *Maps and Dreams*. Vancouver: Douglas and McIntyre, 1981.

– *The People's Land: Eskimos and Whites in the Eastern Arctic*. London: Penguin, 1975.

Brown, Cassie. *Death on the Ice*. Toronto: Doubleday, 1972.

Brown, E.K. *On Canadian Poetry*. Toronto: Ryerson, 1943.

Brown, Joseph Epes. "Evoking the Sacred through Language, Metalanguage, and the 'Arts' in Native American and Arctic Experience." In *Silence, The Word and the Sacred*. Ed. E.D. Blodgett and H.G. Coward. 141–7. Waterloo: Wilfrid Laurier University Press, 1989.

Brown, Russell. "On Reading for Themes in Canadian Literature." *University of Toronto Quarterly* 70.2 (2001): 168–80.

Brydon, Diana. "Landscape and Authenticity: The Development of National Literature in Canada and Australia." *Dalhousie Review* 61.2 (1981): 278–90.

– "Troppo Agitato: Writing and Reading Cultures." *Ariel* 19. 1 (1988): 13–32.

– "The White Inuit Speaks: Contamination as Literary Strategy." In *Past the Last Post: Theorizing Post-Colonialism and Post-Modernism*. Ed. Ian Adam and Helen Tiffin. 191–203. Calgary: University of Calgary Press, 1990.

Buitenhuis, Peter. "Born Out of Fantasy and Cauled in Myth: The Writer and the Canadian North." In *The Canadian North: Essays in Culture and Literature*. Ed. Jorn Carlsen and Bjorn Streijffert. 1–13. Lund, Sweden: University of Lund Press, 1989.

Burnford, Sheila. *One Woman's Arctic*. Toronto: McClelland and Stewart, 1973.

Butler, Judith. *Gender Trouble: Feminism and the Subversion of Identity*. New York: Routledge, 1990.

Campbell, Lydia. *Sketches of Labrador Life*. Happy Valley, NF: Them Days, 1980.

Canada. Minister of Supply and Services. "Our Future Together: An Agreement for Constitutional Renewal." 1992.

Carpenter, Edmund, ed. *Anerca*. Toronto: J.M. Dent, 1959.

– Introduction to *I Breathe a New Song: Poems of the Eskimo*, edited by Richard Lewis. New York: Simon, 1971.

– *The Story of Comock the Eskimo: As Told to Robert Flaherty*. Conneticut: Fawcett, 1972.

Cascardi, Anthony, ed. *Literature and the Question of Philosophy*. Baltimore: Johns Hopkins University Press, 1987.

Caulfield, Mina Davis. "Culture and Imperialism: Proposing a New Dialectic." In *Reinventing Anthropology*. Ed. Dell Hymes. 182–211. New York: Pantheon, 1972.

Chapman, Rowena, and Jonathan Rutherford, eds. *Male Order: Unwrapping Masculinity*. London: Lawrence and Wishart, 1988.

Chatterjee, Partha. *Nationalist Thought and the Colonial World: A Derivative Discourse*. London: Zed, 1986.

Christian, Edgar. *Death in the Barren Ground*. Ed. George Whalley. Ottawa: Oberon, 1980.

Clarke, Austin. *The Origin of Waves*. Toronto: McClelland and Stewart, 1997.

Clifford, James. "On Ethnographic Authority." *Representations* 1 (1983): 118–46.

– *The Predicament of Culture: Twentieth Century Ethnography Literature, and Art*. Cambridge: Harvard University Press, 1988.

Clifford James, and George Marcus, eds. *Writing Culture: The Poetics and Politics of Ethnography*. Berkeley: University of California Press, 1986.

Coates, Kenneth. *Canada's Colonies: A History of the Yukon and Northwest Territories.* Toronto: James Lorimer, 1985.

Coates, Kenneth, and William Morrison, eds. *For Purposes of Dominion: Essays in Honour of Morris Zaslow.* North York, ON: Captus, 1989.

– eds. *Interpreting Canada's North: Selected Readings.* Toronto: Copp Clark Pitman, 1989.

– eds. *Land of the Midnight Sun: A History of the Yukon.* Edmonton: Hurtig, 1988.

– "Writing the North: A Survey of Contemporary Canadian Writing on Northern Regions." *Essays on Canadian Writing.* Special issue edited by Sherrill Grace. 59 (1996): 5–25.

Coates, Kenneth, and Judith Powell. *The Modern North: People, Politics and the Rejection of Colonialism.* Toronto: James Lorimer, 1989.

Code, Lorraine. "Taking Subjectivity into Account." In *Feminist Epistemologies.* Ed. Linda Alcoff and Elizabeth Potter. 15–48. New York: Routledge, 1992.

Cole, Sally. "Anthropological Lives: The Reflexive Tradition in a Social Science." In *Essays on Life-Writing: From Genre to Critical Practice.* Ed. Marlene Kadar. 113–27. Theory and Culture 11, ed. Linda Hutcheon and Paul Perron. Toronto: University of Toronto Press, 1992.

Cole, Sally, and Lynne Phillips. "The Work and Politics of Feminist Ethnography: An Introduction." In *Ethnographic Feminisms: Essays in Anthropology.* Ed. Sally Cole and Lynne Phillips. 1–19. Ottawa: Carleton University Press, 1995.

Coleman, Daniel. "'Playin' 'mas,' Hustling Respect: Multicultural Masculinities in Two Stories by Austin Clarke." In *Masculine Migrations: Reading the Postcolonial Male in "New Canadian" Narratives.* 29–51. Toronto: University of Toronto Press, 1998.

Colombo, John Robert, ed. *Poems of the Inuit.* Ottawa: Oberon, 1981.

– ed. *Songs of the Great Land.* Ottawa: Oberon, 1989.

Cook, Ramsay. "Imagining a North American Garden: Some Parallels and Differences in Canadian and American Culture." *Canadian Literature* 103 (1984): 10–23.

Cournoyea, Nellie. "Everybody Likes the Inuit." In *Northern Voices: Inuit Writing in English.* Ed. Penny Petrone. 286. Toronto: University of Toronto Press, 1988.

Courtauld, Augustine, ed. *From the Ends of the Earth: An Anthology of Polar Writings.* London: Oxford University Press, 1958.

Cowan, Susan, ed. *We Don't Live In Snow Houses Now: Reflections of Arctic Bay.* Canadian Arctic Producers Limited, 1975.

Cox, Bruce, ed. *Cultural Ecology: Readings on the Canadian Indians and Eskimos.* The Carleton Library 65. Toronto: McClelland and Stewart, 1973.

Craig, John. *Zach.* New York: Coward, McCann, and Geohagen, 1972.

Crowe, Keith J. *A History of the Original Peoples of Northern Canada.* Montreal: McGill-Queen's University Press, 1974.

Cruikshank, Julie. "Legend and Landscape: Convergence of Oral and Scientific Traditions in the Yukon Territory." *Arctic Anthropology* 18.2 (1981): 67–93.

– "Oral Traditions and Written Accounts: An Incident from the Klondike Goldrush." *Culture* 9.2 (1989): 25–31.

Cruikshank, Julie, Angela Sidney, Kitty Smith, and Annie Ned. *Life Lived Like a Story: Life Stories of Three Yukon Native Elders.* Vancouver: University of British Columbia Press, 1990.

Crusz, Rienzi. "In the Idiom of the Sun." In *Insurgent Rain: Selected Poems 1974–1996.* Selected and introduced by Chelva Kanaganayakam. 69. Toronto: Tsar, 1997.

Daly, Kerry. "Re-Placing Theory in Ethnography: A Postmodern View." *Qualitative Inquiry* 3.3 (September 1997): 343–65.

Dauenhauer, Nora Marks, and Richard Dauenhauer. *Haa Shuka, Our Ancestors: Tlingit Oral Narratives.* Seattle: University of Washington Press, 1987.

Davey, Frank. "English-Canadian Literature Periodicals: Text, Personality, and Dissent." *Open Letter* 8.5–6 (1993): 67–78.

Davidson, Arnold. "Will the Real R. Mark Madham Please Stand Up: A Note on Robert Kroetsch's *Gone Indian.*" *Studies in Canadian Literature* 6.1 (1981): 135–9.

Davis, Richard. "Fluid Landscape/Static Land: The Traveller's Vision." *Essays on Canadian Writing* 34 (1987): 140–56.

– *Rupert's Land: A Cultural Tapestry.* Waterloo: Wilfrid Laurier University Press, 1988.

Dawson, Carrie. "Never Cry Fraud: Remembering Grey Owl, Rethinking Imposture." *Essays on Canadian Writing* 65 (1998): 120–40.

Daymond, Douglas, and Leslie Monkman. *Towards a Canadian Literature: Essays, Editorials and Manifestos.* Vol. I & II. Ottawa: Tecumseh, 1984.

de Lauretis, Teresa. "Desire in Narrative." In *Alice Doesn't: Feminism, Semiotics, Cinema.* 103–57. Bloomington: Indiana University Press, 1984.

– ed. *Feminist Studies/Critical Studies.* Theories of Contemporary Culture 8. Bloomington: Indiana University Press, 1986.

– *Technologies of Gender: Essays on Theory, Film, and Fiction.* Bloomington: Indiana University Press, 1987.

Delphy, Christine. *Close to Home. A Materialist Analysis of Women's Oppression*. London: Hutchinson, 1984.

Demers, Patricia. "'Youngsters 'in the Great Lone Land': Early Canadian Adventure Stories," *Children's Literature Association Quarterly* 8.3 (1983): 16–18.

Dennis, Philip A, and Wendell Aycock, eds. *Literature and Anthropology*. Lubbock: Texas Tech University Press, 1989.

Denzin, Norman K. "The Standpoint Epistemologies and Social Theory." *Current Perspectives in Social Theory* 17 (1997): 39–76.

de Poncins, Gontran. *Kabloona*. 1941. Introduction by Lewis Galantière. Chicago: Time-Life, 1965.

Desbarats, Peter, ed. *What They Used to Tell About: Indian Legends from Labrador*. Toronto: McClelland and Stewart, 1969.

De Staël, Germaine. *De la littérature considérée dans ses rapports avec les institutions sociales*. 1800. Édition critique par Paul van Tieghem. Tome I. Génève: Librairie Droz, 1959.

Dewart, Edward Hartley. *Selections from Canadian Poets*. Montreal: J. Lovell, 1864.

Dickason, Olive Patricia. "Three Worlds, One Focus: Europeans Meet Inuit and Amerindians in the Far North." In *Rupert's Land: A Cultural Tapestry*. 51–78. Waterloo: Wilfrid Laurier University Press, 1988.

Dickinson, Peter. "Documenting North in Canadian Poetry and Music." *Essays on Canadian Writing*. Special issue edited by Sherrill E. Grace. 59 (1996): 105–22.

Diprose, Rosalyn, and Robyn Ferrell, eds. *Cartographies: Poststructuralism and the Mapping of Bodies and Spaces*. Sydney, Australia: Allen & Unwin, 1991.

Di Stefano, Christine. *Configurations of Masculinity: A Feminist Perspective on Modern Political Theory*. Ithaca: Cornell University Press, 1991.

Djwa, Sandra. "'New Soil and a Sharp Sun': The Landscape of a Modern Canadian Poetry." *Modernist Studies* 2 (1977): 3–29.

Donaldson, Laura E. *Decolonizing Feminisms: Race, Gender and Empire-Building*. Chapel Hill: University of North Carolina Press, 1992.

Dosman, Edgar J. ed. *The Arctic in Question*. Toronto: Oxford University Press, 1976.

– *The Northern Interest: The Politics of Northern Development, 1968–1975*. Canada in Transition Series. Toronto: McClelland and Stewart, 1975.

Doyle, James "The Post-Ultimate Frontier: American Authors in the Canadian West, 1885–1900." *Essays on Canadian Writing* 22 (1981): 14–26.

Dragland, Stan. *Floating Voice: Duncan Campbell Scott and the Literature of Treaty 9*. Toronto: Anansi, 1994.

Drotner, Kirsten. *English Children and Their Magazines, 1751–1945*. New Haven: Yale University Press, 1988.

Drummond, Robbie Newton. *Arctic Circle Songs*. Waterloo: Penumbra, 1991.

Dunae, Patrick A. "Boy's Literature and the Idea of Empire, 1870–1914." *Victorian Studies* 24.1 (1980): 105–21.

– "Boy's Literature and the Idea of Race, 1870–1900." *Wascana Review* (1977): 84–107.

Dwyer, Kevin. "The Dialogic of Ethnology." *Dialectical Anthropology* 4 (1979): 205–24.

– "On the Dialogic of Fieldwork." *Dialectical Anthropology* 2 (1977): 143–51.

Eagleton, Terry, Frederic Jameson, and Edward Said. *Nationalism, Colonialism and Literature*. Minneapolis: University of Minnesota Press, 1990.

Eber, Dorothy, and Peter Pitseolak. *People from Our Side*. Edmonton: Hurtig, 1975.

Edwards, Brian, ed. *Literature and National Cultures*. Typereader Publications 3. Victoria: Centre for Studies in Literary Education and Deakin University Press, 1988.

Eggleston, Wilfred. *The Frontier and Canadian Letters*. Toronto: McClelland and Stewart, 1977.

Egoff, Sheila A. *Children's Periodicals of the Nineteenth Century*. Pamphlet 8. London: Library Association, 1951.

Eisenstein, Hester. *Contemporary Feminist Thought*. Boston: Keagan Paul & Hall, 1983.

Ekogatok, Bernard. *Naraye, Anarktee, and Other Stories*. Yellowknife: Department of Education, 1974.

Ekoomiak, Norman. *Arctic Memories*. Toronto: NC, 1988.

Eliade, Mircea. *Rites and Symbols of Initiation: The Mysteries of Birth and Rebirth*. Trans. Willard R. Trask. New York: Harper, 1958.

Ells, S.C. *Northland Trails*. N.p.: n.p., 1938.

Engel, Marian. *Bear*. Toronto: McClelland and Stewart, 1976.

Engler, Bernd, and Kurt Muller, eds. *Historiographic Metafiction in Modern American and Canadian Literature*. Paderborn, Germany: Schöningh, 1994.

Enslin, Elizabeth. "Beyond Writing: Feminist Practice and the Limitations of Ethnography." *Cultural Anthropology* 9.4 (November 1994): 537–68.

Evans, Hubert. *Mist on the River*. Toronto: Copp Clark, 1954.

Fabian, Johannes. *Time and the Other: How Anthropology Makes Its Object*. New York: Columbia University Press, 1983.

Faris, Wendy B. "Writing In/Of/On the New World: Metafictional Dimensions of Land Use in North and South American Fiction." 151–8. *Proceedings of the XIIth Congress of the International Comparative Literature Association*. Ed. Roger Bauer et al. Munich: Iudicium, 1990.

Fee, Margery. "Romantic Nationalism and the Image of Native People in Contemporary English-Canadian Literature." *The Native in Literature*. Ed. Thomas King, Cheryl Calver, and Helen Hoy. 15–33. Toronto: ECW, 1987.

– ed. *Silence Made Visible: Howard O'Hagan and* Tay John. Toronto: ECW, 1992.

Felski, Rita. *Beyond Feminist Aesthetics: Feminist Literature and Social Change*. Cambridge: Harvard University Press, 1989.

Fichte, Johann Gottlieb. *Addresses to the German Nation*. 1806–1815. Ed. George Armstrong Kelly. New York: Harper, 1968.

Field, Edward, ed. *Eskimo Songs and Stories*. New York: Delacorte, 1975.

Fienup-Riordan, Ann. *The Nelson Island Eskimo: Social Structure and Ritual Distribution*. Anchorage: Alaska Pacific University Press, 1988.

Flax, Jane. *Thinking Fragments: Psychoanalysis, Feminism, and Postmodernism in the Contemporary West*. Berkeley: University of California Press, 1990.

Flynn, Elizabeth A., and Patrocinio P. Schweickart, eds. *Gender and Reading: Essays on Readers, Texts, and Contexts*. Baltimore: Johns Hopkins University Press, 1986.

Folkenflik, Vivian, trans. *An Extraordinary Woman: Selected Writings of Germaine de Staël*. New York: Columbia University Press, 1987.

Forbush, William Byron. *Pomiuk: A Waif of Labrador*. Boston: Pilgrim Press, 1903.

Foster, W.A. *Canada First; or, Our New Nationality; An Address*. Toronto: Adam, Stevenson, 1871.

Franklin, Captain John. *Narrative of a Journey to the Shores of the Polar Sea in the Years 1819, 20, 21, and 22*. Edmonton: Hurtig, 1969.

Fredrickson, Olive A. with Ben West. *The Silence of the North*. Toronto: General, 1972.

Freeman, Minnie Aodla. *Life Among the Quallunaat*. Edmonton: Hurtig, 1978.

Freeman, Victoria. "The Baffin Writer's Project." In New, *Native Writers*. 266–271.

French, Alice. *My Name is Masak*. Winnipeg: Peguis, 1976.

French, Donald G., ed. *Famous Canadian Stories Re-Told for Boys and Girls*. Rev. ed. Toronto: McClelland and Stewart, 1931.

Friis-Baastad, Erling, and Patricia Robertson, eds. *Writing North: An Anthology of Contemporary Yukon Writers*. Whitehorse: Beluga, 1992.

Fry, Alan. *Come a Long Journey*. Toronto: Doubleday, 1971.
– *How a People Die*. Toronto: Doubleday, 1970.
Frye, Northrop. *The Bush Garden: Essays on the Canadian Imagination*. Toronto: Anansi, 1971.
– "Conclusion." *The Literary History of Canada*. Ed. Carl F. Klinck et al. Toronto: University of Toronto Press, 1965.
– *Divisions on a Ground: Essays on Canadian Culture*. Ed. James Polk. Toronto: Anansi, 1982.
Fullbrook, Kate. *Free Women: Ethics and Aesthetics in Twentieth-Century Women's Fiction*. Philadelphia: Temple University Press, 1990.
Fuss, Diana. *Essentially Speaking: Feminism, Nature, and Difference*. New York and London: Routledge, 1989.
Fussell, Edwin. *Frontier: American Literature and the American West*. Princeton: Princeton University Press, 1965.
Gedalof, Robin, ed. *Paper Stays Put: A Collection of Inuit Writing*. Edmonton: Hurtig, 1980.
– "Publishing Eskimo Literature: Developments in the Circumpolar World." *Phaedra* 1985: 45–8.
Geddes, Gary, ed. *Skookum Wawa: An Anthology of the Canadian Northwest*. Toronto: Oxford University Press, 1975.
Geertz, Clifford. "'From the Native's Point of View': On the Nature of Anthropological Understanding." In *Meaning in Anthropology*. Ed. K.H. Basso and H.A. Selby. 221–37. Albuquerque: University of New Mexico Press, 1976.
– "Thick Description: Toward an Interpretive Theory of Culture." In *The Interpretation of Cultures*. 3–30. London: Hutchinson, 1975.
– *Works and Lives: The Anthropologist as Author*. Stanford: Stanford University Press, 1988.
Gellner, Ernest. *Culture, Identity and Politics*. Cambridge: Cambridge University Press, 1987.
– *Nations and Nationalism*. Oxford: Blackwell, 1983.
Gerry, Thomas M.F. "'Green Yet Free of Seasons': Gwendolyn MacEwen and the Mystical Tradition of Canadian Poetry." *Studies in Canadian Literature* 16.2 (1991): 147–61.
Giffen, Naomi Musmaker. *The Roles of Men and Women in Eskimo Culture*. Chicago: University of Chicago Press, 1930.
Gilman, Sander. *Difference and Pathology: Stereotypes of Sexuality, Race, and Madness*. Ithaca: Cornell University Press, 1985.
Glickman, Susan. *The Picturesque and the Sublime: A Poetics of the Canadian Landscape*. Montreal: McGill-Queen's University Press, 1998.

Godard, Barbara, ed. *Talking About Ourselves: The Literary Productions of Native Women of Canada.* Ottawa: Canadian Research Institute for the Advancement of Women, 1985.

Godsell, Jean W. *I Was No Lady ... I Followed the Call of the Wild.* Toronto: Ryerson, 1959.

Goldie, Terry. "Fresh Canons: The Native Canadian Example." *English Studies in Canada* 17.4 (1991): 373–84.

Goldman, Marlene. "Go North Young Woman: Representations of the Arctic in the Writing of Aritha van Herk." In *Echoing Silence: Essays on Arctic Narrative.* Ed. John Moss. 153–62. Ottawa: University of Ottawa Press, 1997.

Goodwill, Jean, comp. *Speaking Together: Canada's Native Women.* Ottawa: Secretary of State, 1975.

Goudie, Elizabeth. *Woman of Labrador.* Agincourt, ON: The Book Society of Canada, 1982.

Grace, Sherrill. "Comparing Mythologies: Ideas of West and North." In *Borderlands: Essays in Canadian-American Relations.* Ed. Robert Lecker. 243–62. Toronto: ECW, 1991.

– "Gendering Northern Narrative." In *Echoing Silence: Essays on Artic Narrative.* Ed. John Moss. 163–81. Ottawa: University of Ottawa Press, 1997.

– "Introduction: Representing North (or, Greetings from Nelvana)." *Essays on Canadian Writing.* Special issue edited by Sherrill Grace. 59 (1996): 1–4.

– "'Mapping Inner Space': Canada's Northern Expressionism." In *The Canadian North: Essays in Culture and Literature.* Ed. Jorn Carlsen and Bjorn Streijffert. 61–71. Lund, Sweden: University of Lund Press, 1989.

– "A Northern Modernism, 1920–1932: Canadian Painting and Literature." *Literary Criterion* 14. 3–4 (1984): 105–24.

– "Quest for the Peaceable Kingdom: Urban/Rural Codes in Roy, Laurence, and Atwood." In *Women Writers and the City: Essays in Feminist Literary Criticism.* Ed. Susan Merrill Squier. 193–209. Knoxville: University of Tennessee Press, 1984.

– *Regression and Apocalypse: Studies in North American Literary Expressionism.* Toronto: University of Toronto Press, 1989.

Grace, Sherrill, Eve d'Aeth, and Lisa Chalykoff, eds. *Staging the North: Twelve Canadian Plays.* Toronto: Playwrights Canada Press, 1999.

Graff, Gerald. *Professing Literature: An Institutional History.* Chicago: University of Chicago Press, 1987.

Graham, Lorrie, and Tim Wilson. "Questions of Being: An Exploration of *Enduring Dreams.*" In *Echoing Silence: Essays on Arctic Narrative.* Ed. John Moss. 137–43. Ottawa: University of Ottawa Press, 1997.

Granofsky, Ronald. "The Country of Illusion: Vision, Change, and Misogyny in Howard O'Hagan's Tay John." In *Silence Made Visible: Howard O'Hagan and* Tay John. Ed. Margery Fee. 109–27. Toronto: ECW, 1992.

– "Western Myth and Northern History: The Plains Indians of Berger and Wiebe." *Great Plains Quarterly* 3.3 (1983): 146–56.

Grant, Agnes. *Our Bit of Truth: An Anthology of Canadian Native Literature.* Winnipeg: Pemmican, 1990.

Grant, S.D. "Myths of the North in the Canadian Ethos." *Northern Review* 3/4 (1989): 15–41.

Grant, Shelagh D. *Sovereignty or Security? Government Policy in the Canadian North, 1936–1950.* Vancouver: University of British Columbia Press, 1988.

Green, Martin. "Adventurers Stake Their Claim: The Adventure Tale's Bid for Status, 1876–1914." In *Decolonizing Tradition: New Views of Twentieth-Century "British" Literary Canons.* Ed. Karen R. Lawrence. 70–87. Chicago: University of Illinois Press, 1992.

– *The Adventurous Male: Chapters in the History of the White Male Mind.* University Park: Pennsylvania State University Press, 1993.

– *The Great American Adventure.* Boston: Beacon, 1984.

Green, Paul, and Abbe Abbot. *I Am Eskimo-Aknik My Name.* Juneau: Alaska Northwest, 1959.

Green, Rayna. *That's What She Said: Contemporary Poetry and Fiction by Native American Women.* Bloomington: Indiana University Press, 1984.

Greene, Gayle, and Coppelia Kahn, eds. *Making a Difference: Feminist Literary Criticism.* London: Methuen, 1985.

Greenfield, Bruce. "The Rhetoric of British and American Narratives of Exploration." *Dalhousie Review* 65.1 (1985): 56–65.

Grenfell, Wilfred. *Off the Rocks: Stories of the Deep-Sea Fisherfolk of Labrador.* 1906. Freeport: Books for Libraries, 1970.

– *Vikings of To-Day: Or Life and Medical Work Among the Fishermen of Labrador.* London: Marshall Brothers, 1905.

Grey Owl. *The Men of the Last Frontier.* London: Country Life, 1931.

Griffiths, Franklyn. "Beyond the Arctic Sublime." In *The Politics of the Northwest Passage.* Ed. Franklyn Griffiths. Montreal: McGill-Queen's University Press, 1987.

Guillory, John. *Cultural Capital: The Problem of Literary Canon Formation.* Chicago: University of Chicago Press, 1993.

Gunew, Sneja, ed. *Feminist Knowledges: Critique and Construct.* London and New York: Routledge, 1990.

Gwynn, Richard. *Nationalism Without Walls: The Unbearable Lightness of Being Canadian.* Toronto: McClelland and Stewart, 1995.

Haliburton, R.G. *The Men of the North and Their Place in History.* Montreal: John Lovell, 1869.

Hall, Tony. "A Canadian Perspective in Native Studies." *Canadian Review of Studies in Nationalism.* 20.1–2 (1993): 79–86.

Hamelin, Christine. "John Moss: Consciousness as Context." *Studies in Canadian Literatures* 20.1 (1995): 160–8.

Hamelin, Louis-Édmond. *Canadian Nordicity: It's Your North, Too.* Trans. William Barr. Montreal: Harvest, 1978.

– "Images of the North." In *Interpreting Canada's North: Selected Readings.* Ed. Kenneth Coates and William Morrison. 7–17. Toronto: Copp Clarke Pitman, 1989.

Hammersley, Martyn. *What's Wrong With Ethnography?* London: Routledge, 1992.

Hammersley, Martyn, and Paul Atkinson. *Ethnography: Principles in Practice.* London: Tavistock, 1983.

Haraway, Donna. *Primate Visions: Gender, Race and Nature in the World of Modern Science.* London: Routledge, 1989.

– *Simians, Cyborgs, and Women.* New York: Routledge, 1991.

Harding, Sandra, ed. *Feminism and Methodology: Social Science Issues.* Milton Keynes: Open University Press, 1987.

Hardy, E.A., ed. *Selections from the Canadian Poets.* Toronto: Macmillan, 1920.

Harlow, Robert. *Scann.* Victoria: Sono Nis, 1972.

Harper, Kenn. *Give Me My Father's Body: The Story of Minik, the New York Eskimo.* Frobisher Bay: Blacklead, 1986.

Harry, Margaret. "Literature in English by Native Canadians (Indian and Inuit)." *Studies in Canadian Literature* 10.1/2 (1985): 146–53.

Hartsock, Nancy. "Rethinking Modernism." *Cultural Critique* 7 (1987): 187–206.

Harvey, David D. "The Lure of the North: American Approaches to the Canadian Wilderness." *Canadian Review of American Studies* 17.1 (1986): 35–50.

Hay, Elizabeth. *The Only Snow in Havana.* Dunvegan, ON: Cormorant, 1992.

Hearne, Samuel. *A Journey from Prince of Wales's Fort in Hudson's Bay to the Northern Ocean 1769 1770 1771 1772*. 1795. Ed. Richard Glover. Toronto: Macmillan, 1958.

Hedican, Edward J. *Applied Anthropology in Canada: Understanding Aboriginal Issues*. Toronto: University of Toronto Press, 1995.

Heilbrun, Carolyn G. *Hamlet's Mother and Other Women*. Gender and Culture. Ed. Carolyn G. Heilbrun and Nancy K. Miller. New York: Columbia University Press, 1990.

Heilbrun, Carolyn G., and Margaret R. Higonnet, eds. *The Representation of Women in Fiction*. Baltimore: Johns Hopkins University Press, 1983.

Heinimann, David. "Latitude Rising: Historical Continuity in Canadian Nordicity." *Journal of Canadian Studies* 28.3 (1993): 134–9.

Heller, Dana A. *The Feminization of the Quest-Romance: Radical Departures*. Austin: University of Texas Press, 1990.

Henderson, Heather. "North and South: Autobiography and the Problems of Translation." In *Reflections: Autobiography and Canadian Literature*. Ed. K.P. Stich. 61–8. Ottawa: University of Ottawa Press, 1988.

Herbert, Wally. *Hunters of the Polar North*. Amsterdam: Time Life Books, 1981.

Heyne, Eric, ed. *Desert, Garden, Margin, Range: Literature on the American Frontier*. New York: Twayne, 1992.

Hirsch, Marianne, and Evelyn Fox Keller, eds. *Conflicts in Feminism*. New York: Routledge, 1990.

Hjartarson, Paul. "Of Inward Journeys and Interior Landscapes: Glenn Gould, Lawren Harris, and 'The Idea of North.'" *Essays on Canadian Writing*. Special issue edited by Sherrill Grace. 59 (1996): 65–86.

Hlus, Carolyn. "The Changing Fictional Images of Women on the North American Landscape." *Canadian Review of American Studies* 17.3 (1986): 347–54.

Hobsbawm, Eric J. *Nations and Nationalism since 1780: Programme, Myth, Reality*. Cambridge: Cambridge University Press, 1990.

Hodgins, Bruce. "The Canadian North: Conflicting Images, Conflicting Historiography." *Voyageur: Collected Papers and Proceedings of the Work-in-Progress Colloquium*. Peterborough: Trent University, 1979–80.

Hodgins, Bruce, J. Benidickson, and R.P. Bowles, eds. *The Canadian North: Source of Wealth or Vanishing Heritage?* Scarborough, ON: Prentice-Hall, 1977.

Hodgins, Jack, ed. *The Frontier Experience*. Toronto: Macmillan, 1975.

Hodgson, Maurice. "The Exploration Journal as Literature." *The Beaver* 298 (1967): 4–12.

- "Initiation and Quest: Early Canadian Journals." *Canadian Literature* 38 (1968): 29–40.
Hoeppner, Kenneth. "The Spirit of the Arctic or Translating the Untranslatable in Rudy Wiebe's *A Discovery of Strangers*," In *Echoing Silence: Essays on Arctic Narrative*. Ed. John Moss. 145–52. Ottawa: University of Ottawa Press, 1997.
Horwood, Harold. *Tales of the Labrador Indians*. St John's, NF: Harry Cuff, 1981.
- *White Eskimo: A Novel of Labrador*. Markham, ON: Paperjacks, 1973.
Housser, F.B. *A Canadian Art Movement: The Story of the Group of Seven*. Toronto: Macmillan, 1926.
Houston, James. *Frozen Fire: A Tale of Courage*. Toronto: McClelland and Stewart, 1977.
- *Spirit Wrestler*. New York: Harcourt, 1980.
- *The White Dawn: An Eskimo Saga*. New York: Harcourt, 1971.
- *Whiteout*. Toronto: General, 1988.
Howe, Joseph. *Acadia*. 1874. Ed. M.G. Parks. London, ON: Canadian Poetry, 1989.
Hubbard, Mina. *A Woman's Way Through Unknown Labrador*. St John's, NF: Breakwater, 1983.
Huggan, Graham. "Maps, Dreams, and the Presentation of Ethnographic Narrative: Hugh Brody's 'Maps and Dreams' and Bruce Chatwin's 'The Songlines.'" *Ariel* 22.1 (1991): 57–69.
Hulan, Renée. "Blurred Visions: The Interdisciplinarity of Canadian Literary Criticism." *Essays on Canadian Writing* 65 (1998): 38–55.
- "'A Brave Boy's Story for Brave Boys': Adventure Narrative Engendering." In *Echoing Silence: Essays on Arctic Narrative*. Ed. John Moss. 183–90. Ottawa: University of Ottawa Press, 1997.
- "Literary Field Notes: The Influence of Ethnography on Representations of the North." *Essays on Canadian Writing* Special issue edited by Sherrill Grace. 59 (1997): 147–63.
- *Representing the Canadian North: Stories of Gender, Race, and Nation*. Diss. McGill University, 1996.
Hutcheon, Linda. *The Canadian Postmodern: A Study of Contemporary English-Canadian Fiction*. Toronto: Oxford University Press, 1988.
- *The Politics of Representation in Canadian Art and Literature*. North York, ON: York University Press, 1988.
Innes, Hammond. *The Land God Gave Cain*. Glasgow: Collins, 1958.
Ipellie, Alootook. *Arctic Dreams and Nightmares*. Penticton, BC: Theytus Books, 1993.

Jacobson, David. *Reading Ethnography.* Albany: State University of New York Press, 1991.

Jameson, Anna. *Winter Studies and Summer Rambles in Canada.* Toronto: McClelland and Stewart, 1923.

Jenness, Diamond. *Arctic Odyssey: The Diary of Diamond Jenness, Ethnologist with the Canadian Arctic Expedition in North Alaska and Canada, 1913–1916.* Hull, QC: Canadian Museum of Civilisation, 1991.

– *The Indians of Canada.* 1932. 7th ed. Toronto: University of Toronto Press, 1977.

– *The Life of the Copper Eskimos.* New York: Johnson Reprint, 1970.

– *People of the Twilight.* New York: Macmillan, 1928.

Jiles, Paulette. *North Spirit: Travels Among the Cree and Ojibway Nations and Their Star Maps.* Toronto: Doubleday, 1995.

– *Song to the Rising Sun: A Collection.* Vancouver: Polestar, 1989.

– "The Spontaneously Created People." *Southwest Review* 78.2 (1993): 267–75.

Johnson, Jay. "The Age of Brass: Drummond, Service, and Canadian 'Local Colour.'" *Canadian Poetry* 23 (1988): 14–30.

Jones, D.G. *Butterfly on Rock.* Toronto: University of Toronto Press, 1970.

Juneja, Om P., and Chandra Mohan, eds. *Ambivalence: Studies in Canadian Literature.* New Delhi: Allied, 1990.

Kalluak, Mark. *How Kabloonat Became and Other Inuit Legends.* Yellowknife: Program Development Division, Government of the Northwest Territories, 1974.

Kamboureli, Smaro. *On the Edge of Genre: The Contemporary Canadian Long Poem.* Toronto: University of Toronto Press, 1991.

Kane, Elisha Kent. *Arctic Explorations: The Second Grinnell Expedition in Search of Sir John Franklin 1853, '54, '55.* Vol. 1. Philadelphia: Childs and Peterson, 1856.

Kapferer, Bruce. "The Anthropologist as Hero: Three Exponents of Post-Modernist Anthropology." *Critique of Anthropology* 8.2 (1988): 77–104.

Kappi, Leoni, ed. *Inuit Legends.* Illus. Germaine Arnaktauyok. Yellowknife: Department of Education, 1977.

Keith, W.J. *Canadian Literature in English.* London: Longman, 1985.

– *A Sense of Style: Studies in the Art of Fiction in English-Speaking Canada.* Toronto: ECW, 1989.

Kelley, Thomas P. *Rat River Trapper.* Don Mills, ON: Paperjacks, 1972.

Kelly, M.T. *Country You Can't Walk In.* Moonbeam, ON: Penumbra, 1979.

– *A Dream Like Mine.* Toronto: Stoddart, 1987.

– *The Ruined Season*. Windsor, ON: Black Moss, 1982.

Kelly, Robert A. "Outlaw and Explorer: Recent Adventurers in the English-Canadian Long Poem." *Antigonish Review* 79 (1989): 27–34.

Kertzer, Jonathan. *Worrying the Nation: Imagining a National Literature in Canada*. Toronto: University of Toronto Press, 1998.

Kimmel, Michael, ed. *Changing Men: New Directions in Research on Men and Masculinity*. New York: Sage, 1987.

King, Bruce. *The New English Literatures: Cultural Nationalism in a Changing World*. New York: St Martin's, 1980.

King, Thomas, ed. *All My Relations: An Anthology of Contemporary Canadian Native Fiction*. Toronto: McClelland and Stewart, 1990.

– "Introduction: An Anthology of Native Fiction." *Canadian Fiction Magazine* 60 (1987): 4–10.

King, Thomas, Cheryl Calver, and Helen Hoy, eds. *The Native in Literature*. Oakville, ON: ECW, 1987.

Klinck, Carl. *Robert Service: A Biography*. Toronto: McGraw-Hill Ryerson, 1976.

Kolodny, Annette. "Honing a Habitable Languagescape: Women's Images for the New World Frontiers." In *Women and Language in Literature and Society*. Ed. Sally McConnell-Ginet and Ruth Borker. 188–204. New York: Praeger, 1980.

– *The Land Before Her: Fantasy and Experience of the American Frontiers, 1620–1860*. Chapel Hill: University of North Carolina Press, 1984.

– *The Lay of the Land: Metaphor as Experience and History in American Life and Letters*. Chapel Hill: University of North Carolina Press, 1975.

Korte, Barbara. "In Quest of an Arctic Past: Mordecai Richler's *Solomon Gursky Was Here*." In Engler and Muller.

Koven, Seth. "From Rough Lads to Hooligans: Boy Life, National Culture and Social Reform." In *Nationalisms and Sexualities*. Ed. Andrew Parker, Mary Russo, Doris Sommer, and Patricia Yaeger. 365–91. New York: Routledge, 1992.

Kroetsch, Robert. *But We Are Exiles*. Toronto: Macmillan, 1965.

– *Gone Indian*. Toronto: New, 1973.

– *A Likely Story: The Writing Life*. Red Deer, AB: Red Deer College, 1995.

– *The Lovely Treachery of Words: Essays Selected and New*. Toronto: Oxford University Press, 1989.

Kroetsch, Robert, and George Bowering. "Writer Writing, Ongoing Verb." Ed. Betty A. Schellenberg. In *Future Indicative: Literary Theory and Canadian Literature*. Ed. John Moss. 5–24. Ottawa: University of Ottawa Press, 1987.

Krupat, Arnold. "An Approach to Native American Texts." *Critical Inquiry* 9.2 (1982): 323–38.

– *Ethnocriticism: Ethnography, History, Literature.* Berkeley: University of California Press, 1992.

– "Native American Literature and the Canon." *Critical Inquiry* 10.1 (1983): 145–71.

Kuester, Martin. "Tales Told in the Bathtub: Robert Kroetsch's Historiographic Metafiction." In Engler and Muller, 399–410.

Lacombe, Michèle. "Theosophy and the Canadian Idealist Tradition: A Preliminary Exploration." *Journal of Canadian Studies* 17.2 (1982): 100–18.

Langevin, André. *Le temps des hommes.* Ottawa: Cercle du Livre de France, 1956.

Lauritzen, Philip. *Oil and Amulets Inuit: A People United at the Top of the World.* St John's, NF: Breakwater Books, 1983.

Laut, Agnes C. *Lords of the North.* Toronto: W. Briggs, 1900.

Lecker, Robert. *Making It Real: The Canonization of English-Canadian Literature.* Toronto: Anansi, 1995.

– "'A Quest for the Peaceable Kingdom': A Narrative in Northrop Frye's Conclusion to the Literary History of Canada." *PMLA* 108.2 (1993): 283–93.

– *Robert Kroetsch.* Boston: Twayne, 1986.

Lewis, Paula Gilbert. *Traditionalism, Nationalism, Feminism: Women Writers of Quebec.* Westport, CN: Greenwood, 1985.

Lewis, Richard, ed. *I Breathe a New Song: Poems of the Eskimo.* New York: Simon, 1971.

Lighthall, William Douw. *Songs of the Great Dominion: Voices from the Forests and Waters, the Settlements and Cities of Canada.* London: Walter Scott, 1889.

Lincoln, Yvonna S. "Self, Subject, Audience, Text: Living at the Edge, Writing in the Margins." In *Representation and the Text: Re-Framing the Narrative Voice.* Ed. William G. Tierney and Yvonna S. Lincoln. 37–55. Albany: State University of New York Press, 1997.

Litteljohn, Bruce, and Jon Pearce, eds. *Marked by the Wild.* Toronto: McClelland and Stewart, 1973.

Livingston, Paisley. "Why Realism Matters: Literary Knowledge and the Philosophy of Science." In *Realism and Representation: Essays on the Problem of Realism in Relation to Science, Literature and Culture.* Ed. George Levine. 134–54. Madison: University of Wisconsin Press, 1993.

Lloyd, Genevieve. *The Man of Reason: 'Male' and 'Female' in Western Philosophy.* London: Methuen, 1984.

Lopez, Barry. *Arctic Dreams: Imagination and Desire in a Northern Land-scape*. Toronto: Bantam, 1987.

Lotz, James. *Northern Realities: The Future of Northern Development in Canada*. Toronto: New, 1970.

Lowenstein, Thomas. *Eskimo Poems from Canada and Greenland, from Material Originally Collected by Knud Rasmussen*. London: Anchor, 1973.

Lyall, Ernie. *An Arctic Man: Sixty-Five Years in Canada's North*. Edmonton: Hurtig, 1979.

MacCormack, Carol P., and Marilyn Strathern, eds. *Nature, Culture and Gender*. Cambridge: Cambridge University Press, 1980.

MacDonald, Malcolm. *Down North*. London: Oxford University Press, 1943.

MacEwen, Gwendolyn. "Terror and Erebus." *Afterworlds*. Toronto: McClelland and Stewart, 1987. Reprinted in *Staying the North: Twelve Canadian Plays*. Ed. Sherrill Grace, Eve d'Aeth, and Lisa Chalykoff. Toronto: Playwrights Canada Press, 1999. 115–133.

Machar, Agnes Maule. *Lays of the True North and Other Poems*. 1899. Toronto: Copp, 1902.

– *Marjorie's Canadian Winter: A Story of the Northern Lights*. Boston: Lothrop, 1892.

MacKay, James. *Vagabond of Verse: Robert Service, a Biography*. Edinburgh: Mainstream, 1995.

Mackenzie, Alexander. *Voyages from Montreal through the Continent of North America to the Frozen and Pacific Oceans in 1789 and 1793*. Vols I & II. 1801. Toronto: George N. Morang, n. d.

MacKinnon, Catharine A. *Toward a Feminist Theory of the State*. Cambridge and London: Harvard University Press, 1989.

MacLaren, I.S. "The Aesthetic Map of the North, 1845–59." *Arctic* 38.2 (1985): 89–99.

– "The Aesthetic Mapping of Nature in the Second Franklin Expedition." *Journal of Canadian Studies* 20.1 (1985): 39–56.

– "David Thompson's Imaginative Mapping of the Canadian Northwest 1784–1812." *Ariel* 15.2 (1984): 89–106.

– "Retaining Captaincy of the Soul: A Response to Nature in the First Franklin Expedition." *Essays on Canadian Writing* 28 (1984): 57–92.

– "Samuel Hearne and the Landscapes of Discovery." *Canadian Literature* 103 (1984): 27–40.

– "Samuel Hearne's Accounts of the Massacre at Bloody Falls, 17 July 1771." *Ariel* 22.1 (1991): 25–51.

MacLulich, T.D. *Between Europe and America: The Canadian Tradition in Fiction*. Toronto: ECW, 1988.

- "The Explorer as Hero: MacKenzie and Fraser." *Canadian Literature* 75 (1977): 61–73.
- "Reading the Land: The Wilderness Tradition in Canadian Letters." *Journal of Canadian Studies* 20.2 (1985): 29–44.
- "Thematic Criticism, Literary Nationalism, and the Critic's New Clothes." *Essays on Canadian Writing* 35 (1987): 17–36.

MacMechan, Archibald. *Headwaters of Canadian Literature.* New Canadian Library 107. Toronto: McClelland and Stewart, 1924.

MacMillan, Miriam. *I Married an Explorer.* London: Hurst and Blackett, 1951.

Maillard, Keith. "An Interview with Howard O'Hagan." In Fee, 21–38.

Mair, Charles. *Dreamland and Other Poems and Tecumseh, a Drama.* Toronto: University of Toronto Press, 1974.

Mallet, Thierry. *Glimpses of the Barren Lands.* New York: Révillon Frères, 1930.

Mandel, Eli. "The Inward, Northward Journey of Lawren Harris." *Artscanada* October–November (1978): 17–24.

Manera, Matthew. "The Act of Being Read: Fictional Process in *Places Far from Ellesmere.*" *Canadian Literature* 146 (1995): 87–94.

Manning, Mrs Tom (Ella W.). *Igloo for the Night.* Toronto: University of Toronto Press, 1946.

Mansbridge, Francis. "The Voyage That Never Ends: The Poetry of Paulette Jiles." *Essays on Canadian Writing* 43 (1991): 153–63.

Marchant, Bessie. *A Daughter of the Ranges.* London: Blackie, 1905.

Marcus, George E. *Ethnography Through Thick and Thin.* Princeton: Princeton University Press, 1998.

Marcus, George E., and Dick Cushman. "Ethnographies as Texts," *Annual Review of Anthropology* 2 (1982): 25–69.

Markoosie. *Harpoon of the Hunter.* Montreal: McGill-Queen's University Press, 1970.

Marshall, Tom. *Harsh and Lovely Land: The Major Canadian Poets and the Making of a Canadian Tradition.* Vancouver: University of British Columbia Press, 1979.

Mascia-Lees, Frances E., Patricia Sharpe, and Colleen Ballerino Cohen. "The Postmodernist Turn in Anthropology: Cautions from a Feminist Perspective." *Signs* 15.1 (1989): 7–33.

Matthews, J.P. *Tradition in Exile.* Sydney: F.W. Cheshire, 1962.

Matthiasson, John S. *Living on the Land: Change Among the Inuit of Baffin Island.* Peterborough, ON: Broadview, 1992.

Maud, Ralph. "Ethnographic Notes on Howard O'Hagan's *Tay John.* In *Silence Made Visible: Howard O'Hagan and Tay John.* Ed. Margery Fee. 92–6. Toronto: ECW Press, 1992.

McCarthy, Dermot. "Early Canadian Literary Histories and the Function of a Canon." In *Canadian Canons: Essays in Literary Value*. Ed. Robert Lecker. 30–45. Toronto: University of Toronto Press, 1991.

McConnell-Ginet, Sally, Ruth Borker, and Nelly Furman, eds. *Women and Language in Literature and Society*. New York: Praeger, 1980.

McGrath, Robin Gedalof. *Canadian Inuit Literature: The Development of a Tradition*. Ottawa: National Museums of Canada, 1984.

– "Editing Inuit Literature: Leaving the Teeth in the Gently Smiling Jaws." In *Cross-Culturalism in Children's Literature: Selected Papers from the Children's Literature Association, May 14–17, 1987*. 31–35. New York: Pace, 1988.

– "Introduction." *More Tales from the Igloo* by Agnes Nanogak. Edmonton: Hurting, 1986.

– "Inuit Literature in the South." *Canadian Review of Comparative Literature* September–December (1989): 700–5.

– "Oral Influences in Contemporary Inuit Literature." In King, Calver, and Hoy, 159–73.

– "Reassessing Traditional Inuit Poetry." In New, *Native Writers*. 19–28.

McGrath, Robin Gedalof, and Penny Petrone. "Native Canadian Literature." In *Studies on Canadian Literature: Introductory and Critical Essays*. Ed. Arnold E. Davidson. 309–22. New York: MLA, 1990.

McLachlan, Alexander. *The Poetical Works of Alexander McLachlan*. Toronto: Briggs, 1900.

McMillan, Alan B. *Native Peoples and Cultures of Canada: An Anthropological Overview*. 2nd ed. Vancouver: Douglas and MacIntyre, 1995.

McNeilly, Kevin. "Listening, Nordicity, Community: Glenn Gould's 'The Idea of North.'" *Essays on Canadian Writing*. Special issue edited by Sherrill Grace. 59 (1996): 87–104.

Melzack, Ronald, ed. *The Day Tuk Became a Hunter and other Eskimo Stories*. Toronto: McClelland and Stewart, 1967.

– ed. *Raven, Creator of the World: Eskimo Legends Retold*. Toronto: McClelland and Stewart, 1970.

Merchant, Carolyn. *The Death of Nature: Women, Ecology and the Scientific Revolution*. New York: Harper and Row, 1980.

Metayer, Maurice, ed. and trans. *Tales from the Igloo*. Edmonton: Hurtig, 1972.

Metcalf, John. "Travelling Northward." In *On Middle Ground*. Ed. Douglas Daymond and Leslie Monkman. 287–337. Toronto: Methuen, 1987.

Meyer, Carolyn. *Eskimos: Growing Up in a Changing Culture*. New York: Atheneum, 1977.

Meyers, Jeffrey. *Fiction and the Colonial Experience.* Ipswich: Boydell, 1973.

Millman, Lawrence. *A Kayak Full of Ghosts: Eskimo Tales.* Santa Barbara: Capra, 1987.

Mills, Elizabeth. "A Manual of Etiquette: An Interview with Paulette Jiles." *Southwest Review* 78.2 (1993): 245–66.

Minh-ha, Trinh T. *When the Moon Waxes Red: Representation, Gender and Cultural Politics.* New York: Routledge, 1991.

– *Woman, Native, Other.* Bloomington: Indiana University Press, 1989.

Mitcham, Allison. *The Northern Imagination: A Study of Northern Canadian Literature.* Moonbeam, ON: Penumbra, 1983.

Mitchell, Marybelle. *From Talking Chiefs to a Native Corporate Elite: The Birth of Class and Nationalism among the Canadian Inuit.* Montreal: McGill-Queen's University Press, 1996.

Moi, Toril. *Sexual/Textual Politics: Feminist Literary Theory.* New Accents. Ed. Terence Hawkes. London and New York: Routledge, 1985.

Monkman, Leslie. *A Native Heritage: Images of the Indian in English-Canadian Literature.* Toronto: University of Toronto Press, 1981.

Moore, Henrietta. "Interior Landscapes and External Worlds: the Return of Grand Theory in Anthropology." *Australian Journal of Anthropology* 8.2 (1997): 125–44.

Morley, Patricia. "Canadian Art: Northern Land, Northern Vision." In Juneja and Mohan, 22–38.

Morton, W.L. "The 'North' in Canadian Historiography." *Transactions of the Royal Society of Canada* (Series 4) 8 (1970): 31–40. Reprinted in *Contexts of Canada's Past: Selected Essays of W. L. Morton.* Ed. A.B. McKillop. 229–39. Carleton Library 123. Toronto: Macmillan, 1980.

Moses, Daniel David, and Terry Goldie, eds. *An Anthology of Canadian Native Literature in English.* Don Mills, ON: Oxford University Press, 1992.

Moss, John, ed. *Echoing Silence: Essays on Arctic Narrative.* Reappraisals: Canadian Writers 20. Ottawa: University of Ottawa Press, 1997.

– *Enduring Dreams: An Exploration of Arctic Landscape.* Concord, ON: Anansi, 1994.

– *A Reader's Guide to the Canadian Novel.* Toronto: McClelland and Stewart, 1981.

– ed. *Future Indicative: Literary Theory and Canadian Literature.* Reappraisals: Canadian Writers 13. Ed. Lorraine McMullen. Ottawa: University of Ottawa Press, 1987.

– "Imagining the Arctic: From Frankenstein to Farley Mowat, Words Turn the Arctic Landscape into Unreality." *Arctic Circle* 1.5 (1990): 32–40.

– *Patterns of Isolation in English Canadian Fiction*. Toronto: McClelland and Stewart, 1974.

Mosse, George L. *Formations of Nations and People*. London: Routledge, 1984.

– *Nationalism and Sexuality: Middle-Class Morality and Sexual Norms in Modern Europe*. Madison: University of Wisconsin Press, 1985.

Mott, Asta. "Aritha van Herk's *Places Far from Ellesmere*: The Wild and Adventurous North?" *Canadian Literature* 157 (1998): 99–111.

Mowat, Farley. *Canada North*. Toronto: McClelland and Stewart, 1967.

– *Canada North Now: The Great Betrayal*. Toronto: Little Brown, 1976.

– *The Curse of the Viking Grave*. Boston: Little Brown, 1966.

– *Lost in the Barrens*. Boston: Little Brown, 1956.

– *Ordeal by Ice*. Boston: Little Brown, 1961.

– *The Snow Walker*. Toronto: McClelland and Stewart, 1975.

– *Tundra: Selections from Great Accounts of Arctic Land Voyages*. Toronto: McClelland and Stewart, 1973.

Mowat, William, and Christine Mowat, eds. *Native Peoples in Canadian Literature*. Toronto: Macmillan, 1975.

Moyles, R.G. "A 'Boy's Own' View of Canada." *Canadian Children's Literature* 34 (1984): 41–56.

Mukherjee, Arun. *Towards an Aesthetic of Opposition: Essays on Literature Criticism and Cultural Imperialism*. Stratford, ON: Williams-Wallace, 1988.

– "Whose Post-Colonialism and Whose Postmodernism?" *World Literature Written in English*. 30.2 (1990): 1–9.

Munn, Captain Henry Toke. *Prairie Trails and Arctic By-Ways*. London: Hurst, 1932.

Nanogak, Agnes. *More Tales from the Igloo*. Edmonton: Hurtig, 1986.

Nasgaard, Roald. *The Mystic North: Symbolist Landscape Painting in Northern Europe and North America 1890–1940*. Toronto: University of Toronto Press, 1984.

– *Tales from the Igloo*. Edmonton: Hurtig, 1972.

Nash, Roderick. *Wilderness and the American Mind*. 3rd edition. New Haven: Yale University Press, 1982.

Nelson, Claudia. *Boys Will be Girls: The Feminine Ethic and British Children's Fiction, 1857–1917*. New Brunswick, NJ: Rutgers University Press, 1991.

Nelson, Richard K. *Shadow of the Hunter: Stories of Eskimo Life*. Chicago: University of Chicago Press, 1980.

Neuman, Shirley. "Unearthing Language: An Interview with Rudy Wiebe and Robert Kroetsch." In *A Voice in the Land: Essays by and about Rudy Wiebe*. Ed. W.J. Keith. 226–47. Edmonton: NeWest, 1981.

New, W.H. *Land Sliding: Imagining Space, Presence, and Power in Canadian Writing*. Toronto: University of Toronto Press, 1997.

– ed. *Native Writers and Canadian Writing*, Special Issue of *Canadian Literature*. Vancouver: University of British Columbia Press, 1990.

Nicol, C.W. *The White Shaman*. Toronto: McClelland and Stewart, 1979.

Nischik, Reingard M. "Narrative Technique in Aritha van Herk's Novels." In *Gaining Ground: European Critics on Canadian Literature*. Ed. Robert Kroetsch and Reingard M. Nischik. 107–20. Western Canadian Literary Documents Series 7. Edmonton: NeWest, 1985.

Norman, Howard, ed. *Northern Tales: Traditional Stories of Eskimo and Indian Peoples*. New York: Pantheon, 1990.

Norris, Frank. "Popular Images of the North in Literature and Film." *Northern Review* 8–9 (1992): 53–72.

North, Dick. *The Mad Trapper of Rat River*. Toronto: Macmillan, 1972.

Nuligak. *I, Nuligak*. Trans. Maurice Metayer. Toronto: Peter Martin Associates, 1966.

Nungak, Zebedee, and Eugene Arima, eds. *Unikkaatuat sanaugarngnik atyingnaliit Puvirgni turngmit/Eskimo Stories from Povungniyuk, Quebec*. Ottawa: Queen's Printer, 1969.

Oehlschlaeger, Fritz. "Civilization as Emasculation: The Threatening Role of Women in the Frontier Fiction of Harold Bell Wright and Zane Grey." In *Gender Studies: New Directions in Feminist Criticism*. 177–86. Bowling Green, OH: Bowling Green University Popular Press, 1986.

O'Hagan, Howard. *The School-Marm Tree*. Vancouver: Talonbooks, 1977.

– *Tay John*. 1939. New Canadian Library Series 105. Ed. Malcolm Ross. Introduction by Patricia Morley. Toronto: McClelland and Stewart, 1974.

– *Wilderness Men*. 1958. Vancouver: Talonbooks, 1978.

Oman, Lela Kiana. *Eskimo Legends*. Anchorage: Alaska Methodist University Press, 1975.

Oppel, Frank, comp. *Tales of the Canadian North*. Secaucus, NJ: Castle, 1984.

Oquilluk, William A., and Laurel L. Bland. *People of Kauwerak: Legends of the Northern Eskimo*. Anchorage: Alaska Pacific University Press, 1981.

Owens, Craig. "Representation, Appropriation and Power." *Art in America* 70.5 (1982): 9–21.

Owens, Louis. *Other Destinies: Understanding the American Indian Novel*. Norman: University of Oklahoma Press, 1992.

Oxley, J.M. "The Romantic Story of a Great Corporation: The Hudson's Bay Trading Company." N.p.: n.p., 1890.

– *The Wreckers of Sable Island*. London: n.p., 1894.

Parker, Andrew, Mary Russo, Doris Sommer, and Patricia Yaeger, eds. *Nationalisms and Sexualities*. New York: Routledge, 1992.

Patten, Harris. *Wings of the North*. Chicago: Goldsmith, 1932.

Perreault, Jeanne, and Joseph Bruchac, eds. Special Issue *Ariel* 25.1 (1994).

Perreault, Jeanne, and Sylvia Vance, eds. *Writing the Circle: Native Women of Western Canada, An Anthology*. Edmonton: NeWest, 1990.

Person, Leland S., Jr. "The American Eve: Miscegenation and a Feminist Frontier Fiction." *American Quarterly* 37.5 (1985): 668–85.

Petersen, Kirsten Holst, and Anna Rutherford, eds. *A Double Colonization: Colonial and Post-Colonial Women's Writing*. Oxford: Dangeroo, 1986.

Petrone, Penny, ed. *Northern Voices: Inuit Writing in English*. Toronto: University of Toronto Press, 1988.

Phillips, R.S. "Space for Boyish Men and Manly Boys: The Canadian Northwest in Robert Ballantyne's Adventure Stories." *Essays on Canadian Writing*. Special issue edited by Sherrill E. Grace. 59 (1996): 46–64.

Pitseok, Peter. *People From Our Side*. With Dorothy Eber. Edmonton: Hurtig, 1975.

Pitseolak, Peter. *Peter Pitseolak's Escape from Death*. Toronto: McClelland and Stewart, 1977.

Pryde, Duncan. *Nunaga: My Land My People*. Edmonton: Hurtig, 1971.

Purdy, Alfred. *Naked With Summer in Your Mouth*. Toronto: McClelland and Stewart, 1994.

– *North of Summer: Poems from Baffin Island*. Toronto: McClelland and Stewart, 1967.

– *The Purdy-Woodcock Letters: Selected Correspondence 1964–1984*. Ed. George Galt. Toronto: ECW, 1988.

– *Reaching for the Beaufort Sea: An Autobiography*. Ed. Alex Widen. Madeira Park, BC: Harbour Books, 1993.

– *Wild Grape Wine*. Toronto: McClelland and Stewart, 1968.

Querengesser, Neil. "Canada's Own Dark Heart: F.R. Scott's 'Letters from the Mackenzie River.'" *Essays on Canadian Writing* 47 (1992): 90–104.

Rabinow, Paul. "Representations are Social Facts: Modernity and Post-Modernity in Anthropology." In Clifford and Marcus, 234–61.

Radhakrishnan, R. "Nationalism, Gender, and the Narrative of Identity." In Parker et al., 77–95.

Radley-Walters, Maureen, and Peter Watson. *The Arctic: Canada's Last Frontier*. Don Mills, ON: Nelson, 1973.

Rapp, Rayna Ritter, ed. *Towards an Anthropology of Women*. New York: Monthly Review, 1975.

Rasmussen, Knud, ed. *Eskimo Poems from Canada and Greenland*. Trans. Tom Lowenstein. Pittsburgh: University of Pittsburgh Press, 1973.

Ray, Anne Chapin. *Janet: Her Winter in Quebec*. London: Frowde, 1908.

Readings, Bill. *The University in Ruins*. Cambridge: Harvard University Press, 1996.

Reed, Helen. *Amy in Acadia*. Toronto: Morang, 1905.

Relke, Diana M.A. *Greenwor(l)ds: Ecocritical Readings of Canadian Women's Poetry*. Calgary: University of Calgary Press, 1999.

Renan, Ernest. "Qu'est-ce qu'une nation?" 1882. *Œuvres complètes*. 887–906. Vol. 1. Paris: Calmann-Lévy, 1947–61.

Reynolds, Jan. *Frozen Land: Vanishing Cultures*. New York: Harcourt Brace, 1993.

Richler, Mordecai. *The Incomparable Atuk*. London: André Deutsch, 1963.

– *Solomon Gursky Was Here*. Markham, ON: Viking, 1989.

Ridington, Robin. *Trail to Heaven: Knowledge and Narrative in a Northern Native Community*. Vancouver: Douglas and McIntyre, 1988.

Rink, Heinrich Johannes, ed. *Tales and Traditions of the Eskimo*. Edinburgh: William Blackwood and Sons, 1875.

Rohner, Ronald P., and Evelyn C. Rohner. "Introduction: Franz Boas and the Development of North American Ethnology and Ethnography." Trans. Hedy Parker. *The Ethnography of Franz Boas*. Ed. Ronald P. Rohner. Chicago: University of Chicago Press, 1969.

Ross, James A. *Canada First and Other Poems*. Toronto: Macmillan, 1920.

Ross, W. Gillies. *This Distant and Unsurveyed Country: A Woman's Winter at Baffin Island, 1857–1858*. Montreal: McGill-Queen's University Press, 1997.

Roth, Lorna. "(De)Romancing the North." *Border/Lines* 36 (1995): 36–43.

Rowley, Graham H. *Cold Comfort: My Love Affair with the Arctic*. Montreal: McGill-Queen's University Press, 1996.

Roy, Gabrielle. *La petite poule d'eau*. Montréal: Beauchemin, 1966.

– *La rivière sans repos*. Montréal: Beauchemin, 1970.

Ruffo, Armand Garnet. *Grey Owl: The Mystery of Archie Belaney*. Regina: Coteau, 1996.

Said, Edward. "Representing the Colonized: Anthropology's Interlocutors." *Critical Inquiry* 15.2 (1989): 205–25.

Sanders, Clinton R. "Stranger than Fiction: Insights and Pitfalls in Post-Modern Ethnography." *Studies in Symbolic Interaction* 17 (1995): 89–104.

Sarris, Greg. "Keeping Slug Woman Alive: The Challenge of Reading in a Reservation Classroom." *The Ethnography of Reading*. Ed. Jonathan Boyarin. 238–69. Berkeley: University California Press, 1992.

Satzewich, Vic, and Terry Wotherspoon. *First Nations: Race, Class, and Gender Relations*. Scarborough, ON: Nelson, 1993.

Saul, Joanne. "Enduring Themes?: John Moss, the Arctic, and the Crisis in Representation." *Studies in Canadian Literature* 24.1 (1999): 93–108.

Saul, John Ralston. "Subversion in the North." *Writing Away: The PEN Canada Travel Anthology*. Ed. Constance Rooke. Toronto: McClelland, 1994.

– *The Unconscious Civilization*. Toronto: Anansi, 1995.

Schäfer, Jürgen. "A Farewell to Europe: Rudy Wiebe's The Temptations of Big Bear and Robert Kroetsch's Gone Indian." In *Gaining Ground: European Critics on Canadian Literature*. Ed. Robert Kroetsch and Reingard M. Nischik. 79–90. Edmonton: NeWest, 1985.

Schaffer, Kay. *Women and the Bush: Forces of Desire in the Australian Cultural Tradition*. Cambridge: Cambridge University Press, 1988.

Scheman, Naomi. *Engenderings: Constructions of Knowledge, Authority, and Privilege*. New York: Routledge, 1993.

Schenk, Susan J. "'Let Me Begin Again': Women and Storytelling in the Poetry of Paulette Jiles." *Canadian Poetry: Studies, Documents, Reviews* 20 (1987): 67–79.

Schlegel, August Wilhelm von. *A.W. Schlegel's Lectures on German Literature from Gottsched to Goethe*. 1833. Ed. H.G. Fiedler. Oxford: Basil Blackwell, 1944.

Schroeder, Andreas, and Rudy Wiebe, eds. *Stories from Pacific and Arctic Canada*. Toronto: Macmillan, 1974.

Schultz-Lorentzen, Finn. *Arctic*. Toronto: McClelland and Stewart, 1976.

Schwarz, Herbert. *Elik and Other Stories of the MacKenzie Eskimos*. Toronto: McClelland and Stewart, 1970.

Schwenger, Peter. *Phallic Critiques: Masculinity and Twentieth Century Literature*. London: Routledge, 1984.

Scott, Duncan Campbell. "The Last of the Indian Treaties." 1906. *The Circle of Affection and other Pieces of Prose and Verse*. 109–22. Toronto: McClelland, 1947.

Sedgwick, Eve Kosofsky. *Between Men: English Literature and Male Homosocial Desire*. Gender and Culture. Ed. Carolyn G. Heilbrun and Nancy K. Miller. New York: Columbia University Press, 1985.

Seidler, Victor. *Recreating Sexual Politics: Men, Feminism, and Politics*. London: Routledge, 1991.

– *Rediscovering Masculinity: Reason, Language and Sexuality.* London: Routledge, 1989.

Senkpiel, Aron. "From the Wild West to the Far North: Literary Representations of North America's Last Frontier." In Heyne, 133–42.

Service, Robert. *The Collected Poems of Robert Service.* New York: Dodd Mead, 1966.

Seton, Ernest Thompson. *Two Little Savages: Being the Adventures of Two Boys who Lived as Indians and What They Learned.* New York: Grosset, 1903.

Seton-Watson, Hugh. *Nations and States: An Enquiry into the Origins of Nations and the Politics of Nationalism.* London: Methuen, 1977.

Shemie, Bonnie. *Houses of Snow, Skin and Bones.* Native Dwellings: The Far North. Plattsburgh, NY: Tundra, 1989.

Shields, Rob. *Places on the Margin: Alternative Geographies of Modernity.* London: Routledge, 1991.

Showalter, Elaine, ed. *Speaking of Gender.* New York: Routledge, 1989.

Shrive, Norman. Introduction to *Dreamland and Other Poems and Tecumseh, a Drama*, by Charles Mair. Toronto: University of Toronto Press, 1974.

Sidney, Angela. *Tagish Tlaagu. Tagish Stories.* Whitehorse: Angela Sidney, 1982.

Siska, Heather Smith. *People of the Ice: How the Inuit Lived.* Illus. Ian Bateson. Vancouver: Douglas & McIntyre, 1980.

Sissons, Jack. *Judge of the Far North.* Toronto: McClelland and Stewart, 1968.

Slemon, Stephen, and Helen Tiffin, eds. *After Europe: Critical Theory and Post-colonial Writing.* Australia: Dangaroo, 1989.

Slemon, Stephen, Helen Tiffin, and Jo-Ann Wallace. "Into the Heart of Darkness?: Teaching Children's Literature as a Problem in Theory." *Canadian Children's Literature* 63 (1991): 6–23.

Slotkin, Richard. *The Fatal Environment: The Myth of the Frontier in the Age of Industrialization 1800–1890.* New York: Atheneum, 1985.

– *Regeneration Through Violence: The Mythology of the American Frontier, 1600–1860.* Middleton, CN: Wesleyan University Press, 1973.

Smith, Henry Nash. *Virgin Land: The American West as Symbol and Myth.* New York: Random, 1961.

Smith, Sidonie, and Julia Watson, eds. *De/colonizing the Subject: The Politics of Gender in Women's Autobiography.* Minneapolis: University of Minnesota Press, 1992.

Smyth, Heather. "Sexual Citizenship and Caribbean-Canadian Fiction: Dionne Brand's *In Another Place, Not Here* and Shani Mootoo's *Cereus Blooms at Night.*" *Ariel* 30.2 (1999): 141–60.

Söderlind, Sylvia. *Margin/Alias: Language and Colonization in Canadian and Québécois Fiction*. Toronto: University of Toronto Press, 1991.

Spalding, Alex, and Thomas Kusugak. *Stories from Pangnirtung*. Edmonton: Hurtig, 1976.

– *Eight Inuit Myths*. Ottawa: National Museums, 1979.

Spector, Judith, ed. *Gender Studies: New Directions in Feminist Criticism*. Bowling Green, OH: Bowling Green State University Press, 1986.

Spelman, Elizabeth V. *Inessential Woman: Problems of Exclusion in Feminist Thought*. Boston: Beacon, 1988.

Spillers, Hortense J., ed. *Comparative American Identities: Race, Sex and Nationality in the Modern Text*. New York: Routledge, 1991.

Spivak, Gayatri Chakravorty. "Can the Subaltern Speak?" In *Marxism and Culture*. Ed. Cary Nelson and Lawrence Grossberg. 271–313. Urbana: University of Illinois Press, 1988.

– *In Other Worlds: Essays in Cultural Politics*. New York: Methuen, 1987.

– "The New Historicism: Political Commitment and the Postmodern Critic." In *The New Historicism*. Ed. H. Aram Veeser. London: Routledge, 1989.

St Maur, Gerald. *Odyssey Northeast: A Trilogy of Poems on the Northwest Passage*. Edmonton: University of Alberta Press, 1983.

Stables, Gordon. *Wild Adventures Around the Pole*. London: Hodder, 1888.

– *Off to Klondike*. London: Nisbet, 1890.

Stacey, Robert. "From 'Icy Picture' to 'Extensive Prospect': The Panorama of Rupert's Land and the Far North in the Artist's Eye, 1770–1830." In *Rupert's Land: A Cultural Tapestry*. Ed. Richard C. Davis. 147–93. Waterloo: Wilfrid Laurier University Press, 1988.

Staines, David, ed. *The Canadian Imagination: Dimensions of a Literary Culture*. Cambridge: Harvard University Press, 1977.

Stephansson, Vilhjalmur. *The Friendly Arctic*. New York: Macmillan, 1921.

– *Kak the Copper Eskimo*. Toronto: Macmillan, 1924.

– *My Life with the Eskimo*. 1913. New York: Collier, 1971.

– *Unsolved Mysteries of the Arctic*. New York: Macmillan, 1938.

Stephen, A.M. *The Golden Treasury of Canadian Verse*. Toronto: J.M. Dent, 1928.

Stouck, David. "The Art of the Mountain Man Novel." *Western American Literature* 20 (1985): 211–22.

Strathern, Marilyn. "An Awkward Relationship: The Case of Feminism and Anthropology." *Signs* 12.2 (1987): 276–92.

– *Partial Connections*. Lanham, MD: Rowman and Littlefield, 1991.

Sullivan, Rosemary. "Beyond Colonialism: The Evolution of Canadian Literature." In *The Colonial and the Neo-Colonial Encounters in Commonwealth Literature*. Ed. H.H. Anniah Gowda. 71–82. Mysore: University of Mysore, 1983.

Surette, Leon. "Creating the Canadian Canon." In *Canadian Canons: Essays in Literary Value*. Ed. Robert Lecker. 17–29. Toronto: University of Toronto Press, 1991.

– "Here Is Us: The Topocentrism of Canadian Literary Criticism." *Canadian Poetry* 10 (Spring/Summer 1982): 44–57.

Swinton, George. Introduction to *Shadows* by Armand Tagoona. Ottawa: Oberon, 1975.

Symons, R.D. *North by West: Two Stories from the Frontier*. Markham, ON: Paperjacks, 1974.

– *Still the Wind Blows*. Saskatoon: Prairie Books, 1971.

Tagoona, Armand. *Shadows*. Ottawa: Oberon, 1975.

Tanner, Ella. *Tay John and the Cyclical Quest: The Shape of Art and Vision in Howard O'Hagan*. Toronto: ECW, 1990.

Taussig, Michael. *Mimesis and Alterity: A Particular History of the Senses*. New York: Routledge, 1993.

Taylor, George Rogers, ed. *The Turner Thesis Concerning the Role of the Frontier in American History*. 3rd ed. Lexington, MA: D.C. Heath, 1972.

Thériault, Yves. *Agaguk*. Toronto: Ryerson, 1963.

– *Agoak: L'héritage d'Agaguk*. Montréal: Editions Quinze, 1975.

– *Ashini*. Montréal: Fides, 1960.

Thomas, Peter. *Robert Kroetsch*. Studies in Canadian Literature. Vancouver: Douglas & McIntyre, 1980.

Thompson, David. *David Thompson's Narrative 1784–1812*. 1916. Ed. Richard Glover. Toronto: Publications of the Champlain Society, 1962.

Thompson, Stith. *Tales of the North American Indians*. Bloomington: Indiana University Press, 1968.

Thrasher, Anthony Apakark. *Thrasher...Skid Row Eskimo*. Toronto: Griffin House, 1976.

Threadgold, Terry, and Anne Cranny-Francis, eds. *Feminine/ Masculine and Representation*. London: Allen and Unwin, 1990.

Tiffin, Helen. "Commonwealth Literature and Comparative Methodology." *World Literature Written in English* 23.1 (1984): 26–30.

– "Post-Colonialism, Postmodernism and the Rehabilitation of Post-Colonial History." *Journal of Commonwealth Literature* 23.1 (1988): 169–81.

Tolson, Andrew. *The Limits of Masculinity: Male Identity and the Liberated Woman*. New York: Harper, 1977.

Toye, William, ed. *The Oxford Companion to Canadian Literature*. Toronto: Oxford University Press, 1983.

Trehearne, Brian. "Influence, Aestheticism, Modernism." In *Aestheticism and the Canadian Modernists: Aspects of a Poetic Influence*. 3–21. Kingston: McGill-Queen's University Press, 1989.

Trigger, Bruce G. "The Historian's Indian: Native Americans in Canadian Historical Writing from Charlevoix to the Present." *Canadian Historical Review* 77. 3 (1986): 315–42.

Tulurialik, Ruth Annaqtuusi, with David Pelly. *Qikaaluktut: Images of Inuit Life*. Toronto: Oxford University Press, 1986.

Turner, Frederick Jackson. *The Frontier in American History*. 1920. New York: Holt, Rinehart and Winston, 1962.

Turner, Lynnette. "Feminism, Femininity, and Ethnographic Authority." *Women: A Cultural Review* 2.3 (1991): 238–54.

Tyler, Stephen. "PostModern Ethnography: From Document of the Occult to Occult Document." In Clifford and Marcus, 122–40.

van Herk, Aritha. *In Visible Ink: Crypto-Frictions*. Edmonton: NeWest, 1991.

– *No Fixed Address: An Amorous Journey*. Toronto: McClelland and Stewart, 1986.

– *Places Far from Ellesmere*. Red Deer, AB: Red Deer College, 1990.

– *The Tent Peg: A Novel*. Toronto: McClelland and Stewart, 1981.

Van Maanen, John. *Tales of the Field: On Writing Ethnography*. Chicago: University of Chicago Press, 1988.

Van Rys, John. "Alfred in Baffin Land: Carnival Traces in Purdy's North of Summer." *Canadian Poetry: Studies, Documents, Reviews* 26 (1990): 1–18.

van Toorn, Penny. *Rudy Wiebe and the Historicity of the Word*. Edmonton: University of Alberta Press, 1995.

Visweswaran, Kamala. "Histories of Feminist Ethnography." *Annual Review of Anthropology* 26 (1997): 591–621.

Wachowich, Nancy, in collaboration with Apphia Agalakti Awa, Rhoda Kaukjak Katsak, and Sandra Pikujak Katsak. *Saqiyuq: Stories from the Lives of Three Inuit Women*. Montreal: McGill-Queen's University Press, 1999.

Wadden, Marie. *Nitassinan: The Innu Struggle to Reclaim their Homeland*. Vancouver: Douglas & McIntyre, 1991.

Walzer, Michael. *Spheres of Justice: A Defense of Pluralism and Equality*. New York: Basic, 1983.

Warwick, Jack. *The Long Journey: Literary Themes of French Canada*. University of Toronto Romance Series 12. Toronto: University of Toronto, 1968.

Waterston, Elizabeth. *Children's Literature in Canada*. Twayne's World Authors Series 823. Ed. Ruth K. MacDonald. New York: Twayne, 1992.

Webb, Melody. *The Last Frontier*. Albuquerque: University of New Mexico Press, 1985.

Webster, Steven. "Ethnography as Storytelling." *Dialectical Anthropology* 8 (1983): 185–205.

– "Realism and Reification in the Ethnographic Genre." *Critique of Anthropology* 6 (1986): 39–62.

Whitaker, Muriel, ed. *Stories from the Canadian North*. Edmonton: Hurtig, 1980.

Whitlock, Gillian. "The Bush, the Barrack-yard and the Clearing: 'Colonial Realism' in the Sketches and Stories of Susanna Moodie, C.L.R. James and Henry Lawson." *Journal of Commonwealth Literature* 20.1 (1985): 36–48.

– "Unreliable Citizens: Gender, Nation, Interpretation." *Australian-Canadian Studies* 8 (1990): 109–17.

Wiebe, Rudy. *A Discovery of Strangers*. Toronto: Knopf, 1994.

– *The Mad Trapper*. Toronto: McClelland and Stewart, 1980.

– "The Naming of Albert Johnson." *Queen's Quarterly* 80 (1973): 370–8. Reprinted in *Stories from Pacific and Arctic Canada*. Ed. Andreas Schroeder and Rudy Wiebe. Toronto: Macmillan, 1974.

– *Playing Dead: A Contemplation Concerning the Arctic*. Edmonton: NeWest, 1989.

– *River of Stone: Fictions and Memories*. Toronto: Vintage, 1995.

– "Western Canada Fiction: Past and Future." *Western American Literature* 6.1 (1971): 29.

– "The Words of Silence Past and Present." In *Silence, The Word and the Sacred*. Ed. E.D. Blodgett and H.G. Coward. 13–20. Waterloo: Wilfred Laurier University Press, 1989.

Wilkinson, Doug. *Sons of the Arctic*. Toronto: Clark, Irwin, 1965.

Williams, Bernard. *Ethics and the Limits of Philosophy*. Cambridge: Harvard University Press, 1985.

Wilson, Robert R. "National Frontiers and International Movements Postmodernism in Canadian Literature." In *Ambivalence: Studies in Canadian Literature*. Ed. Om P. Juneja and Chandra Mohan. 48–61. New Delhi: Allied, 1990.

Wonders, William, ed. *Canada's Changing North*. The Carleton Library 55. Toronto: McClelland and Stewart, 1971.

Woodcock, George. *George Woodcock's Introduction to Canadian Fiction*. Toronto: ECW, 1993.

Woodman, David C. *Unravelling the Franklin Mystery: Inuit Testimony.* Montreal: McGill-Queen's University Press, 1991.

Wright, Allen. *Prelude to Bonanza: The Discovery and Exploration of the Yukon.* Sidney, BC: Gray's Publishing, 1976.

Wynne, May. *Two Girls in the Wild.* London: Blackie, 1920.

York, Lorraine. "The Ivory Thought: The North as Poetic Icon in Al Purdy and Patrick Lane." *Essays on Canadian Writing* (1993): 45–56.

York, Thomas. *The Musk Ox Passion.* Toronto: Doubleday, 1978.

– *Snowman.* Toronto: Doubleday, 1976.

Young, Egerton Ryerson. *Three Boys in the Wild North Land.* Toronto: W. Briggs, 1897.

– *Winter Adventures of Three Boys in the Great Lone Land.* New York: Eaton and Mains, 1899.

Zaslow, Morris. *The Northwest Territories 1905–1980.* Canadian Historical Association Historical Booklet No. 38. Ottawa: Canadian Historical Association, 1984.

– *The Opening of the Canadian North 1870–1914.* Toronto: McClelland and Stewart, 1971.

Zeller, Suzanne. "Encompassing the North." In *Inventing Canada: Early Victorian Science and the Idea of a Transcontinental Nation.* 161–80. Toronto: University of Toronto Press, 1987.

Index